Praise for *Don't Talk About Politics*

'This book changed the way I talk about politics.'

Grace Blakeley, author of *Vulture Capitalism*

'A very timely book indeed, full of wise, hopeful, sometimes sad, sometimes funny truths, about how we have reached the place we are in. It asks to put aside so much of what we think we know in the name of a more realistic assessment of how politics, language, communities and beliefs really work. Eye opening and necessary.'

Alain de Botton, author of *The Consolations of Philosophy* and *Essays in Love*

'A timely and hopeful critique of today's political culture, Sarah Stein Lubrano challenges us to rethink politics – placing interpersonal activism and community-building above performative outrage.'

Alice Cappelle, author of *Collapse Feminism: The Online Battle for Feminism's Future*

'A rare combination of cognitive science and critical theory... Sarah Stein Lubrano is an exceptionally erudite and thoughtful veteran activist. A skillful, meticulous dismantling of debate culture.'

Sophie Lewis, author of *Abolish the Family* and *Enemy Feminisms*

'[A] thought-provoking debut work.'

Daily Mail

To Deb and Mike, who provided the love
(and also the infrastructure).

DON'T TALK ABOUT POLITICS

HOW TO CHANGE 21ST-CENTURY MINDS

SARAH STEIN LUBRANO

BLOOMSBURY CONTINUUM
LONDON · OXFORD · NEW YORK · NEW DELHI · SYDNEY

BLOOMSBURY CONTINUUM
Bloomsbury Publishing Plc
50 Bedford Square, London, WC1B 3DP, UK
Bloomsbury Publishing Ireland Limited,
29 Earlsfort Terrace, Dublin 2, D02 AY28, Ireland

BLOOMSBURY, BLOOMSBURY CONTINUUM and the Diana logo are trademarks
of Bloomsbury Publishing Plc

First published in Great Britain 2025

Paperback 2026

Copyright © Sarah Stein Lubrano, 2025

Sarah Stein Lubrano has asserted her right under the Copyright, Designs and Patents
Act, 1988, to be identified as Author of this work

For legal purposes the Acknowledgements on pp. 250–1 constitute an extension of
this copyright page

All rights reserved. No part of this publication may be: i) reproduced or transmitted in
any form, electronic or mechanical, including photocopying, recording or by means of
any information storage or retrieval system without prior permission in writing from
the publishers; or ii) used or reproduced in any way for the training, development
or operation of artificial intelligence (AI) technologies, including generative AI
technologies. The rights holders expressly reserve this publication from the text and
data mining exception as per Article 4(3) of the Digital Single Market Directive
(EU) 2019/790

Bloomsbury Publishing Plc does not have any control over, or responsibility for, any
third-party websites referred to or in this book. All internet addresses given in this
book were correct at the time of going to press. The author and publisher regret any
inconvenience caused if addresses have changed or sites have ceased to exist, but can
accept no responsibility for any such changes

A catalogue record for this book is available from the British Library

Library of Congress Cataloguing-in-Publication data has been applied for

ISBN: PB: 978-1-3994-1393-0; eBook: 978-1-3994-1394-7; ePDF: 978-1-3994-1391-6

2 4 6 8 10 9 7 5 3 1

Typeset by Lumina Datamatics Ltd
Printed and bound in Great Britain by Clays Ltd, Elcograf S.p.A.

To find out more about our authors and books visit www.bloomsbury.com
and sign up for our newsletters

For product safety related questions contact productsafety@bloomsbury.com

CONTENTS

Introduction: The Requirement   1

1. Don't Enter the 'Market' for Ideas   15
2. Don't Debate It   41
3. Act First, Think Later   69
4. Think with Your Friends   107
5. Take Back Twitter (and Other Infrastructure)   137
6. Fight Social Atrophy   179
7. Loving and Leaving the Liberal Ideal (or, To My Fellow Lovers of Ideas)   221

Further Reading   247
Acknowledgements   250
Notes   252
Index   275

INTRODUCTION

THE REQUIREMENT

One day in 2016, shortly after Donald Trump had been chosen as the Republican nominee in the US Presidential election, I went out for ice cream with some friends. As we sat with our cones, one friend asked, 'Do you guys remember when Donald Trump's campaign manager was fired for punching a woman in the face?'

We did not.* But perhaps the remarkable thing was that so many wild things had happened in that election period alone that this particular tale was already buried in a distant media cycle, overshadowed by revelations about porn stars and Trump's boasts of pussy-grabbing. Unless you are reading this in the far distant future, you know political life became mostly ever weirder after that year – less apparently rational, more self-destructive, more dishonest, more violent and more chaotic, in the US and in other countries too.

Not only that, but talking about politics became stranger too, on- and offline. People who appeared to be relatively left or right suddenly switched sides or fell down conspiracy rabbit-holes; there was more yelling, more trolling, more

---

*In fact, the friend had the details wrong, though the gist correct: the assault had in fact happened, but differently, and the man had stepped down, not been fired. Maggie Haberman and Michael M. Grynbaum (2016), 'Corey Lewandowski, Donald Trump's Campaign Manager, Is Charged with Battery', International New York Times, 29 March, available at: www.nytimes.com/2016/03/30/us/politics/trump-campaign-manager-corey-lewandowski.html (accessed 1 October 2024).

fake-things-appearing-real and more real-things-appearing-fake. Today all this is part of a common worry on both right and left: the 'public sphere' seems broken. People worry about cancel culture, 'wokeness', free speech, polarization, echo chambers and conspiracy thinking. They are concerned about people's inability to speak to one another about politics.

Watching this fracturing of public discourse and political life has been one of the most jarring changes of my adult life, and I receive notifications about it all day long on my phone. So I have spent a great deal of time trying to understand it. I try to understand why people on Twitter/X spend so much time bickering, why conspiracy theories always seem to bloom around the latest news story, why family members talk past each other at the dinner table or why politicians can win round voters by fuelling barely comprehensible grudges.

And when I think about this – why the public sphere is so divided, confusing and stymied – I have come to wonder at the assumption that discourse could work easily in the first place. I particularly wonder that it ever seemed that a good idea or powerful argument should be enough to change your mind, even if you only hear it once. And then I think about the Spanish Requirement of 1513.

The *Requerimiento*, as it was called, was a declaration that Spanish settlers were supposed to proclaim when they encountered new groups of indigenous people. It explained that the land they had been living on for thousands of years was actually Spanish because the pope had 'made donation of these isles' to the king and queen, 'as is contained in certain writings which passed upon the subject as aforesaid, which you can see if you wish'.[1] Citations available upon request! Indigenous people were asked 'that you consider what we have said to you, that you take the time that shall be necessary to understand and deliberate upon it' and then to acknowledge the Church, pope and king and queen as their sovereigns. If they accepted their new overlords, the Spanish colonizers claimed (untruthfully) that they would be treated well. If not,

> we shall take you and your wives and your children, and shall make slaves of them, and as such shall sell and dispose of them as their Highnesses may command; and we shall take away your goods, and shall do you all the mischief and damage that we can ... and we protest that the deaths and losses which shall accrue from this are your fault.

This was an ultimatum, phrased as information in order to absolve those speaking of further obligation. The whole process was haphazard; typically, a small group of indigenous people would be gathered on the beach where the Spanish boats landed and read the text on behalf of all the inhabitants on the island, even if (as regularly happened) it was read to them without translation.[2] And if they did not immediately understand and accept, then violence, slavery and general plunder followed and were considered to be justified. According to the *Requerimiento*, any deaths or losses were, in fact, entirely the Natives' own fault.

It was the whitewashing of its time, an attempt to make something unjust look less so by vaguely nodding to consent and discourse and ethical values. It was in large part constructed as a response to those in Spain who, even then, dissented from the murderous acts perpetuated by the colonizers. But, of course, it was hardly an improvement on, or justification for, the genocide about to take place.

Yes, it's an extreme historical example. But the idea that we are at fault if we're not immediately converted by the 'truth' is not so unusual. While there is a lot of theological debate on the matter, to this day many Christians believe that those who have never heard the Gospel get some special consideration in the next life. But for the rest of us, it is believed, who have heard of the Gospel, even briefly, even badly translated, even just once, we have our mortal souls on the line, our eternal fate dependent on our response.[3]

You shouldn't need to tell people twice – that's the idea.

I've always found this notion, that someone talking to you could sway your understanding of the structure of the universe (compared with the weight of all your own experiences, your family and relationships, your personal convictions and your previous commitments), terribly ambitious. (Perhaps it's that I'm Jewish, and we don't proselytize.) And yet, this is the premise of our modern political culture. We are given access to media and debates, and then we have the chance to vote. We're told that a little 'critical thinking' should be enough to furnish a democracy, and encouraged to focus on that, even by the psychologists and commentators who probably know that that's not how people really behave, especially when it comes to politics.

Meanwhile, trust in society and interest in politics have hit a nadir in many countries around the globe. Perhaps that's because discourse, which is so highly valued in theory in our society, appears so ineffective in practice. Or perhaps it's because politics simply feels too sinister and hopeless to many of us, too unfixable. We might sense that the politicians that 'consult' us for our views already have their own plans firmly in place, that our neighbour is being fed disinformation by bots at a speed we could never counter, that something about our newsfeed is targeting us like a sniper. Trying to engage with these odds stacked against us can feel fruitless. Talking more with those near us often is not only deeply frustrating, but also diverts our energy from other solutions to the world's most pressing problems. It can be much easier to disengage. And while we do, those in power do as they like.

INTRODUCTION

In short, our political culture today, with its emphasis on discourse and the airing of opinions and debates, is not fair or effective in helping people think through political issues – just as the *Requerimiento* wasn't fair and didn't make colonialism any more just 500 years ago. A great deal of the public sphere is, in fact, just gestures. And sometimes it's whitewashing for something worse.

Something about political discourse has always actually troubled me, but it took me a long time to understand what exactly was troubling about it. I grew up in Washington, DC, surrounded by endless conversations about politics. I always loved books and ideas, and for many years I imagined that, if I got an impressive education and read as many books as I could, that alone would prepare me to do good in the world. I thought people found truth through entertaining abstract ideas. This assumption was the bedrock of the world I was raised in – yes, people could be irrational but they could also, over time, be exposed to ideas, take them on board and change their lives for the better.

It wasn't until I began to study psychology and sociology that a different picture of human beings emerged – one where people certainly did reason and change their minds, but mostly for reasons outside their conscious perception. I discovered that the two disciplines I was most passionate about, politics and psychology, had conflicting ideas of how people operate. I wanted to understand how to reconcile these two visions of humanity, and the political worlds they implied. This took me through a PhD in political theory and cognitive science, especially the study of cognitive dissonance (more on that term soon). And eventually, it brought me to writing this book.

The problems described above (and other problems related to discourse, such as cancel culture, echo chambers, polarization and more) share a common underlying feature: they rely on faulty models of what it means to think about politics. For our society has two deeply flawed models of how politics works: first, that it is effectively commerce ('the marketplace of ideas'); and second, that it is effectively war (as with 'debate' when we let ideas clash). Sometimes we hold both these models in our understanding at the same time. From these two flawed models (in this book I call them *reasoning-as-commerce* and *reasoning-as-war*), we have built some of the least effective forms of communication: debates that go nowhere, conversations that stoke antagonism and reinforce existing beliefs and interventions that overload people with information. The result is hostility and derision that lead many of us to disengage from politics altogether. Unfortunately, these models drive a great deal of how our society structures reasoning and communication, from school essays to presidential debates to Supreme Court rulings. We're individually and structurally stuck in old, bad models of thinking and conversing. In the first two chapters of this book, I look at these myths and the reality of whether simply talking about ideas in these ways is likely to cause political change. Spoiler: no.

However, all is not lost. People do change their minds all the time, just not for the reasons we might instinctively imagine. As I show over the next two chapters (Three and Four), change in our interpersonal relationships or our own actions often *does* change our politics, sometimes powerfully. This means that political reasoning is an interdependent, not independent, activity. Our thoughts are formed through our social world. Our ability to reason about politics is also shaped by the opportunities we have. If our lives are limited and narrow, it's likely that our ability to reason about new ideas will be so too. Right now, we live in a particularly socially isolated and action-limited age in countries like the US and the UK, and this is harming our ability to think about politics together.

The upside of this insight is that there's an opportunity amid the crisis: if we could enable people to interact with a wider range of people, share their political concerns and explore new activities and ways of living, then they would be in a much better position to reason well about politics. Equipped with this understanding, we can (and hopefully will) build a better-functioning public sphere, by which I generally mean one where people can still come to understand each other and their shared world better, build a more just future and steer the world away from the ecological and economic precipice on which we currently stand. In Chapter Five, I outline the need for infrastructure that can help expand people's possibilities for action and their social life. In Chapter Six, I look at a specific contemporary crisis related to interpersonal reasoning, social atrophy. And in Chapter Seven, I return to the question of how to understand political reasoning in our current moment, and how to go beyond existing liberal sentiments in this area and reach a more true and promising understanding of what it means to think and act about politics (not just talk about it).

We have to face the long-term systematic challenges that threaten democracy and public reasoning. Someone has already made this point, many years ago in fact: a German intellectual named Jürgen Habermas. Habermas was born in Germany in 1929 with a cleft palate that required multiple surgeries, a circumstance which he has explained made him think deeply and seriously about the importance and difficulty of human communication.[4] When he was a child, the Nazis rose to power, and he was drafted into the Hitler Youth. After the war came to an end, he spent much of his career working to make sense of the aftermath of German fascism and genocide, directly and indirectly, including confronting the philosopher Martin Heidegger about his support for the Nazi party. As of the time of writing, he is, amazingly, still alive and writing, and a celebrity of sorts, frequently published in newspapers and widely known even to those outside his academic field.[5]

Habermas is perhaps best known for his theories about the 'public sphere', a term he coined to describe the arenas in which citizens come together to discuss matters of public interest. (In the original German it's *Öffentlichkeit*, which rolls off the tongue a little less easily.) Habermas argued that in eighteenth-century Europe there was a sudden proliferation of spaces that were neither private homes nor parts of the state nor parts of the church (in other words, what we call 'third spaces' today). These were often coffee houses. (Europeans had just gained access to coffee, first through the Middle East and later through various colonies; it was an exciting and over-caffeinated time.) According to Habermas, the tradition of public discussion began not with political debates but with long conversations about novels. At the same time as Samuel Richardson was publishing his latest page-turners, growing markets fed by colonial territories and financial speculation required more accurate and regular information. Soon, the first regular news-sheets and newspapers also sprang into circulation, allowing an increasingly literate public to learn about and opine on local and world affairs after they'd had their winding conversations about fiction. The result was a flourishing of both commerce-related activity and political discussion. Here the forces of the market, combined with public spaces and a rise in literacy, led to the public sphere.[6]

This public sphere is the area, literal or metaphorical, where common affairs (the environment, the economy, our culture, our health, war, social norms and so on) can be discussed openly. Habermas calls it 'society engaged in critical public debate', but I rather like Hannah Arendt's related poetic line about 'the public realm': it is 'the common world' that 'gathers us together and yet prevents our falling over each other'. A place where, ideally, we can gather and learn how to do better by each other in our social and political life.

It is, in other words, a beautiful idea. But even Habermas himself is quick to acknowledge that most of our world does not look like this today. Indeed his work on the public sphere suggests that it has been, in some ways, a victim of its own success. In the eighteenth century, for example, the public sphere contributed to Enlightenment thinking and helped lead to the rise of science, technology and modern democracy.[*] But in the long run this heady mix of technology, media, markets and colonialism also meant that the world became much harder for the average person to understand and influence. Consider what it would require for a citizen to form a thoughtful critique of tax policy today: it is not impossible, but it is a Herculean task even for a well-educated person to untangle the complex bureaucracy, specialized expertise and opaque lobbying that shapes the way we pay our taxes. More than this, perhaps, we're now entangled in endless notifications from apps owned by billionaires, all intended to get us to open the platform, see ads and buy things. We're also exhausted from the mental load of work. No wonder so many people cannot imagine wanting to sit

---

[*] In fact, both Lloyd's of London (later Lloyd's Insurance) and the New York Stock exchange began as coffee houses; the same conditions that allowed people to gather to discuss literature and politics also allowed them to do business in an age of growing capitalism. See, for example, E. Wesley Reynolds (2022), Coffeehouse Culture in the Atlantic World, 1650–1789, Bloomsbury Publishing.

down for a long, slow, thoughtful chat about politics. It no longer feels as though we have access to the ideal coffee house for such an endeavour – or the collective wherewithal to use one. The capitalist and bureaucratic world that was in part created in these coffee shops has eaten away at the democratic life also generated there. As Habermas puts it, the 'system' of capitalism and its attendant bureaucracies have pathologically 'colonized' the 'lifeworld' in which we live. (Just think about what has happened to universities in the past few decades, as they have become increasingly monetized and bureaucratized at the same time, to the detriment of the educational experience.[7])

This is part of the problem I examine throughout this book, with an eye towards the ever-expanding, specific crises of the twenty-first century and a plethora of psychological and sociological research. Like Habermas, I am by training a 'critical theorist', which means that I am engaged in a practice of attempting to discern and uncover the power structures in society and the social, historical and ideological forces that support them. I care deeply about the question of democracy, but unlike many liberal theorists, I am not persuaded that the most important strategy in politics is to persuade others with words. Still, in the right context, with a range of other democratic structures in place (including rights protections for minorities and for dissent, and relatively egalitarian economies), discourse has its place in politics: thoughtful informed consent, understanding and consensus is desirable even amid the genuine and sometimes irreconcilable conflicts of interest at stake in every modern society. In other words: I care about this problem of the public sphere, but, perhaps more than Habermas, I don't see democracy as primarily a matter of talking.

A bit about this word, 'liberal'. Some of my readers, especially Americans, may associate the word with the left half of the political 'Overton window', with politicians like Barack Obama or Alexandria Ocasio-Cortez. Readers in other countries may think about liberals as those belonging to specific political parties, such as the Liberal Democrats in the UK. But I use the term throughout this book to mean the political philosophy that emphasizes the individual and individual rights, private property, freedom of expression, freedom from state or religious interference, consent of the governed and equality before the law. There are many good aspects of liberalism; of the list I've just given, I particularly like the last three. But there are also significant downsides, profound and hidden problems, with some of what liberalism and its long legacy have to offer – particularly, as I shall argue, the private ownership of capital and the way markets can come to dominate the rest of our lives, as well as the way an emphasis on 'free' speech can mask a real difficulty in people being able to understand their political world. As some theorists have noted, societies founded on supposedly liberal principles often have surprisingly illiberal outcomes, like slavery and genocide. At the theoretical level there are problems, too: liberal theorists tend to ask questions about politics without taking full account of economic power, which sometimes leaves them asking the wrong questions altogether.

In addition, the cultural trappings of liberalism come with a wealth of problems. For while some of the official aspects of liberal ideology are commendable, liberalism is not just a legal system or a set of political commitments. It has also become a sensibility, a cultural lens on the world, a set of expectations about how social interactions should be structured. As I shall show throughout this book, some of the culture that has come with liberalism, such as a 'debate culture', has led to harmful and unproductive forms of politics.

In recent years, I've noticed, many who until now had broadly admired liberal ideas have begun to waver in their admiration. Some have moved rightward or become reactionary, some have simply not been sure how to respond, some have come leftward, ever more critical of the economic system. This book is written in part for those who are disillusioned about some aspects of liberalism, but who also see the beauty of some of its ideals. It's for those who know the current system won't work but are unsure about how to understand the world we're facing in the twenty-first century, a world characterized by social isolation, low social trust, spiralling economic and climate crises and a rise in authoritarian leaders in supposed democracies. This book seeks to provide an answer that isn't just a return to an 'illiberal' world, but which instead takes what is promising in liberalism (ideas around equality and autonomy, for example) and marries it to a set of material considerations that might allow those values to be better realized in practice. You'll also notice in this book that I don't always sound like other people in the critical theory tradition, as they often focus mostly on high-level concepts and theories, while I am happy to draw on research and studies that show us how things work in practice. I tend to write in an empirically informed way, and a historically informed way, about how and what people actually do and think and what this might tell us about the challenges at hand. This more empirical, even scientific, approach is not without its challenges and problems. Most people conducting research are not looking to answer the same questions I am. To write this book I have taken a highly interdisciplinary and somewhat speculative approach, drawing on other people's data and applying it to questions they rarely considered directly.

Another methodological note: I am very much the product of 'the Global North': I grew up in the very centre of political life in the United States, attended elite American institutions, then moved to the UK and attended elite institutions there. I have never lived outside the Global North. In this book, I write about what I know, and make no pretence of speaking more widely. The problems I describe, and even the solutions that might help, are aimed at precisely the kinds of places I'm from, especially the US and the UK.

In all this, my aim is to address politics in its broadest sense: the difficult, artful, necessary means by which humans conduct life in common. This is a book about how we can reason better so as, ultimately, to live well and justly together. We will be able to think better about politics when we can belong together more equally and live enabled, rather than constrained, by our material world and social norms.

And to get to that point, we'll have to take apart the myth that words alone will change the world. This is true not least of all because much political communication, like the words of the *Requerimiento*, is coercion more than communication. Of course discourse can be an invitation to a real discussion, but it can also be a formality, an expression that really means: 'I've given you a fair chance by exposing you to this right idea, one any right mind would have responded to, and now I can use force to get my way.' At its worst, discourse does what the *Requerimiento* did, which is to provide a cover for the structures of power and domination to go on as they were always going to anyway, with the convenient excuse that a discussion has happened. 'Things are fine, fair and democratic', those in power can say, 'because everyone is free to say and believe whatever they want!'

Discussion of political reasoning and public opinion has long been limited by the same old metaphors of war and commerce. We can do better than relying on these metaphors and endlessly discussing politics. We can get to the heart of what it really means to think about politics by considering the underlying forces that shape the way we think, from economics to our social lives to technologies. We can do more than just talk: we can build a diverse social fabric, change the daily possibilities for people's lives, organize politically, and use this expanded world to think together, differently and better. With better models of communication we can come to work through the contradictions of political life not with arguments or force but through action and imagination.

1

Don't Enter the 'Market' for Ideas

On the same continent as the distribution of the *Requerimiento*, nearly half a millennium later, I was a teenager. Like most teenagers, I did not like waking up for school, so every morning my father would turn on the radio and leave it on, loud, until I came downstairs for breakfast. And so it was that I spent my formative years waking up to advertisements for military planes and helicopters.

Each ad tended to start with a moment of pulsing, dramatic music, followed by the sounds of missiles and explosions, and all of them went a bit like this:

> Raytheon's collaborative team of the miniature air launch decoy (or 'MALD'), Joint Stand-Off Weapon (or 'JSOW') and High-Speed Anti-Radiation Missile (or 'HARM') is a proven, affordable response to the proliferation of A2AD enablers. MALM, JSOW, and HARM complement each other's attributes, providing synergy to disrupt and

overwhelm an advanced adversary across multiple domains, while protecting launch platforms.*

If you did not grow up near Washington, DC, at this point you might be a bit confused. Not only by all the acronyms but also that an ad for such an expensive and deadly set of products would play after the daily weather report. Second amendment notwithstanding, surely the average American consumer cannot purchase an assault helicopter?

But as a teenager I was not confused. It was normal, as were the ads in the metro for defence companies. It's not that I thought they were targeting me personally, exactly, but I didn't question why they were there either. It was only a decade later that I paused to consider what these ads were doing. And the answer was simple, in a way: defence contractors are not legally allowed to wine and dine federal employees, so they had to look for other ways to win the attention of the relevant decision-makers. What's $10,000 in local radio ads if your whole proposal cost a full million to put together? 'It's very important to get information out to the acquisition board', one contractor spokesperson said when interviewed, 'Just like Coke or Pepsi does marketing, it's important for us to create awareness about our business.'[1]

These ads are not meant to influence the average voter. No one is likely to write to their congressional representatives and urge them to purchase the decoy, weapon and missile package

---

*In fact, to avoid in any way misrepresenting the thing I am talking about, I have here just lifted lines from a real Raytheon advertisement that I found on the internet, one that comes with animations that are remarkably video-game-like. The ad I found online, like all the ads I listened to growing up, is narrated by a strong 'manly' voice, in an almost cheerful manner. Military.com (2024), *JSOW, MALD & HARM vs. Threats*, available at: www.military.com/ video/defense-systems/air-defense/jsow-mald-harm-vs-threats/3176191229001 (accessed 8 October 2024).

(not least because a set of 250 air launch decoys alone cost $96 million). But nor are these ads just there in case the guys in the Pentagon get inspired while eating their cereal. No, I'd like to suggest the ads work better when they're broadcast publicly because they create the illusion that there is an informed public, somewhere, that *might* have an opinion about which defence contractors should receive contracts. It gives the impression that the decision-makers might be subject to peer pressure, judgement or even social reward – depending on their choice. It works to 'prepare' the way consciously and unconsciously for the lobbyists who descend on Capitol Hill to reach the handful of guys on our planet (and they are mostly guys) who decide what kind of missiles we 'need'. These lobbyists will think about their own radio alarm clock experience and commute, and feel pressure to purchase in line with the opinions of an imagined micro-public of their peers.

These strategies appear to work. Raytheon won the contract for these 'collaborative' devices, and many others besides. The ads have an impact on the wider public too, making it seem as though the main political question at stake is not whether we should buy assault helicopters at all but rather whether we should buy them from Raytheon or Lockheed Martin. Or Northrop Grumman, a company with a very catchy, entirely meaningless, slogan, one my brother and I can still recite in unison: 'Northrop Grumman. *Defining the Future!*'

The missile-pushing radio ads are effective and escaped my early scrutiny, in part because of a myth deeply embedded in American, and indeed Western, culture. It is a myth that few people believe in explicitly or in full, but which is nevertheless the basis for much of our political system and our personal behaviour. The myth goes like this: if ideas are proposed in an open 'marketplace', they will be duly and truly considered by citizens who will then select the best ideas and pressure their governments to enact policies that reflect them. The myth suggests that, as long as the public is continuously exposed to ideas, and can discuss them, politics will more or less function well. All you have to do is browse the available options and purchase the right one – it is a kind of consumerism, it is *reasoning-as-commerce*.

This chapter is about this myth, which is often associated with the term 'marketplace of ideas', and the belief that such a marketplace can help solve our political problems. Even if you haven't heard this term, you might recognize the intuition in the idea that 'sunlight is the best disinfectant' or that every idea must be given a fair hearing. Even though there's very little truth in this myth empirically (as I'll show below), the assumption that the free airing of ideas is enough for democracies to function – even with all the money and power hidden in the background – is one we can't seem to shake off. The idea has structured our government, institutions, laws, media and political parties. It has seeped into our personal intuitions, relationships and conversations. So why has this idea, indeed this ideal, been so enduring, appealing and (even when we spot its numerous flaws) inescapable?

The term 'the marketplace of ideas' comes from a Supreme Court decision in 1919. Justice Oliver Wendell Holmes coined it to defend the rights of Jewish radicals who were criticizing US wartime policies during the First World War. He wrote about the importance of having a 'free trade in ideas' within 'the competition of the market'.[2] In 1953 Justice William O. Douglas used the phrase yet more neatly to defend a dissident publisher being pressured into releasing the names of their customers, writing, 'This publisher bids for the minds of men in the marketplace of ideas.'[3] In 1969 it was further enshrined in free speech laws that limited what the government could censor – in this instance, upholding the right of the Ku Klux Klan to publish. It was eventually used by Justice Kennedy of the US Supreme court as part of the justification in the Citizens United ruling, a Supreme Court ruling that held that corporations and unions cannot have restrictions placed on their political spending on causes and candidates, as this would constitute a violation of their right to free speech. Money itself became a legally recognised form of speech, making the myth of a marketplace of ideas a strange, perverse American reality.[4]

But the general idea of the marketplace of ideas is much older. The ancient Greeks prided themselves on their *agora*, a central civic meeting place that was both a marketplace and somewhere people could gather to discuss politics. (Those who look to tech as a solution for societal problems often like to imagine that places like X, the site formerly known as Twitter, can be our modern agora.[5]) Political theorists influenced by the Enlightenment, such as John Stuart Mill and Thomas Jefferson, wrote that free speech was necessary for the best ideas to win in the long arc of history, although they did not rely on the metaphor of the marketplace.[6] Today a certain amount of cynicism has eaten away at the idea – but it's not uncommon to hear think tanks and economists using the metaphor of the marketplace to think through how they might help 'sell' the most advantageous ideas.[7]

When most people use the term 'marketplace of ideas', they don't just mean a market where speech can flourish free from government censorship or regulation. Like Thomas Jefferson, they have something grander in mind – a conviction that the market will, if it's honest and efficient, allow the best ideas to win. As the philosopher Olúfẹ́mi O. Táíwò puts it, 'Much like the mythical market, mythical liberal democracy is supposed to be self-correcting and self-justifying by definition.'[8] The claim, in short, is that markets create a certain kind of justice when it comes to economics and that they can do this for political ideas, too.

Both these ideas are questionable. Markets create inequalities and injustices, even when it comes to goods, services and wealth. And while few of us want heavy censorship, does it follow that we should simply leave things to a 'marketplace'? Can we trust a conceptual 'marketplace' and the kind of talking it implies to create the best of all possible future political worlds?

Let's consider this proposition – that what is required for good politics is a 'marketplace of ideas' – a few different ways: first, as a claim that serves the interests of those in power, then through the lens of psychology, then laid out against our economic reality, then as a question of what would be politically desirable and then finally, to zoom out, as an idea that is seductive because it appeals to very particular emotional attachments that many of us carry.

Looked at the other way, we might consider the marketplace of ideas to be merely a legitimizing myth, one that supports the winners of history and alienates the marginalized. The American law professor Stanley Ingber has sounded a more ominous note on this tendency for the marketplace to allow those whose ideas are already popular to claim their ideas are popular *because* they are right: 'the marketplace model provides a dominant group with a basis for its self-serving belief that the dominance of its perspectives is justified.'[9] He suggests that the myth of the marketplace of ideas has become so pervasive because it allows those who hold mainstream views to feel justified that their ideas have already been proven best. At the same time, dissidents are more likely to distrust the concept of the marketplace of ideas, seeing it as a tool of those in power, ironically widening the distance between the two groups so that they are less interested in exchange than before. Indeed, in the 1960s the spokespeople for the 'New Left' movement concluded that the first amendment in the US, which guarantees free speech, was 'a meaningless sop, designed to siphon off protest and delude the populace into believing it has a participating voice'.[10]

When it doesn't crown the historical victors and alienate the losers, the myth that a marketplace of ideas might ultimately allow for the best historical outcome also allows people across the political spectrum to perform a sort of conceptual hand-waving gesture. If, for example, you believe an important idea has 'won' (say, that women should be able to vote, or gay people to marry), the idea that the best ideas always win in the end not only helps explain how a groundbreaking shift in public opinion happened but also proves that the idea must have been right all along, since only the best ideas win. It is certainly a neater explanation than the messy, material realities of generations of painful, often apparently fruitless, struggle against oppression that actually underlie advances in feminism and gay rights. And, of course, if you believe in something but it hasn't yet 'won', it's comforting to think that it will eventually come out on top in a marketplace of ideas – and you're just ahead of the tide. Sure, the idea suggests, we live in a world of increasing inequality, imminent ecological collapse and rising authoritarianism, but there is another mechanism out there that works to keep that in check. Just wait!

In everyday life I see this implicit belief that simply exposing each other to ideas can help when people say things like 'We need to talk about x' or 'We don't talk about y enough.' Sometimes x and y are emotional, therapeutic things, such as male vulnerability or post-natal depression, in which case the move is meant to make people feel less shame or ask for interpersonal support. And sometimes (as with the #metoo campaign) it can begin a conversation that then leads to active political organizing.[11] But often the underlying assumption is that just talking about the issue will somehow make it better. Perhaps we think that, if we talk about it enough, we'll prove that it's the better product – a best-selling idea. It's probably not entirely a coincidence that, as more and more of our lives have been shaped by market forces, people have begun to conceptualize reasoning in terms of being a consumer (or seller!) of ideas.

Perhaps the main clue that 'the marketplace of ideas' is a bad model for a healthy public sphere is that it relies on the idea that people easily identify the best ideas when comparing them to others, and then change their minds as necessary. Yet one recent survey found that only 14 per cent of people had changed their minds on any issue in the last year as a result of something they saw on social media.[12] And forget data: most of us know many people that are not like this. In fact, most *of us* are not like this, most of the time. Most of us rarely change our minds about the big things, and are often too busy to consider the small ones. This is true across much of life, of course: which sports team we predict to win, what we think of our neighbours and colleagues, what to make of conspiracy theories about pop stars ... but it is perhaps nowhere more evident than when it comes to politics.

If one consults the best available psychology research (and I have), one discovers that, when it comes to political issues, in particular, minds are remarkably difficult to sway with new ideas, and especially new ideas about emotional issues. (This lies, for the most part, in contrast to the lofty, hopeful assumptions of many of the political philosophers I read during my graduate study, who imagined relative ease for those deliberating in democracies.) Study after study shows that simply being exposed to new ideas and facts, at least in areas where people already hold strong beliefs, does not change people's minds. For example, a regularly tested phenomenon called 'confirmation bias' leads people to weigh information that confirms their existing views more strongly and weigh information that might disprove their view less strongly, reinforcing their existing ideas.[13] I experience confirmation bias whenever I nod at the sagacity of those I already follow (often while scrolling social media). I experience it whenever I tell myself that whatever data is presented by the 'other side' is probably cherry-picked, without questioning the same feature in my own sources.[14] Indeed, confirmation bias also occurs when people stop listening to whole news sources entirely, if those trouble their worldview. Similarly, rationalizations lead people to come up with very clever (but nevertheless misleading and ultimately irrational) justifications for why they should continue to think the way they do. I tend to rationalize travelling by plane with 'but only structural changes can fix climate change anyway', and I rationalize not going for a run with 'the weather isn't great and I might fall and slip'. But neither of these rationalizations really explains why I have made the choices I have. Cognitive dissonance, a term that is used colloquially in a variety of ways, is in psychology the discomfort that emerges when our actions contradict our beliefs (for instance, when someone terrified by the climate crisis books a seat on a flight) or when two of our beliefs contradict one another. I use the term throughout this book in this formal, scientific way. Cognitive dissonance makes us engage in both these types of thinking (confirmation bias and rationalizations) more often, as we strive to reduce our discomfort with contradictions in our worldview. We can see cognitive dissonance and its effects at work when people rapidly 'reason' in ways that are really attempts to mitigate their discomfort with new information about strongly held beliefs. For example, before Donald Trump was convicted of various serious crimes in 2024, only 17 per cent of Republican voters believed that felons should be able to be elected president; directly after his conviction, that number rose to 58 per cent.[15] To reconcile two contradicting beliefs (that presidents shouldn't do x, and that Trump should be president) an enormous number of Republican voters simply changed their mind about the former. In fact, Republican voters shifted their views on more or less all the things Trump had been convicted of: fewer of them, for example, felt it was immoral to have sex with a porn star, pay someone to stay silent about an affair, falsify a business record or pay someone to stay silent in order to influence election results.[16] In short, we rationalize what we need to in order to hold on to the beliefs that let us keep operating in the world, which, for these people, was that voting for Trump would improve their lives.

Cognitive dissonance and its relationship to political reasoning was the subject of my PhD research at Oxford University, and after five years of wading through all the research I could find on the topic, what ultimately struck me most was not that it was some strange glitch or outlier in human reasoning, but rather how ubiquitous it is, and in some sense how central to the process of human reasoning. After all, who doesn't want to feel they have a coherent worldview? And who really has the time or ability to do all the work to create one? Is it even possible to live without contradictions?

Beyond dissonance too there are many, many other common and well-documented systematic 'errors' of human reasoning. Many are the results of the 'biases and heuristics' that have recently become popular areas of study in fields such as behavioural psychology. I have put 'errors' in quotation marks here because, while these forms of reasoning may lead to faulty conclusions and annoy academics and social media users alike, they do serve a function for the people experiencing them.

Many of these 'errors' stem from our attachment to a sense of agency, belonging and identity, by which I mean our understanding of how we might meaningfully act in the world, belong in our social groups and maintain our sense of self, including the ways in which we are 'good'.* Indeed, many of our political beliefs, right or wrong, contain these attributes. If, for example, I believe in a certain kind of economy because it encourages 'personal responsibility', that is tied to my understanding of how I should act each day as I go to work and raise my children (my meaningful actions), what sorts of people I can be honourably grouped with (my sources of belonging) and why I am a good person (my sense of self). Sometimes this insistence on seeing ourselves as having agency and being on the right side gets in the way of our ability to shift our views in line with new information or meaningful counterarguments. It is frequently our attachment to our belief that we are competent and good that gets in our own way, in other words; as law professor Ozan Varol puts it, 'When your beliefs are entwined with your identity, changing your mind means changing your identity. That's a really hard sell.'[17] It matters a lot to us whether we think we're a good feminist, a baby-killer, an anti-racist, a 'productive citizen' or a 'welfare leech'. Precisely because we

---

*I don't doubt there are other common characteristics, but I'll focus on these for now, as they are especially relevant to the topic of political discourse.

care so much about these questions of identity, agency and belonging, however, they tend to systematically distort how we see political issues, in ways that are difficult for us to notice for ourselves or admit when confronted.[18]

One telling study on the matter was conducted by Jonas T. Kaplan, Sarah I. Gimbel and Sam Harris.* The authors ascertained people's views on a number of issues, some with clear political implications (such as whether there should be further restrictions on gun ownership in the US), some with little to no political implications (such as who invented the light bulb). They then exposed the participants to data (some faked!) that should weigh in the balance of their views and perhaps change their mind (e.g. evidence that the US had fewer nuclear weapons than Russia was used to increase support for a larger military budget, or it turns out Thomas Edison did not invent the light bulb but rather several others pioneered versions before him). For topics without political dimension, people changed their minds quite a bit. For those with political dimension, people hardly changed their minds at all. Brought back to revisit the topic weeks later, the findings held up: people had new beliefs about light bulbs but they had refused to shift their beliefs or preferences in line with new information about political topics. (For example, even if legal gun ownership did not, for instance, have this or that negative effect, they still were just as strongly against it.) In other words, we're pretty good at changing our views when they don't affect our sense of agency, belonging and identity; but once beliefs

---

*Yes, the third author on this study is the well-known philosopher, author and neuroscientist often considered one of the 'Four Horsemen of Atheism'. That I disagree with his views on many political subjects and am therefore made uncomfortable by appreciating his psychology study is arguably itself an example of cognitive dissonance. This is from Jonas T. Kaplan, Sarah I. Gimbel and Sam Harris (2016), 'Neural Correlates of Maintaining One's Political Beliefs in the Face of Counterevidence', Scientific Reports 6: 39589.

involve these factors (as political beliefs always do), it's all much more challenging to shift.

This makes sense really. It would be costly if we changed our views easily. We might struggle to know what to do next, or have to change our social role and relationships completely. For this reason, perhaps, we are very good at maintaining our 'big' political beliefs even when this means acting inconsistently. The result is that, as Dan Kahan, a theorist of 'cultural cognition', describes, people often use their strong reasoning skills to adapt their beliefs to fit with others and their values. Thus conservative farmers are pretty capable of adjusting their practical beliefs, such as 'It's been kinda dry the last few years, let's buy some drought-resistant seed', without changing their 'identity-forming belief' that there is no man-made climate change.[19] (Here, as elsewhere, cognitive dissonance applies its pressure, and rationalizations do their work.) Our reasoning processes are not adapted to get at this or that specific truth, after all, but are meant to help us thrive in the world, especially with other people. In this way, our views may realistically be formed not so much in exchange as in coordination with others, adjusted to help the group as a whole get along.[20] With these strong motivations it should be no surprise that we cannot easily shift our beliefs whenever we encounter otherwise persuasive information.

It's not just our brains that don't fit the mould required for a 'marketplace of ideas' to work well. Precisely because ideas operate in real economic markets, it's often not possible to convey ideas thoughtfully or well. Today, the most obvious example of this is perhaps the way technological changes are ravaging the media industry, especially when it comes to reporting, which of course serves a crucial political function. At the time of writing, mainstream publications are folding and firing staff right, left, and centre. The problem is particularly dire for digital newsrooms, as much of their revenue has disappeared now that digital news largely is read on, or accessed via, social media – which means the revenue goes to the social media sites rather than the newspapers. In 2018, for example, Google alone made nearly $5 billion from their news content, nearly as much as every news organization in the US, combined, made from digital ad revenue.[21] That year, Facebook and Google together took 60 per cent of digital ad revenue, much of which would otherwise have gone to journalism producers instead. Sixty per cent of journalism jobs, about 30,000 newspaper jobs, disappeared between 1990 to 2016, according to government statistics. And needless to say, similar results are present in other countries around the world. At the same time, more than 350 newspapers failed in the first few years of the pandemic in the US alone, and many more have done so since.[22] The imperatives of digital media lead to other consequences too: expensive paywalls, more clickbait and gossip, less serious long-form reporting. Indeed, profit incentives mean that what it does more reliably is sell ads – and this does not maximize our exposure to new and varied ideas.

Of course, another problem with the mediasphere is that it has fractured into many tiny media landscapes, in large part owing to the internet. There are, in effect, a lot of smaller 'marketplaces' of ideas now, each selling such specialized wares that people in one marketplace have no idea what is being sold in the others. I am likely to see mostly what left-wing middle-class people see on my social media timeline, and am accordingly always absolutely baffled by what counts as news for right-wing publications such as Britain's *Sun* or America's *Fox News*. The problem with these media micro-climates is psychological as much as infrastructural: it's both that we see more of what we agree with and that, with little common ground between news sources, we can more easily dismiss what dissent we do see, and return to our 'home beliefs' feeling sure that other mediaspheres are simply for loonies. All these mediaspheres and echo chambers, of course, defeat some of the ideal purpose of having a marketplace of ideas. They mean that people cannot find a shared starting point for conversation with others; they mean that we cannot weigh ideas in some objective way, that we are not really able to consider all the options of what to believe before we choose and invest deeply. Of course, in a way there have always been echo chambers in people's individual communities or newspaper selections, but the internet has made this problem more intense.

The way media functions on the internet does funny things to our brains too. There is the regularly made point about our shortened attention spans – although research is fuzzy on whether this is actually the case or whether we are now simply engaged in tasks that require shorter bursts of attention. But it's not just about the length of our attention spans. Some technologies that are theoretically meant to help us focus our attention can actually have the opposite effect. The remote control for the TV, for example, often puts people in a strange reverie of automatically flipping between channels while barely thinking. Social media scrolling is similar. When I am tired, bored or unhappy with my lot, I often scroll listlessly, and I cannot say that I necessarily am ingesting the content that passes through my line of sight. There's simply something addictive about searching for more. As the writer Jia Tolentino notes, this kind of social media use is often due to the psychological tendency to respond to the 'intermittent reinforcement' of the occasional dopamine hit that happens when we finally find something good: 'It is *essential* that social media is mostly unsatisfying. That is what keeps us scrolling, pressing our lever over and over again in the hopes of getting some fleeting sensation – some momentary rush of recognition, flattery, or rage.'[23] Hardly the kind of thoughtful, deliberate mindset that would lead us to be wise consumers of what we see.

The rise of digital media has also meant that news can happen at any moment, and it will appear on our phones, which are at our fingertips. That leads to all kinds of strange outcomes: a world where the most recent thing seems like the most important, a certain hypervigilance attached to all our news consumption and, of course, our total exhaustion, at times, in the face of the 24-hour news cycle. The average amount of screen time globally is about six or seven hours a day; and much of this is spent clicking and scrolling and checking and shaping one's brain to these profit-driven behaviours, without any of it necessarily looking like a truly free and open forum for ideas.[24]

The way much of our media is consumed in a social manner also means that many of us feel pressure to tell everyone our opinions (even though we are rarely able to do this in a meaningful way). After all, on social media we repost things we have read and have our own thoughts on, or are prompted by the platform to say something every time we open the page. On the one hand, this encourages people to be active participants (even 'producers') in this apparent marketplace of ideas, foraging our own 'hot takes' as products. But, on the other hand, some of the most popular hot takes are simply goofy jokes or 'shitposts', designed to stir up ire from others. We are not necessarily producing what we think are the best ideas, nor are we equipped or incentivized to do so. The format of online communication often means that it's the silliest takes that seem to really take off. This may be because we are living in an age of what Jonah Peretti, founder of Buzzfeed, calls 'contagious media', or media that 'you immediately want to share with all your friends ... you take pleasure in consuming the media but also pleasure in the social process of passing it on.'[25] This means that we are all being prompted to write whatever might be fun to pass around like hot gossip, often on issues that we might have mulled over in greater depth.

The idea that communications networks are or even really could be entirely open, egalitarian, horizontally structured places for the democratic exchange of ideas neglects many of the built realities of how networks, communications technologies and even human relationships more broadly work. Inequality is built into networked interactions, perhaps unavoidably – that's why, while most people have 200 or so followers on Twitter, Katy Perry has over 100 million. Some people are just more popular than others, on and offline. And networks, digital or otherwise, tend to make things go viral, increasing these popularity disparities over time. However, there is no doubt that we are living in a particularly dystopian version of what is possible: online systems structured like networks exacerbate certain kinds of inequalities, and popularity there can often be purchased and manipulated in even more sudden and striking ways than it can be in the real world. The web, in short, is nothing like a 'level playing field' where the best ideas are likely to win out. Sure, occasionally a nobody's tweet goes viral, but most of the time what is received are messages from a few powerful nodes.

We're currently in a world that has technologies that make it feel like we're in an open marketplace for the exchange of ideas. But since this isn't really how the technologies work, nor how our brains work, this illusion only makes everything more difficult.

It's not just that technology and actual markets distort our thinking, or that our brains are poorly set up to consider things objectively. It's also not obvious that we really could consider political ideas in the same way as we choose commodities, or that we should even want to. To start with, we all begin any political consideration with a fairly hefty dose of preconceived ideas, a problem that has always both troubled and inspired political theorists. When philosopher John Rawls sought to imagine how we might come to better political judgements, he suggested that we should begin as if from behind a 'veil of ignorance' – thinking as though temporarily ignorant of our self or social position in society – and then devise a social arrangement that we would be willing to adopt without knowing where we would end up within that social order.[26] In this way, Rawls suggested, we might be able to judge the best social arrangements, away from prejudices and self-interest.

But (apologies to Rawls) this is, of course, precisely what real human beings do not and cannot do. Theorists in my specific discipline, political theory, have noted that political reasoning is by its very nature situated: we always start from where we are. This is true with regard to 'obvious' markers such as those included in 'diversity and inclusion' trainings: class, race, gender, age, sexuality and so on. But it is also true in terms of the traditions that mould our thinking, even unconsciously. Not only are *we* situated in a particular part of society, but so is our concept of the 'good'. What is hopelessly oppressive in one society is simply sensible and community-minded in another, for example. When it comes to the marketplace of ideas, we may simply be 'buying' what we are buying because, well, our mother always bought it, and other products just seem weird.

This does not, of course, imply that some social positions are not better 'standing grounds' than others for understanding the world. As feminist 'standpoint theorists' have suggested, some groups, especially those who experience oppression first hand and then try to combat it, are best placed to understand how a system works.[27] Women are generally best placed to come to understand the nature of the patriarchy, or black people the nature of racial oppression. But 'come to' is key here: such a political standpoint is always an achievement, the result of assiduous work, work that is largely done with others, part of active struggle. Good political beliefs, this type of theory suggests, are not simply adopted because they sound right during an intellectual shopping excursion; they are the result of our labour and our lives, built, carved, refined through collective toil.

All this underlines just how impoverished and curious the metaphor of 'the marketplace of ideas' really is when it comes to how we think. Indeed, as David Graeber notes in his book *The Democracy Project*, we've long thought of reasoning as a much more sterile and straightforward activity than it really is – and this way of thinking about politics has favoured one group of people in particular.[28] Starting in the Western tradition with Aristotle, many political theorists assumed that only those with significant property (and generally those free and male) could exercise full rationality, because only they were sufficiently disinterested and thus able to choose for the well-being of the whole. Put another way, the theory was that the wisest consumers would be the loaded ones, because rich people are surely not tempted to impulse-buy a special deal from a politician who promises them a bit more. The obvious problem with this is that rich people are often tempted by things politicians have to offer them, and have frankly not been good decision-makers for everyone else, if history is anything to judge by.

There is, however, yet another problem with this metaphor. As Graeber puts it, 'to be rational in this tradition has everything to do with the ability to issue commands: to stand apart from a situation, assess it from a distance, make the appropriate set of calculations, and then tell others what to do.'[29] The assumption is that to be rational is to see things from the outside, as a controlling force, like a conductor facing the orchestra. But many ideas, especially political ones, might not be things we best judge from the outside.

For in truth, in many ways, we don't have ideas, they have us. Ideas are not commodities and, properly understood, they are not much like them. They are not inspectable entities that we can assess from the outside and trade in and out of our lives. We do not really command them. They often transform us. Most of us know this when it comes to the very big ideas that govern our lives, ideas about (say) fairness, helping others or being true to who we are. These kinds of ideas, the kinds that tend to be bound up in our political judgements, are not mere rational propositions. They are only made fully comprehensible and 'real' when we live them out, day to day. Consider what it means to experience romantic or parental love, for example: much of that cannot be understood without living it. Or we may only feel that we 'get' what depression means, or what perseverance requires, when we have been through real difficulty. So it is too when we try to explain what it means not to have control over one's working hours, to experience sexual harassment, to be the target of political violence. One can be biased 'from the inside' too, but a solely outside perspective on many political issues is simply too far away to grant one understanding.

The fact that ideas often have to be lived to be understood is perhaps yet another reason why people strongly resist efforts to change their minds. Studies show that, faced with a series of arguments for a different view, people often experience 'reactance': an unpleasant motivational state that occurs when people encounter a threat to their free behaviour. In other words, reactance is our allergic reaction to the sense that someone else is limiting or controlling us, trying to steer our ideas away from the way we already experience the world, or limit our ability to make up our minds for ourselves. The strength of reactance is one reason why, as journalist David McRaney puts it when summarizing the best research on the topic, 'all persuasion is *self*-persuasion': when people do change their minds, it is generally because they have avoided any attempts by others (which they will view as coercion) and instead altered their views according to what they see as their own reasons, reasons that accord with their own perceived interests or metrics.[30] We are not blank slates, open to easy inscription by others. We experience ideas by encountering their realities ourselves, and resist the approaches of new ideas when they come from others with some good reason – we want to maintain our autonomy and think according to what we have deeply felt.

For all these reasons, political reasoning is not and generally cannot be the same type of reasoning as that involved in purchasing goods. The 'marketplace of ideas' that is so often put forth as a force for good is, in fact, full of relatively close-minded consumers, starting from their own situated positions, averse to any obvious attempts to change their minds and often just filling their shopping carts with the same thing again and again. More than this, in some ways we are the product of ideas, rather than ideas being products we can purchase. For we are first shaped by the world and then select ideas accordingly; we do not choose from a neutral position.

Even the liberal economists of the 1950s, the great proponents of the marketplace, weren't convinced that people could be good consumers of ideas in the same way they could be consumers of, say, microwaves. They thought that, when it came to politics, people were too influenced by their culture, social circle, personal biases and own interests to ever recognize the 'best' ideas (which, as you can imagine, they thought were theirs).[31] And in our current age, more and more people have become sceptical too. The *Financial Times* is a newspaper founded to support markets, but its columnist Stephen Bush agrees that the 'marketplace of ideas' just doesn't work: '[t]here are numerous problems with this. The biggest is that all the data we have suggests that people do not treat ideas in the same way they do other goods ... most of us do look out for information that validates our previously held opinions.'[32] The best freedom of speech can offer, Bush notes, is the right to dissent – as for people coming round to 'the right' ideas, people are only likely to change their views about a policy after it has been implemented and they have tried the ideas out in practice.

The most interesting question here is perhaps not why the 'marketplace of ideas' or reasoning-as-commerce are poor models, but why the model of reasoning they present has persisted in the structure of public understanding all the same. One reason for this myth's appeal and persistence may be that the 'marketplace of ideas' fits in with the ideals that make many middle-class people feel better about their lives and especially about the work they spend their lives doing, work that is done with the mind more than the body. This work is in practice frequently boring, logistical, over-supervised and under-inspiring (as so many going to work on a Monday morning can tell you). But believing that generating words and similar intellectual forms of labour is the most powerful thing one can do grants those of us who hunch over laptops a bit of cultural value and status. The idea of a functioning 'marketplace of ideas' may help us think that we meaningfully contribute to politics and the world in the kind of work we do, whether or not that is true. The myth of a well-functioning 'marketplace of ideas' also fits with many of our culturally popular professional aspirations. Doesn't every start-up story begin with a good idea? Isn't every best-seller premised on one? Even as the middle class is in many ways declining across the West, owing to rising inequality, the ideal involved in a middle-class idea of success probably lingers on, even for those who cannot achieve it.[33] In other words, it might be hard for us to move on from the logic of the 'marketplace of ideas' because doing so involves abandoning a common intuitive sense of what is valuable and desirable not only for society but also for ourselves.

There are other sacred cows at risk too. The assertion that ideas are not enough is hard for liberals because it clashes with some of their closest intuitions about free speech leading to free societies. It makes conservatives worry that private or, at least, limited institutions such as the family, church and education system are not sufficient to support people in thinking well, nervous that someone will suggest that further government intervention is required. Many left-leaning people feel discouraged hearing about all this because they harbour the hope (sometimes only half-consciously) that, if they just explain oppression clearly enough, people will be motivated to overthrow it. Realising that the logic involved in political belief and the logic involved in shopping are different forces us all to reconsider the claim, frequently made by those in favour of capitalism, that democracy and capitalism rely on each other and go hand in hand. Others worry that to deny that a 'marketplace of ideas' works in the realm of politics is an attack on intellectual life as a whole, or even an attack on science.

Yet science involves one kind of truth: factual statements about the world (however politically relevant). Politics, in contrast, involves other, trickier forms of assertions, assertions about what is right, good, just or desirable. To say that human beings think about these aspects of politics in a particular and particularly tricky way in no way suggests that we should not engage in scientific thinking when it comes to science.[34] Nor does it mean we cannot ever accept new intellectual ideas. It's just that political ideas may come with their own particular challenge: they are so profoundly tied to our sense of self, belonging and agency that simply considering ideas in the abstract rarely leads to profound changes in belief.

That's not to say that there's nothing to be said for this idea about the exchange of ideas happening via a marketplace. There are probably limited circumstances in which this is the right metaphor for what is desirable or at stake. It is, after all, good to resist censorship, all other things being equal, and the marketplace generally brings to mind an open forum, where anyone can, at least theoretically, bring anything to sell or buy. It's also meaningful that marketplaces are generally peaceful places where all parties look for something that will benefit them, which suggests an aspiration for the public sphere where the exchange of ideas can happen without violence, and sometimes even to everyone's mutual advantage. That is a nice goal, whether or not it is true of any literal or metaphorical marketplace in our current age. A 'marketplace' for ideas is a metaphor about 'frictionless' competition, as my friend the political theorist Shai Agmon puts it – where ideas win not simply by attacking other ideas but by having merits in their own right.[35] And while that may not always be how ideas work or how ideas win, in an age of digital screaming and the breakdown of social trust it is still a nice thought that we might try to build spaces where ideas compete without merely descending into mutual attack mode. In other words, the marketplace is largely useful when it points us in the direction of certain goals for people's behaviour, should they choose to engage in discourse: relatively peaceful exchange and a lack of censorship.

And, sure, 'marketplaces' in the sense of open fora for exchange and the generation of many points of view might yet be beneficial in limited ways, with the right supports and infrastructure in place, and we should continue to enable these for that reason (also because censorship is annoying and morally odious). Though I'd suggest it is rare, sometimes people do not yet have entrenched sets of beliefs and identity tied to a particular political issue, and they can then possibly be persuaded. I wonder whether houses becoming uninsurable during climate change might, for example, be such a subject, where traditional political affiliations do not yet provide an automatic response for people on either 'right' or 'left'. After all, it combines issues of the state and private property, as well as environmental damage and who is responsible for it. Sometimes, despite everything written here, the marketplace of ideas does provide a genuinely new idea for policymakers to try. Sometimes the marketplace even serves as an exchange of ideas that leads to the creation of social movements. As a general mechanism for political change, however, there are significant reasons why simply generating and dispersing ideas into a 'marketplace' of consumers is not very effective, and can often be counterproductive. A great deal else is also needed for humans to think well and make good ideas powerful in the world, individually and together, especially when it comes to political and social issues.

The metaphor of the marketplace of ideas, as it has been used in law, and also as it has seeped into our public consciousness, similarly obscures the power relations involved in politics and political thinking and communication. Many of the gains of the long arc of history are to do not just with exposure to new ideas but also with fearsome generations-long social struggles, from the feminist movement to the gay rights movement. Some of their efforts involved persuasion-via-dissemination, of course, but other efforts included protest, property destruction and the use of new technologies such as the birth control pill. In other words, the changes can hardly be attributed to a 'marketplace of ideas' on its own, and in some cases cannot really be traced to that kind of structure at all. And in the meantime, the idea that ideas win on their own can cover a myriad of other sins – providing legitimacy to those in power, and perhaps distracting those who want a more just world from fighting for it in other ways.

So we must reject the metaphor of public life as a 'marketplace', and understand politics differently. To do this, we first have to overcome our own sometimes faulty intuitions about what reasoning really is, and cease imagining it as a form of commerce or marketplace exchange, rejecting the myth of a marketplace of ideas now deeply imbued in our cultural sensibilities. We need to stop thinking that talking about politics is the same thing as truly engaging in it, because all the evidence suggests that simply presenting one another with ideas changes very little. Instead, doing politics means taking new actions and building relationships – as I shall demonstrate throughout the rest of this book. One day, I hope, we will have a different set of cultural sensibilities about what it means to think well about politics (one I shall try to outline in this book). If that ever happens, I suspect we will look back at the idea that taking in new ideas is anything like buying commodities with curiosity and disbelief. The idea that we might individually go and 'buy' an idea after simply hearing it once, without further interaction, without rearranging our life or our relationships, will seem as curious and implausible as the idea that we might individually choose to purchase the MALM, JSOW and HARM system. We both should and must reason very differently when it comes to making decisions about the most important questions we face together.

2

Don't Debate It

On both sides of the Atlantic a curious trend has emerged over the last few years: politicians are dropping out of debates. Admittedly, that might not be the first thing you remember about debates in recent history. That will probably be ex-President Joe Biden dropping out of the US presidential election after appearing, well, old when debating President Donald Trump. But perhaps that excruciating moment tells us something about why politicians across the country and even around the world have been dodging debates in remarkable ways, left, right and centre. Trump refused to engage in any of the Republican primary debates. Then his rival Nikki Haley refused to attend any either, and soon those televised debates were entirely cancelled.[1] The Brookings Institution, a centre-right think tank in the United States, reports that the number of debates in competitive US Senate races declined in the years between 2010 and 2022.[2]

Meanwhile, across the ocean, dropping out of debates is hardly foreign to the UK political scene either. In Britain, during the September 2022 Conservative Party leadership contest, candidates (including the two front-runners, Liz

Truss and Rishi Sunak) pulled out of the last round without providing much in the way of explanation.[3]

Refusing to debate is not – shall we say? – a great look. It might suggest a lack of confidence in one's ideas or an inability to perform under pressure. Yet today politicians are turning away from debate in a way that would once have been suicidal and sacrilegious. The question is, why? Before we can figure that out, we need to ask why we expect them to debate at all. It is, after all, possible to imagine a world where politicians could present their ideas without attacking each other. (The nerd in me wonders: perhaps they could simply compare policy positions with charts?)

Advocates of debate argue that rigorous conflict helps us to rebut false claims, policies and ideas so that we can decide what to believe. In this way, debate is understood essentially as a wrestling competition between ideas.

For the last half a century or so, debate has appeared to deliver on this democratic ideal, or at least to wield powerful influence. In the US, the history of modern political debate arguably began with the televised debate between John F. Kennedy and Richard Nixon in September 1960. Analysis of this usually focuses on how Nixon's failure to look good – he had lost a lot of weight, owing to health problems, wore bad make-up and generally lacked telegenic qualities – propelled Kennedy to an unexpected victory.[4] At the time, these televised debates seemed incredibly persuasive: half of all voters said they were influenced by what they'd seen, and 6 per cent of voters claimed the debate had been the decisive factor in their choice.[5]

Afterwards, politicians were increasingly expected to debate one another on live television if they wanted to have a chance of winning an election. It became a standard, vital process in the US. Larry Sabato, director of the Center for Politics at the University of Virginia, nostalgically notes: 'I watched all four of the Kennedy–Nixon debates and you could hear a pin drop anywhere you went. Everybody was watching. In fact, over 70 million watched and the number of votes that year? 70 million.'[6] Televised debates slowly spread around the world. Germany and Canada got theirs in the 1960s, and France in the 1970s. (In Germany, the term for the debate between party leaders is, delightfully, *Elefantenrunde*, or 'Elephants' round table', to reflect the weightiness of the people in the room.[7]) Mexico had its first in the 1990s and, oddly, perhaps because of the long tradition of parliamentary debate, televised leaders' debates only hit the UK in 2010. It's now a tradition in most major democracies.

Debates grew and grew, and so did the implicit assumption that they mattered and changed people's minds. Then, in 2019, researchers Caroline le Pennec and Vincent Pons analysed the effects of 56 TV debates on 31 elections in the US, Canada, New Zealand and Europe from 1952 to 2017.[8] The study tracked nearly 100,000 respondents day by day to see when people made their final choices, looking at whether debates helped undecided voters change their minds or caused decided voters to switch teams. Pons and Le Pennec found no evidence for either. 'I was surprised,' Pons admitted. 'If you look at the numbers of people watching TV debates and all the media attention around debates, you would think debates matter.'[9] In 2012 reporter Dylan Matthews ran an analysis for the *Washington Post* about whether debates influenced election outcomes, drawing on several studies done by a variety of political scientists. As he put it, 'In short, the effects of debates on eventual votes are likely mild, and, in most cases, effectively nil. Moreover, what effects do exist are often caused by factors wholly beyond the candidates' control, like media coverage, attractiveness, and whether voters are watching a Nats [baseball] game in the other panel of their TV.[10] The Nixon–Kennedy debate threw us off. Perhaps it was just more influential than most debates, or it only appeared influential because it was a novelty. Perhaps people even overestimated how much it changed their views but, whatever the reason, overall, debates do not appear to change people's minds.

In fact, even after Biden's disastrous debate performance, voter preferences did not appear to be seriously affected.[11] So why don't the vast majority of debates change minds? We can look to psychology research for some probable reasons. First, our minds crave consistency, especially about our sense of self, which means that we often experience painful cognitive dissonance when we consider new ideas that might make us change our mind. Although we might entertain these new ideas briefly, if they contradict our daily actions (going to church, going to work, driving a gas-guzzling car, having the group of friends that we have) we face acute psychological discomfort until we resolve our beliefs one way or the other – usually in line with whatever matches our lifestyle and the views of our social world. This means that whether we're watching debates or reading arguments against a point of view we hold, we work quickly to rationalize away the arguments and evidence on the other side. We're also likely to distrust sources that contradict our beliefs, while selectively trusting the sources that favour our own views more – what psychologists term 'confirmation bias'.[12] Much of what is happening during debate is less a process of seeking truth and more a process of finding reasons to fit our existing motivation. With this in mind, we should question whether debate is really a form of reasoning at all.

There are other ways in which debates are likely to trip us up psychologically. Much of what 'debate' and 'opinion pieces' do is collapse ambiguities and complexities as they argue for one single side of an issue, rather than helping people conduct the difficult work of grappling with nuance and contradiction. As so many psychological studies demonstrate, people are already inclined to avoid complexity as they get overwhelmed by ambiguity and decision-making, and would much rather artificially make up their mind than stay in the discomfort of uncertainty. Disagreement often leads to painful yet almost addictive conflict. (Analysis shows that online debates make toxic sentiment even more likely.[13]) Given all that, it's easy to imagine how all these tendencies might make debates an ineffective, even counterproductive, way of convincing people to change their minds or accept new ideas.

Even when one isn't running for president, then, debate can be a trap. Donna Zuckerberg, a writer and classicist (who also happens to be Mark Zuckerberg's sister!), noted in an op-ed that she is sometimes hounded by men demanding that she debate them about her claims about the relationship between the far right and the use, and misuse, of Greek and Roman classics. As Zuckerberg points out, what these men want is rarely a true exchange of ideas, least of all from her. 'I've gotten my fair share of "debate me" challenges,' she noted:

> For the most part, the kind of debate these men are asking for isn't a conversation – an exercise in which people generously try to understand each other's point of view. A real conversation doesn't have a 'winner.' ... If I got angry or flustered in a debate, then I would lose by virtue of being emotional and irrational. If I used jokes or sarcasm, I'd lose by virtue of seeming flippant and smug. If I did take the debate seriously and even briefly entertained the points made by my opponent, I would seem conciliatory and weak. And no matter what, my

opponent will have gotten my attention and sucked up my time. The only winning move is not to play.¹⁴

The journalist Miles Klee calls the person who uses this to their advantage the 'debate me' guy, and notes that if you refuse to engage, this too will be taken as an admission of defeat (though at least you won't have wasted your time).* At this point 'debate' is often used as a demand for political theatre, where the demand itself is a form of aggression.

If the 'marketplace of ideas' is meant to be a 'frictionless' form of competition, as described in the last chapter, debate is 'friction-full': opponents take aim at each other. Indeed, fighting and war metaphors abound in our culture when it comes to politics: people 'take aim', 'slam' each other and 'fight back'; they 'gain ground' and sometimes even 'break ranks'. It is reasoning-as-war, and it often seems just as fruitless and destructive as wars can be.

Some commentators, however, have suggested that politicians are avoiding debates precisely because debates *are* effective. David Knight Legg, former political adviser to Canadian politician Jason Kenney and chair of Intelligence Squared, an online and events-based debate platform, wrote an op-ed

---

*Men on the far right seem to have made a special sport of demanding that people debate them: union buster Dave Portnoy demanded that Alexandria Ocasio-Cortez debate him when she criticized his labour practices, and Ben Shapiro even offered her $10,000 for the same (though he has himself turned down debate requests). She refused in both cases, and likened the 'debate-me' challenge to a catcall, unworthy of response. Miles Klee (2024), 'Debate Me, Dudes: Ben Shapiro vs. Alexandria Ocasio-Cortez', *Mel Magazine*, available at: melmagazine.com/en-us/story/debate-me-dudes-ben-shapiro-ocasio-cortez (accessed 13 October 2024).

for *Politico* arguing that debates should be legally mandated because they level the playing field between candidates with very different budgets, disrupt targeted messaging and wreck candidates' carefully constructed images.[15] Don't get me wrong – in many ways, I would love for something as simple as mandated debate to have a profound effect like this. But, as the social-scientific studies cited above demonstrate, historically, debates do not appear to have altered election results.

When broken down via statistics and long-term studies, debates do not seem to help candidates win. Moreover, if they have any significant effect at all it is simply to make people dislike their own candidates, even as they remain on their own 'side'. For example, when Truss and Sunak declined the last debate in 2022, the UK TV channel Sky News put out a statement that read: 'Conservative MPs are said to be concerned about the damage the debates are doing to the image of the Conservative party, exposing disagreements and splits within the party.'[16] It is this analysis that demonstrates the trade-off politicians feel they face when engaging in debate: they do not see an opportunity to win round undecided voters or those who might disagree, but they do see the risk of demotivating those who already roughly agree with them by looking stupid. If one debates well, one motivates one's base to vote (which is not the same as persuading the undecided!); if one debates poorly, one demotivates them. In a sense, then, some politicians are afraid of the outcome of debates – not because debates are effective at changing elections outcomes but because they can affect future enthusiasm among their own base.

This risk is very real. For most politicians, the more they speak, the less we like them. After Liz Truss began to be frequently profiled on television and radio, her popularity among members of her own party took a serious dive. Polls found that in just one month voters had come to see her as less principled, competent, trustworthy, likeable and in touch (among other things). The proportion of the electorate that saw her as competent dropped from 55 per cent to 35 per cent, and those that saw her as likeable dropped from 52 per cent to 31 per cent.[17] Truss may be exceptionally unlikeable for many, but this trend holds for most politicians; for example, over the course of his two terms Obama's approval ratings dipped from 76 per cent to 37 per cent.[18] All US presidents see declines in their approval ratings shortly after they enter office. The more the public sees politicians, the less they like them. Indeed this has been especially true lately. While in 1944 one third of British people saw politicians as 'out for themselves', in 2014 half of all Brits did, and in 2021 that number had risen to nearly two-thirds.[19] Overall, debates are often seen as something that can only really 'hurt you'. One Republican adviser happily told the *Washington Post* that he usually tells his clients to skip them, as they're a waste of time: 'You could be doing a Facebook live. You could be raising money. You could be door-knocking.'[20]

With this in mind, maybe those who defect from debates aren't chickens after all. Perhaps they are being strategic, aware that riling up their base is more effective than trying to speak to the other side (which, unfortunately, seems to be true no matter what views you're trying to get across). They already know that, for most people, debate is not a very effective method of coming to better political conclusions. It does not change minds or help the undecided decide, especially not on the strength of better arguments. Sure, Trump and other debate-dodgers are disengaging in part because there's less of a general sense of accountability in our current mediasphere, but they're also able to do this because these debates don't change minds. Debate-dodgers are motivated not just by the fact that debating would show their weakness to anyone who would otherwise vote for them but also by the belief that it is a waste of political capital and of their time.

Rather than wringing our hands over debate's demise, we should seize the opportunity to rethink our assumptions about what makes for good political conversation. This won't be easy, however. Even if politicians are leaving debate behind, it has already worked its way into the very fabric of how we think.

We now live in a society overrun with debates. Any time there is a political conflict or disagreement it is put up, formally or informally, for debate. Even for issues that might not obviously fit the format, 'debate' creeps in. There are fake media debates over which celebrities one should favour, which products one should buy, whether pineapple should be eaten on pizza, what colour that internet dress is and whether aliens exist. This on its own is all just rather silly, but the insistence on debate extends into political issues as well, even when they are poorly suited to that format. If house prices go up or down, if a minority group wants to live a seemingly peculiar way, if a celebrity does something odd, our media will not only discuss it but will frame it as a two-sided issue and find a way to make it into a debate between opposing viewpoints. The linguist Deborah Tannen believes that Western society in general, and the US in particular, is now in the grips of an 'argument culture':

> The argument culture urges us to approach the world – and the people in it – in an adversarial frame of mind. It rests on the assumption that opposition is the best way to get anything done: The best way to discuss an idea is to set up a debate; the best way to cover news is to find spokespeople who express the most extreme,

polarized views and present them as 'both sides'; the best way to settle disputes is litigation that pits one party against the other; the best way to begin an essay is to attack someone; and the best way to show you're really thinking is to criticize.[21]

Debate culture (or argument culture, if you like) has meant that our de facto sense of what it means to engage in politics is to immediately have a strong, combative opinion whenever asked. Even for politicians this is a difficult task, given that there are so many political issues and each of them can be quite complex. Yet woe to the politician who changes their mind, or does not have an immediate response for a reporter! Lately, perhaps owing to the use of social media and the sudden visibility of others' views, it also feels as though this sort of scrutiny has come to bear on all of us, that we should all already have an opinion about any issue.

I think about this odd aspect of our culture regularly because it has sometimes been my job to inhabit it. While working for a global organization called the School of Life, which offers a philosophical take on life's key questions and moments, I fell into the role of being one of the people who often answered the call from journalists and pundits to speak on key issues. As a result, I have spoken many times on public radio shows and podcasts whose format is almost always, either explicitly or implicitly, a debate. Perhaps the most insidious part of this format is the extent to which we are encouraged to put things in black-and-white, artificially exaggerating the degree of conflict and opposition. I can confirm from my own and others' experiences that it's common to be asked, when preparing for public-facing media shows, to find a disagreement with the other experts on the panel. Sometimes this is challenging, as in many cases the experts might mostly agree on most things but feel themselves pressured into picking an exaggerated position, knowing it is what the programmers, and presumably many viewers, want to hear. Too often debates are a painful simplification and compression of reality.

These conflict-driven formats are not like this by accident. Debates drive viewership and ratings by tapping into our psychological tendency to pay close attention to conflict. Many studies suggest that our brains focus instantly on negative information. We're attracted to debates as spectacle for this reason: we like watching conflict and drama, even though we are rarely influenced by them when it comes to our personal beliefs. One study, run by researcher Dr Tiffany Ito and her colleagues at Ohio State University, found this was true for videos, pictures or text – pretty much any form of media.[22] Compared with a more moderate reaction to positive media, the brain's electrical activity was far higher, suggesting that negative information had a far greater effect on the person's mind. Another study, measuring other physiological reactions, found that the same was especially true, across six continents and 17 countries, when people consumed the news.[23] We find human conflict stimulating, whether it's to do with Parliament, the office drama, a football match or the in-laws at Christmas. Framing a political question as a 'debate', where two sides are actively opposed and one side should win, is a good (if sometimes cheap) way to grab, and retain, viewers' attention.

The conflict of debate is not only attention-grabbing; it is, in effect, replacing a much older form of political conflict. For much of human history politics has been, without pretence, about war. Not just a war between ideas, as our modern democracies appear to be, but the literal destruction of life and limb and rape and pillage and starvation. Even in times of peace much of politics was still about war: class structures were held in place by the threat of war, alliances and strategic marriages were arranged to prevent war and governments held their legitimacy because of their ability to respond to the threat of war. It is perhaps understandable, then, that much of political discourse today operates implicitly like war. The logic of this reasoning-as-war is to win without spilling blood, because your ideas are better: Jürgen Habermas famously encapsulated this by suggesting that the ideal form of political reasoning is in essence a bloodless replacement for war, where one side triumphs due to the 'forceless force of the better argument'.[24] The emphasis is not just on convincing others but on *beating* them by proving the other side wrong definitively, vanquishing them with a counterargument, showing, with great force, not just why your views are better but also why theirs are wrong.

A great deal of our cultural life is implicitly built on this model of political reasoning. Despite many poorly staged and framed debates, these moments of public confrontation are often viewed as a moment of truth for political campaigns, especially when broadcast and televised. Our newspapers and magazines are full of what are, essentially, asynchronous debates via opinion pieces – and our social media feeds are full of not just 'hot takes' but 'takedowns', most of which align broadly with this combative form of reasoning where one side takes on another. A common demand is that we should, regarding a particular issue, 'leave it up for debate' or 'open things for debate'. This points to the (in practice, faulty) assumption that debate will reveal the truth. Our minds, primed for conflict, may well pay attention at first, but in the long run the positioning of political reasoning as a win-or-lose conflict obscures nuance, polarizes populations and leads to immense levels of disengagement about some of the most pressing issues of our time.

In the UK, where I live, debate occurs regularly as part of parliamentary process, at a televised session that airs once a week known as 'Prime Minister's Question Time'. Notably, even those prime ministers who have been judged to be 'good' at competing in that spectacle have hated it. Tony Blair called it 'the most nerve-racking, discombobulating, nail-biting, bowel-moving, terror-inspiring, courage-draining experience' during his time as prime minister, and viewed this type of debate as the 'emotional, intellectual and political depository of all that is irrational'. He was the one who cut the sessions from two to one a week, and said he would have preferred to have his teeth drilled for 30 minutes without anaesthetic.[25] Rishi Sunak had his team work on the event all week, and spent every Wednesday morning rehearsing, with an unlucky aide playing the role of the opposition leader, Keir Starmer. If I thought that these debates were holding these politicians to account, I might take a little sinister joy in how much terror they caused; but seeing what little impact they seem to have, I'm left wondering if they're a good use of the public's time and money.

At its worst, debate is a replacement for the kind of long-term engagement by citizens that would be required for democracies to really work. In 2019 the French president, Emmanuel Macron, declared the need for a *Grand Débat* to include the citizens of France in a conversation about how they should implement the kinds of economic reforms that were, in his view, needed for the country to be financially responsible. The process was also, critics suggest, a way of trying to circumvent the demands of the grassroots protest group the *gilets jaunes*, or 'yellow jackets', who wanted financial reforms of the opposite kind and greater direct democracy.[26]

Of course, Macron was not offering the sort of direct democracy demanded by the *gilets jaunes*; his 'debate' was set up on his terms – quite literally, in fact, because early on the impartial committee supposed to handle the debates bowed out owing to squabbles about salaries and questions to be asked, and the government took the process over. Despite this, it went ahead over the course of two months. There were town hall meetings, complaint books, mobile desks, online suggestion boxes, citizens' assemblies arranged by sortition, and four national stakeholders' meetings. Everything was meant to operate according to the values of transparency, pluralism, inclusion, equality, neutrality and respect. As an overeager political theorist, I was curious to see if something could emerge. But, as with many debates, the 'Great Debate' was mostly a bunch of loud voices from a not particularly representative sample of the French population. As one think tank noted, 65 per cent of those who participated were highly educated, and 75 per cent were homeowners, both above the national average.[27] More strikingly, more than two-thirds were over 50, and just 5 per cent were 25 or younger. Most physical meetings were held in large urban centres. The platforms on which much of this discussion happened were also owned by private companies. The infrastructure, design and outcomes of this process were often poor. Rarely were any conclusions reached or documented. There were not nearly enough independent moderators. Attendance, even in the citizens' assemblies, was irregular.

Just as strikingly, not only did the Great Debate fail to produce any widely absorbed new ideas or useful consensus, but it also did not do much in terms of helping the French people's preferences be implemented in practice. As the same think tank put it, 'Specialists of deliberative democracy warn that, for such forums to be successful, precise questions must be asked, adequate time must be afforded to make an informed and detailed opinion, and assurances must be given on the way conclusions feed into an institutional process. The *Grand*

Débat failed to meet any of these three conditions.' Most of the reforms that were widely favoured did not happen, and most people were dissatisfied with the process.[28]

Several years later, little has changed. In one sense, it's tempting to want to cheer on projects such as the Great Debate, which are at least ostensibly ambitious. But without any process of accountability, without appropriate infrastructure and, perhaps most of all, without any way of overcoming some of the psychological and sociological problems that arise when people debate political issues, it's unclear if something like this could have a positive impact. Instead, it seems to have briefly made Macron more popular without leading to any long-term structural changes to French society. (Some even accused Macron of using the process as a way of campaigning for his next term in office.) This is just one, particularly large-scale, particularly French example, but it happens more generally – the presence of 'debate' can whitewash things, making them appear to involve democratic, free and fair discussion, even as real accountability (via policy change) or political progress remains elusive. The underlying struggle for power continues as it would regardless.

———

The modelling of reason as debate, as reasoning-as-war, goes far deeper than our media. It is drilled into us from a young age, starting in school with essay-writing. In secondary school you were probably taught that you should choose a single, authoritative position and defend it, while taking down other points of view. Of course, much of the time in these exercises you might not really have yet developed your own point of view, so you'd have to artificially choose an opinion to defend. And, if the studies on cognitive dissonance described in the previous chapter are right, you'd end up coming to believe what you were arguing for, or at least believing it more. (Which, intriguingly, suggests that asking people to defend an opposing argument, even as an intellectual exercise, may be a way for people to change their minds, a sort of anti-debate process.) In short, being right by showing that others are wrong will probably change your own mind more than anyone else's. Debate's function is to draw the battle lines ever more starkly, so that people must choose a side, and this is not the same thing as thinking clearly about an issue, or developing one's views.

I have myself performed this specific exercise hundreds of times as part of my education, and never felt comfortable with it. My teachers and professors were always asking me to draw things to an ever sharper point, to take more of a stance, to find arguments against my position and rebut them – artificially forming an opinion before I had one. I felt that there might, somehow, be a way of structuring thinking so that it embraced more ambiguity, more uncertainty. (And there is – but it is not commonly taught in my experience.) I also wished for a form of analysis less associated with aggression, as 'argument' often is. (And this does exist but, again, it is not commonly taught.) Classrooms can often involve a good deal of fruitless conflictual arguments; I still think frequently about a particular seminar where our professor (an exceptionally kind, timid man) asked us to read and then discuss the section of Hegel's *Phenomenology of Spirit* about the family unit. I was one of only two women in the room, so I decided it was on me to point out the possible feminist objections to this concept of the family. (Among other things, Hegel assigns rather different roles to men and women.) At that point an outspoken German man interrupted and suggested that my frustration was a woke twenty-first-century phenomenon. I responded by pointing out that Lou Andreas-Salomé, a nineteenth-century intellectual (and my historical crush), had agreed with me. When the German student said that she was only really known for her relationships with famous men, I accused him of being blinded by a slut-shaming line of logic. As you can imagine, things only got louder and less productive from there. The whole episode was a particularly asinine exchange, but I still remember it all these years later because, in truth, a great deal of my education felt like a version of that argument, albeit usually less frustrating. I was constantly being asked to find ways to intensify my disagreements with others, rather than find areas of overlap, fruitful comparison, mutual understanding or nuance.

None of this is what good communication or reasoning should look like, of course. But even those who find the warlike nature of debate uncomfortable are trained in higher education to argue more or less constantly. I was a diligent student. I liked to write footnotes and do extra credit activities. Yet I could not stomach the process of taking all the fascinating things I was learning about the world and condensing them into weapons to be used against another point of view. In a classroom with much louder men I increasingly avoided this – Hegel-driven outbursts aside. Even now, some part of me retains a suspicion that debate is often a form of coercion.

Many people who are more marginalized than I with respect to class, race or gender face this issue far more acutely. After all, who really gets to be part of an ideal 'debate'? In the classroom (as in the courtroom, TV studio, Parliament and more) the answer is usually those who are already likely to be listened to. In this way, reasoning is indeed like war, but to its detriment – those who already have an upper hand will continue to accrue strategic advantages. When it comes to the public stage, debates are often set up by those already in power to keep things that way while crafting the appearance of space for dissent.

The aggression that often comes with argumentation and debate did prevent me from thinking as well, or seeing as well, or learning as well, as I might. I am hardly alone. If we wish to bring more people around to thinking through ideas, an entirely different format may be needed.

Reasoning-as-war and debate are appealing for many of the exact same reasons that they are troubling – they are likely to catch our imaginations but they alienate us in the long run. 'Look at my opponents,' the debater says on the floor of congress or Parliament or to the television interviewer, 'look how weak, wrong, unethical, hypocritical, pathetic they are.' And the spectators enjoy watching those they disagree with being put in their place. People who share clips of debate on social media are often speaking not to accounts who might disagree with them but to those who want to see just how right they are. None of this leads to anyone thinking about whether they should change their views; it mainly leads to the quiet, smug enjoyment of being right (and scorning the 'other' side). This tendency chimes with the idea that people do in fact look for arguments that oppose their own opinions, but they do so in order to unpick them.

However compelling they are to watch and even read, if a debate is badly framed, the 'battle' for a better way of thinking may already be lost. George Lakoff, a cognitive theorist long known for his work on 'framing' questions, points out that, if we use a particular frame for an issue, we reinforce it in the minds of those listening and often make it difficult to then see the issue any other way. In the Bush era, for example, even progressive politicians found themselves using the language of 'tax relief', and with it reinforcing the idea that taxes are primarily a burden from which people must seek relief.[29] A debate on 'tax relief' is already, in this sense, far from a fair or neutral way of asking the question of how resources should be distributed in society. Debating whether it is 'fair' to tax rich people more may frame an issue as a matter of undue burden when it might instead be better understood as a matter of shared investment. Similarly, asking about whether we should repay student loans is important, but may distract us from the question of why higher education isn't state-funded in the first place. As writer Shon Faye points out, endless sweat and ink are spilled over a few transgender swimmers or the rare case of a transgender person in a prison or domestic violence shelter, whereas the most pressing issues facing transgender people are lack of employment, healthcare and housing – all issues that are hardly specific to trans people and are indeed crucial for cis women in particular, whose well-being is often held up as a reason for denying trans people recognition or inclusion.[30] So many of our most common debates are not set up to help us access alternative solutions or shift our systematic thinking about issues – instead, they reinforce the same conflict ad nauseam.

A particularly deadly example of this problem has developed in recent years in the debate over how to price medicines. In the US patients often cannot afford insulin and die as a result; in the Netherlands, a key cancer drug, Keytruda, is too expensive for the government, even though the government helped develop it. In England, similarly, the NHS cannot afford a drug for cystic fibrosis, Orkambi. As the pharmaceutical policy expert Melissa Barber puts it, these debates about whether and how to regulate drug prices are framed as 'either "should we kill innovation" or "should we kill patients who can't afford crucial medications"'. We have spiralled into wildly unhelpful false binaries in part because of the constant framing of the issue as a two-sided 'debate', which plays out not only in individual countries but also at international meetings held by the World Health Organization (WHO) and World Trade Organization (WTO), which debate the best policies every year.

The stakes of 'debate' over the cost of pharmaceuticals, as it has been constructed, with innovation pitted against poor people, entails (and results in) the sacrifice of human lives. But it shouldn't have to. As Barber points out, 'how many people is it OK to die to get innovation' is an obscene, deranged way of thinking about this complicated and crucial question. Instead, she believes, 'the correct policy frame is: "it's a terrible idea to have research and development paid for by having some people die because they can't afford their medicines; we should do something different."'[31]

Of course, some advocates for affordable medicine do attempt to reframe this debate, but the framework of debate – two-sided, each side asked to disprove the other rather than concede or collaborate – itself makes it harder to point people towards the idea that innovation is not inherently at odds with poor people having access to affordable medication. And while this may seem like a niche issue now, if medicine prices continue to rise it may not stay that way.

It's also true that debates are often set up only for a very specific audience. As the reporter Thomas Baerthlein put it, 'There is no functional European public sphere.' If there were one, when it came to the Euro crisis and Greece, it 'would for example mean that Greek and German politicians, economists and ordinary citizens would have been able to discuss their differences of opinion about austerity on a joint, unbiased platform such as one TV debate watched in both countries'.[32] Sometimes people tell me that they dream of a wider sense of debate – one that really means collective problem-solving by being willing to entertain multiple points of view on a problem.

It sounds nice, but it would require a great deal of repackaging of problems and reshaping of audiences. It's not obvious that the term 'debate' would even have much to do with the end product of such a radical transformation. In other words, by the time you've fixed all these problems with debate, you've probably got something else altogether on your hands.

Setting up debates can also serve to artificially inflate the importance of issues that are not really worthy of consideration. Indeed, some political theorists have argued that Brexit only became an issue in the mind of the British public because of a series of highly choreographed 'debates'. As one particularly acerbic academic, Raymond Geuss, put it in 2019:

> ten years ago no one, except a handful of fanatics, had any real interest in discussing relations with the EU; they were not on the table, and nothing was any the worse for that. It is only the discussion of the last four years, stoked by a few newspaper owners (many of them not domiciled in the UK at all), a small group of wealthy leftover Thatcherites and some opportunistic political chancers, that generated any interest in the subject at all.[33]

Whatever one thinks of Brexit, it is true that sometimes discourse is created to legitimize and popularize issues that were not originally of obvious importance to anyone else, and that while this could in theory mean that people become more concerned about meaningful problems, it can also mean that they fixate on the wrong thing.

Brexit is also a good case study for how debates can often make issues look more 'even' than they might be. As Emily Maitlis, a former newsreader for the BBC, put it, 'It might take our producers five minutes to find 60 economists who feared Brexit and five hours to find a sole voice who espoused it ...

But by the time we went on air we simply had one of each; we presented this unequal effort to our audience as balance. It wasn't.'[34] In a similar vein, and in more or less bad faith, there are still 'debates' set up about climate change happening, despite widespread scientific consensus. As the science writer and academic Ben Goldacre put it after being asked to speak on the Australian television show *I Can Change Your Mind about ... Climate*, 'I'd rather slam my cock in a door than debate climate change.'[35] On shows like this, Goldacre noted, someone with the weaker scientific argument (in this case a conservative Australian MP) can appear just as strong as someone with the science, precisely because of the two-sided, debate-like format:

> You [the denier] will win every time. You can cherry pick data and there'll be no time to point out the flaws, you can pull out dodgy science and there will be no time to point that out. You can pull out arguments that have already been resolved. You can find one of those [arguments] that the person you're arguing with hasn't heard of and then it will be next Tuesday by the time you have gone off to research it.[36]

Debates can not only make two unequal sides appear equal, but they can also make the 'centre' (or whatever position lies between these artificial poles) appear to be common sense and the obvious solution, even when it isn't. This in turn means that posturing as a centrist can be used in all kinds of potentially nefarious ways. The writer Aaron Huertas describes the trend of 'reactionary centrism', where a reactionary centrist is someone who 'says they're politically neutral, but who usually punches left while sympathizing with the right'.[37] This stance is often taken up by pundits who reject views to both the left and right of themselves, thus describing themselves as neutral, 'reasonable' referees.

Of course, if one has constructed the debate, it's not hard to position oneself as the 'middle' by choosing two 'sides' that are not, in any way, commensurate: it may not be a reasonable compromise, for example, to take a position somewhere between that of an oil and gas executive and a climate change activist. In fact, a climate denier (or these days, more commonly, a 'delayer') has a position that is so radical that this skews the middle ground towards a position which may endanger all life on this planet. In other words, debate often obscures complex power dynamics, and what is 'right' is not always something we can arrive at like Goldilocks. For instance, the only rational response to the climate crisis may be a radical and collective shift in nearly every part of society. 'Debating' whether climate change is real or serious or whether it can be affordably addressed is, from this perspective, itself a distortion of reality. Debate can also be harmful by legitimizing views that in truth should have no real purchase in public life. Nearly the only way to debate something such as 'race science' is to platform the views of racists and spread them, while normalizing extremism. It is similarly undesirable that we should have a 'moderate' amount of human rights.

More than this, debate and reasoning-as-war mistake what it means for people to be more perceptive, open-minded and imaginative in the way they think about politics. To understand political reasoning primarily as a process of war obscures the way that politics may often be about questions where there is no single, correct, persuasive, knockdown argument that allows one side to win. Many political conflicts are intractable because they involve genuinely incompatible sets of human interests, which can realistically only be addressed through compromise or sheer power.

This is why some theorists see the process of politics as largely agonistic: about a struggle for power, not a struggle to be 'right'.[38] For example, if I want to live in a specific peaceful small town and you want the country to finally have high-speed rail, these two desires may be impossible to reconcile if the rail needs to run through my town. No amount of reasoning with the other person is going to bring them around, and indeed it is not obvious that anyone is 'right' in some abstract, provable, logical sense. We cannot defeat each other with reasons; we are simply at odds. Agonistic political theorists see a great deal of political struggle this way, especially when it comes to class interests. It is not in the obvious interests of those who run large companies to pay their employees more, nor is it in the interests of landlords to lower the rent. And no amount of reasoning is going to bring about more than the most moderate of compromises. Hence the historical need to struggle for power instead, from the strike to the guillotine. In cases such as these, those we appear to disagree with are not exactly mistaken; they are (simply put) our adversaries. They want something different from what we want, not because they are 'wrong' logically and we are 'right', but because it is possible for different groups of people in society to have genuinely opposing interests.

Of course, there are potential problems with the logic of agonistic politics as well. Relying on it too heavily may mean that one misses areas where reasoning can lead to beneficial compromises or to new solutions that are actually better for everyone. It constrains our way of thinking about certain issues, as in the reasoning-as-war model, making it difficult to imagine handling political problems through collaboration, innovation, systemic change or compromise. But there are issues where it is the most accurate model of what people want and of what is possible.

In many political questions there may not be a single right answer, and indeed it may be fruitless to imagine that one side can defeat the other with reason. A good deal of politics still works more like actual war, rather than war as a metaphor: we defeat one another not with reasons and rebuttals but with a show of force. And an even more cynical person would say that debates only make it appear as though we have moved beyond fundamental struggles of power, giving false legitimacy to a process that in fact comes down to how many people and resources you can marshal to your side. It teaches people to focus their thinking on a practice that conveniently does very little to challenge the status quo.

What is the debate you've been wanting to win your whole life? Sometimes, in the courses I teach for activists and organizers (with my colleague Max Haiven) we ask this question. Everyone in the room has an answer, usually straight away. Most often, it's a debate with a family member they've been struggling with for near-Freudian reasons. Sometimes it's an ex or a former friend or a teacher or mentor. Almost everyone has at one point shared the same hope that one day, if they could just get this person to listen, they could finally change their mind.

Behind the political ideal of debate I sometimes catch glimpses of a deeply held fantasy that one really good conversation can set things right. Sometimes, especially among my nerdier, more scholarly workshop participants and friends, this dream is all the more powerful because it enlists a sense of personal competence: *I'm really good at convincing people, maybe I can solve this thing if I just take the right approach.* This is unlikely. It's a beautiful fantasy, but it is still a fantasy. It's not how political change works, and it's also probably not how our own lives will go.

In our workshops we try to suggest that we have to move beyond attempting to convince the people we emotionally long to convince (our uncle who is so wrong, or that childhood friend that it hurts to differ from). Instead we should look for people who are persuadable – if we want to engage in one-to-one persuasion at all. For example, there's a conceptual tool called the 'spectrum of allies' that breaks the population up into different categories on any given issue.[39] There are active allies, passive allies, neutral people, passive opponents and active opponents. If persuasion of any kind is to be effective, it's usually with passive allies (to motivate and inform them) or neutral people. Often we focus on convincing our opponents, but most persuasion is about pushing certain persuadable people slightly more towards our position on a spectrum.

In truth, I feel ambivalent about attacking debate, as I do about suggesting that the marketplace of ideas is an ineffective form of politics. I feel *dissonance* about it. I worry that, in an increasingly undemocratic age, it's counterproductive to turn on the limited forms of public discourse that still take a democratic shape. I also feel, though, that if we don't note their shortcomings, it won't be possible to find other forms of democratic life that are more powerful and possible.

So I don't want to discount what does work about these forms, even if what works is limited. There are some merits to debate and reasoning-as-war as a form of public life. To start with, debate is preferable to literal war as a means of addressing disagreement. It commits people to a process of discussion rather than violence, and forces those who engage in it to take a stance on issues when they might obfuscate or refuse to commit to action. Debate brings potentially neglected issues to light via the excitement of the conflict involved. It demonstrates that there are at least two ways of thinking about an issue (even if our faulty brains generally cannot wisely weigh the new ideas they encounter). Though debate may in practice artificially harden people's views, it is true that clarity and taking a stand are significant political virtues.

And of course, to reject debate and reasoning-as-war is not an attack on argumentation in the broader sense of the term. It is possible to construct an argument in a manner that is imaginative rather than warlike: generating as many options as possible, or entirely reframing an issue. And writing arguments and making political points does not always have to be about persuasion either. One of my favourite quotations about politics comes from the posthumously published notebooks of the German physicist and satirist Georg Christoph Lichtenberg, who wrote:

> I ceased in the year 1764 to believe that one can convince one's opponents with arguments printed in books. It is not to do that, therefore, that I have taken up my pen, but merely so as to annoy them, and to bestow strength and courage on those on our own side, and to make it known to the others that they have not convinced us.[40]

Perhaps Lichtenberg would not have been surprised to learn that today elections are more about increasing turnout than about changing minds. Making a strong argument can still be useful for engaging those who agree with you, even if it is unlikely to convince anyone who currently disagrees with you. This is especially true for minority groups and points of view, who take strength from being able to articulate, together, what they believe and why they believe it.

In insisting on looking at what really happens when debates occur (as opposed to what we wish debates could accomplish in theory) I am suggesting a pragmatic approach for addressing political issues. We shouldn't approach politics via an ideal theory, a theory that starts with the ideal, just outcome and then works its way backward. Too often, this means we imagine a path to our ideal outcome that does not exist, or ignore paths towards other interesting points of progress. We have to accept and understand the world as it is now and consider realistically what we should do about it. When it comes to debate, this means it is not good enough to argue that we might construct a hypothetical speech situation where debates would do good. It is more important to think about whether it is reasonably likely, given the world we live in today, that debate-like forms will allow our political life to improve. Given the most pressing issues we face, from climate change to personal freedom and economic fairness, our responsibilities towards justice, other humans beings and the planet are too great for us to invest time poorly. The stakes are too high for us to press on with techniques that are already shown to be ineffective. We have to do better, starting with taking seriously the way things really are.

It's going to be difficult to largely abandon debate and give up on the model of a marketplace of ideas, but doing so will help us find new ideas and to practise living those out in order to reshape our sensibilities, at least partially. In the rest of this book, I will describe various more effective means for political change than debating, or shouting into the void of a 'marketplace' for ideas. To move beyond the idea that reasoning is war or a competitive marketplace, we need to consider what else reasoning might meaningfully entail. I'm going to suggest that thinking through ideas is something that we do by acting in the world, often by collaborating, rather than competing, with others, and while necessarily relying on each other. Let's now turn to those two counter-ideas.

3

Act First, Think Later

In early May 2024 I was walking the streets of Berlin with around 30,000 other people. More precisely, I was yelling over the roar of the nearby drum line to ask my friends: where should we peel off to avoid the police and grab a falafel?

I'd been running a 'May Day Movement Anti-Academy' (yes, 'MDMA' for short) with my colleague Max. In the surrounding days we'd given lectures and facilitated workshops with a group of about 25 activists, exploring the psychology of organizing and activism to understand what makes movements effective. But on 1 May, International Workers' day, Berlin largely shuts down for a full day of left-wing protests, accompanied by sprawling sunny park picnics and all-night clubbing and street parties. On that day we didn't bother with lectures or workshops; we went with our workshop participants to join the big march.

If there is any place on earth to regularly observe the protests of a highly varied plethora of social movements, it is probably Berlin. There was, of course, a large pro-Palestine contingent that year, but there were also Basque separatists, hardcore Marxists, mainstream unions and feminist witches. I shouldn't have been surprised to notice an 'Irish Bloc', but I was. At one point the march came to a brief stop when two people dressed from head to toe in black appeared on a rooftop, shot off fireworks and unravelled enormous banners encouraging everyone to go on strike. There were musical interludes and dogs on leads. Families strapped their kids to their bikes and brought them along. A few counter-protesters lined the streets, but mostly it was a receptive crowd of bystanders. At some point, though, we all knew – especially those with kids or with asthma, or anyone elderly, but really just anyone who was anxious about tear gas – that it was time to peel off. For before the march arrived at Hermannplatz station, there was likely to be violence.

I was grateful to be there, but also a bit uneasy. I always am at protests, for multiple reasons. First, because of the aforementioned threat of violence, of course. Second, because, while I have certainly attended protests in my life, I have mostly done so to show solidarity with (for example) Black Americans and trans people. Beyond such outward signs of solidarity, however, I have always doubted the political effectiveness of protest. *Do we really think anyone is listening?* I used to wonder. And I always felt slightly out of place for having these doubts.

Third, as an actual experience, protests are uncomfortable. They are loud, chaotic and frequently unnuanced. (They remind me of music festivals, another place where my rare shy side kicks in and I largely feel stressed.) Indeed, perhaps it's fair to say that, no matter how well organized, protests are inherently disruptive and messy. Pretty much anyone can show up and say anything. That is the point of them, and their magic; but they can also be tiring, anxiety-provoking and sometimes a real drag (as anyone who has wanted to take away a megaphone can attest). Seeing all these many groups together felt a bit like watching an orchestra tune their instruments – there was certainly coordination, but a lot of dissonance too. Max and I eventually peeled off from the dissonant chaos before Hermannplatz to meet some friends who, as it happens, had already found an excellent falafel shop. And we were lucky with the timing, as it turned out: later, the police cracked down.

What to make of this giant, sprawling, varied, mostly peaceful but sometimes violent protest? Could it have had much of an impact on the German state, or on any major decision-makers? *Did it change anyone's mind?* Do protests work as vehicles for persuasion? Probably not. But that's not to say there's nothing to protests, even if they make me personally feel like I need a lie-down.

At their surface, protests appear to be a form of speech about the issues at hand. They look like demands aimed at fellow citizens, the government or others with power.* However, the effects of protests on any of these groups is at best weak or unclear. Even when protests are frequent or happen at scale, research suggests they are not necessarily effective at influencing governments.[1] Part of this is simply that governments tend to respond to the needs of the wealthy, rather than those of the population as a whole. In the US, for example, public policy statistically barely tracks with public opinion, and instead closely mirrors the views and concerns of wealthy donors to political parties. One study found that the opinions of the

---

*Here, for the purpose of thinking about protests as a form of 'speech' versus other kinds of political action, I'm somewhat artificially using the term to refer to large-scale public demonstrations about an issue – that is, those designed to attract attention – without including analysis of tactics such as strikes or boycotts, which employ further levers of economic power. This is to consider the effects of protest as 'speech'. I am naturally aware that many of the movements I refer to have used other tactics.

Similarly, while protests are, of course, used across the political spectrum, they are perhaps especially favoured by those on the left. Research on established, mostly Western, democracies has repeatedly found that citizens with left-wing political outlooks are substantially more likely to engage in protest behaviour than right-wingers. The reasons for this are complicated: see F. Kostelka, and J. Rovny (2019), 'It's Not the Left: Ideology and Protest Participation in Old and New Democracies', *Comparative Political Studies*, 52(11): 1677–1712.

'bottom' 90 per cent of Americans had no effect whatsoever on Congress's position on any issue. Only the top 10 per cent (and their related political donors and lobbying groups, presumably) appeared to sway how members of Congress voted.[2] So, given this disregard for public opinion, it's hardly surprising that protests rarely have a direct effect on policy. Many politicians are happy to admit this, seeing the concerns of the public as irrelevant: perhaps most famously, George W. Bush responded to the multi-million-people worldwide protests against the Iraq war by saying that being swayed by them would be like allowing his policies to be chosen by 'a focus group'.[3] (With this attitude you can see how defence spending is impacted by the result of strange ads to a few officials but not by any democratic process.) Governments may also wish to show that they are not vulnerable to the demands of protesters as a sign of strength, which means that protests can backfire. Indeed, some climate activists I know worry, in their darkest moments, that one of the main results of all their hard work a few years ago is that the police now have stronger strategies for dealing with protesters.

Many lawmakers view protest as nothing more than background noise to the real business of getting elected. When politicians do listen, it tends to be because they feel under threat. Activists are aware of this, and it's given rise to the not uncommon practice of 'bird-dogging', where activists follow a key policymaker for weeks, turning up and protesting wherever he or she makes public appearances, generally seeking to give the impression that many influential people care deeply about this issue or that it is frequently in the news (when the reality is that only a few people know what the issue is). The tactic can be effective. In fact, it is more or less a version of the technique used by defence contractors. But it is, notably, built on creating the appearance of a lively, engaged public sphere where there is none.

In truth, there is no particular reason why the government or the military or a large corporation should respond to protest on its own. Just because many people disagree with their actions does not really give them a reason to change course; presumably the course they chose in the first place was to their strategic benefit or they would not be pursuing it in the first place. If protest works at all (and here I focus largely on the 'discourse' bit of protest – that is, demonstrations, rather than boycotts or strikes, which work by other means), it works when it represents a threat: that people will prevent things from going ahead as usual if they don't get what they want, that they will shut down labour or business, that they will vote in a significantly different way at scale and so on. Many protests are ineffective because the people involved in them are not or cannot be making a credible threat: either they do not have the power to affect the person in power or they never supported that system in the first place. One reason George W. Bush probably did not fear the Iraq war protesters is that most of them didn't vote for him in the first place.

Protests have very little effect, indeed essentially none at all, on the beliefs of the general public. Vincent Pons, the same researcher who studied debates in the previous chapter, ran a complex statistical analysis of whether protests had any effect on public opinion. He and his co-authors looked at 14 protest movements from the year 2017 to 2022 on topics including immigration, climate change, gun control and racism. They compared similar groups of people who either happened to have intense protests in their area or did not, looking at their voting intentions, online activity, and more. Protests did create a very temporary increase in online activity about topics, as well as interest in them. But these dissipated within two weeks after the start of a protest movement. And the protest movements had essentially no effect on anyone's long-term beliefs. With the exception of the Black Lives Matter movement, which changed Democrats' views on racial issues, every other protest movement had no measurable effect at all on public opinion. (And, as I shall describe in a few pages, nationwide opinion on Black Lives Matter actually polarized over time so that arguably little progress was made).[4] Here, as in so many areas, this mixed record is partially due to the fact that the effects of protest are difficult to measure, particularly when it comes to disentangling correlation and causation. For example, public opinion about police violence changed during the height of the Black Lives Matter movement in the US. But was this because of the protests or because of the police violence that led to the protests? As with so many things in social science, the answer is probably some combination. Another reason the effects of protest are limited is that they seem to change people's minds only (or at least, largely) if they're already in the 'right' political party to hear the message. For example, half of Republicans report concern about climate change, but studies show that it is only Democrats, not Republicans, who have their views changed by climate protests. It may be that Republicans see those protesting as simply unlike them, and this alone makes the protest uninteresting or unpersuasive.[5]

Protests seem largely to reach the choir, so to speak, providing them with at best a motivating spectacle. Indeed, we might think of protests as being a little like advertising, another practice with mixed and uncertain effects. If you're already likely to be persuaded to try a new beer or splurge on a hairdryer, advertising can sometimes get you to do so. If you don't drink or if you're bald, it won't matter. Overall, ads aren't the main thing driving people's spending patterns, and they rarely change the fate of entire industries. Similarly, protests are but one tactic, and work only in limited ways at changing outsiders' minds or public policy.

There's also the question of whether any change to public opinion that does result from protest is likely to 'stick'. Research suggests that, even when protest does have impressive effects on public opinion, these effects generally don't last. In 2020 pollsters were surprised to note that since the first wave of Black Lives Matter protests in the US, the difference between the percentage of people in the country who approved of the movement and those who did not (otherwise known as the net favourability margin) moved up by ten points. Analysts saw evidence that the protests themselves (not just the deaths in police custody) were changing public opinion. This was unusual compared with the effects of other protests. But as time wore on, the numbers went back roughly to where they had been in 2018, when more Americans opposed the movement than supported it.[6]

Some of this probably had to do with a sense of disillusionment when change didn't happen 'fast enough'; some of it may have stemmed from (often false and always politically targeted) negative rhetoric about the group as violent or destructive. But perhaps the most obvious explanation is simply that protests themselves fade, and movements lose momentum. And when they do, the shift in public opinion tends to fade too. This is not a jab at the BLM movement, whose goals I generally support, but instead a broader point about protest. Even very successful protest movements do not appear to move the dial on public opinion permanently, although they may slowly ride a changing tide of opinion.

And yet. Protests do make very powerful changes in hearts and minds in one particular area: the protesters themselves. Those who join movements generally experience profound changes in their views, right across multiple areas of their lives. The scholarly literature that demonstrates this tends to call these effects the 'biographical impacts' of social movements. Generally these impacts are measured by comparing two groups who are otherwise biographically similar, but where one group happened to join social movements (say, because a protest was happening very near them) and the other group, by chance, did not. Over and over, researchers find profound effects on those who join protest movements and social movements more broadly. Those who join protest movements tend to put off marriage, and to get divorced more. They have children less frequently, pursue further education more frequently and choose lower-paying but socially beneficial jobs. They become a little less religious.[7]

Interestingly, those who become members of protest movements, compared with control groups of similar people who don't, seem to have greater self-esteem and well-being. In fact, their well-being may increase the more their activism happens in a directly confrontational way, or is seen as 'actually doing something' – a finding that aligns with a broader field of research that shows that people do better psychologically when they perceive themselves to be active, autonomous and agents for good.[8] They also, of course, become more skilled and knowledgeable. And these changes tend to stick, often for decades. BLM's protests seem to have changed public opinion for just about five years. But the protesters themselves (and Black Lives Matter had between 15 and 26 million participants, making it one of the largest protest movements in human history) are likely to experience a permanent change in their worldview.[9] This is the secret, far more effective, aspect of protest. Zeynep Tufekci, a sociologist and Pulitzer prize finalist, puts it this way: 'protests work because they are often the gateway drug between casual participation and lifelong activism.'[10] They take people casually interested in one issue and get them to take a stand publicly, devoting time and energy to a cause, ultimately making them often committed, lifelong devotees, while arming them with the social networks and skills they made along the way.

In other words, protests may not change the world, but they change their participants.

Some of my friends who have served as missionaries in the Mormon church (the Church of Jesus Christ of Latter-Day Saints) have let me in on a secret: they don't end up baptizing all that many people on their years-long missions. But these missions are still probably incredibly valuable for the church. Why? Because missionaries spend years telling everyone around them that they believe deeply, while acting with great conviction and making deep sacrifices. A member of the church who has been on a mission is therefore almost certainly much more likely to stay in the church and to raise their children in a devout manner. Those who join social movements are probably experiencing a similar effect. Like proselytizers, protesters convince themselves. (And yes, cognitive dissonance theory is at play here, moving people's beliefs towards their actions.)

Part of me, I confess, is annoyed by my own analysis. I would be happier to report that protests do inspire the general public, rather than that they serve as conversion rituals and training camps for the next generation of activists. It sounds much more appealing and glamorous to change the minds of others – more dramatic and, probably, more fun. I also worry that the idea of protests as a training ground for something else risks infantilizing the people on the front lines, a tactic that those who oppose protests use all the time when they say that protesters are just snowflakes or students with too much time on their hands, weirdos who should go get a job.

Nevertheless, this analysis says something profound. Protests are ephemeral, people less so. When the crowd disperses, some of us remain, changed for ever, driven to go do more for the world, able to influence other people in other ways. Protests make us new kinds of political subjects – or, to put it another way, they help us become people who are not just subjects but, ideally, agents.

Why, then, is it the protesters who change? While there are a few different reasons, one of the most profound has to do with a particularly intriguing and repeated finding in studies of human psychology: our actions and experiences change our beliefs, often in ways that we do not fully notice.

For example, people rapidly adapt their beliefs to changes in their lives, especially if these have to do with restrictions on what they can and cannot do. One study tracked the effect of a plastic water bottle ban in the city of San Francisco: before the ban was implemented, many people were against it; just one day later a significant number suddenly supported the ban.[11] This is an interesting finding, because it suggests that people did not change their minds because they had learned to live a new way. Rather, they made a psychological adjustment to the reality of what would be expected going forward.

There are a number of ways to explain this shift: it may be that people experienced cognitive dissonance about not liking the ban (a belief) and yet having to follow it (an action). To reduce this discomfort, people may simply have shifted their beliefs and concluded, 'Actually, this ban isn't so bad.' The researcher who conducted the study on plastic water bottles, Kristin Laurin, found similar results when people in Ontario experienced a ban on smoking in restaurant outdoor areas and parks. People disliked the idea right up until they knew it was inevitable, and then they decided they were actually for it. In fact, Laurin's team noticed that people even changed their memories retrospectively when it came to this smoking ban: after its implementation, they estimated that far less of their smoking time had previously happened in these public spaces. This probably allowed them to think better of themselves even before the ban was implemented. Notably, the kinds of shift in thinking here involved more than passive acceptance. People actively spent time coming up with new ideas, their own ideas, for why a system or change was good or bad. They were thinking, in a way, but this thinking was driven in large part by psychological pressures rather than by the abstract value of any particular set of ideas.

In fact, dissonance research suggests we do this all the time. Adapting with enthusiasm may make us feel more like we have some control over our lives. ('I'm not being forced to work super long hours! I'm a girl-boss!') This strange aspect of human psychology is probably harmless a lot of the time. Call me woke, but I'm not that worried about us all learning to cope without plastic water bottles, or having to smoke further away from other people. However, the adaptation of our beliefs to our actions can also be dangerous if it means we convince ourselves that oppressive parts of our lives are actually just fine. There's something especially perverse about the way that we can see so many people in these studies adapting their beliefs to fit the status quo in order to preserve their sense of agency in the face of their own powerlessness – they learn to like the way things are precisely so they can believe they chose it in the first place.[12] Indeed, those who have lived in less democratic regimes and seen the rise of cheerful adherence to autocratic rule may recognize this kind of human behaviour.

It is this frightening possibility, and the related question of oppression and our adaptation to it, that drove research in the larger field of System Justification Theory, of which Laurin's work is a part. The basic premise of this theory is that people who are harmed by a social or political system may be motivated to justify that system, so they can believe that what they are experiencing is 'fair, legitimate, justifiable and necessary'.

For example, if we have a job with a company that has some negative effects on the world, we will probably experience dissonance about doing this job while knowing its negative effects. To resolve this, we might tell ourselves that if we didn't do this job, someone else would, or that at least we're working to change the system from within. Interestingly, studies in this field suggest those who are more harmed by political and economic systems may sometimes work harder to justify its existence. John T. Jost, who pioneered System Justification Theory, suggests that 'people who are most disadvantaged by the status quo would have the greatest psychological need to reduce ideological dissonance and would therefore be most likely to support, defend, and justify existing social systems, authorities, and outcomes.'[13] Since the actions required to live as an oppressed person are more difficult and require more pain and effort (you may be going to exploitative jobs, being treated with prejudice and perhaps sense that life isn't going to get better), greater ideological justification is required to restore a certain kind of mental coherence. Indeed, Jost and his fellow researchers have shown that

> low income Latinos were more likely to trust in U.S. government officials and to believe that the government is run for the benefit of all than were high income Latinos ... poor and Southern African Americans were more likely to subscribe to meritocratic ideologies than were African Americans who were more affluent and from the North ... low income respondents and African Americans were more likely than others to believe that economic inequality is legitimate and necessary ... people who suffer the most from a given state of affairs are paradoxically the least likely to question, challenge, reject, or change it.[14]

This kind of research suggests that most of us are probably engaged in ways of getting through the world that are not ideal for us, but which we also come to justify to ourselves as a way of getting by psychologically. 'I'm going to work today, so it must be not just necessary but virtuous to work hard long hours, to "grind". 'I'm in this church group, so this must be the one true faith, even if it closes me off from the rest of the world.' And so on. We might even become attached to the very things that tend to cause us pain and suffering. All of which is to say that we should be very suspicious of whether we've chosen our beliefs via careful consideration of arguments or have developed them because they matched actions we had to engage in anyway.

Laurin and her teams' research, and the research behind System Justification Theory, shows what happens when you limit people's possibilities for action. If you shut down the range of possibilities in a person's life, you may well restrict their views and ability to question too.

I want to admit straight away that this idea is, or at least can be, difficult and uncomfortable. We may find it condescending, or it may sound like victim-blaming, to suggest that those who are oppressed don't recognize the true nature of their oppression. Not to mention the fact that most of us know plenty of women furious at the patriarchy or people of colour who are very conscious of the nature of racial oppression. Clearly our actions are just one factor in how people form their understanding of the world, but they do appear to have a measurable impact on how we think. And we can accept this without looking down on people: none of this suggests that people are stupid – only that we are all subject to some psychological pressures towards consistency in an often oppressive world.

There is a range of evidence that (as one sociology paper puts it) 'experiences such as education and travel – which presumably increase openness to new experiences by rendering uncertainty less aversive and the unfamiliar less threatening – may increase the affinity for liberal, progressive, and egalitarian ideas.'[15] Conversely, frightening experiences such as terrorist attacks tend to make people more conservative.[16] Even fairly contingent events in our lives can shift our political views. For example, a group of researchers conducted what they called 'the turnaway study', which looked at what happened to women who sought abortions. A subset of these women were, for essentially logistical and/or bureaucratic reasons, unable to receive desired abortions. (They were often slightly further along in their pregnancy than they realized, and no longer eligible in their particular state.) Controlling for other factors such as class, age and so on, researchers could observe what happened to women who were turned away compared with those who got the abortions they wanted.[17] Getting or being denied an abortion changed some women's political views in arguably surprising ways. We might expect that women who didn't get an abortion that they wanted would think of abortion rights as even more important. After all, they'd just been denied something they wanted, which they could find upsetting, oppressive and/or unfair. But in fact, the turnaway study showed that 'women who had been denied an abortion were more likely than those who had received one to say they had become less supportive of abortion rights (21% vs. 9%), while women who received an abortion were more likely than those turned away to become more supportive of abortion rights (33% vs 6%).'[18] In other words, each group of women became more in favour of what had actually happened to them; they aligned their beliefs about what is best with what they had experienced. (It's worth noting, of course, that the majority of these women still supported access to abortion.) These are not enormous statistical effects (and they are doubtless made sharper by the strange existential experience of coming to love a child one originally chose not to have), but neither are these measurable effects negligible.

Abortion is far from the only example where actions and lived experience appear to change people's views. Evidence shows that, across the political spectrum, those who experience the effects of climate change directly or even vicariously (hearing about these effects from other people) become more convinced that climate change is serious and real.[19] If one considers how events like these must compound over the course of our lives, we can then see how much of what we believe is profoundly influenced not by arguments but by often chance events, experiences and actions we undertake and are often forced to undertake and then integrate into our worldview and sense of self. And this, in turn, is uncomfortable because it shows us just how determined we are by events outside our control – even when it comes to something so deeply rooted and personal as what we believe.

Which is not to say we are entirely determined. In fact, it's probably a good idea to remind ourselves that there are always more options for our lives than we realize, because it appears that it is precisely when we think our circumstances are inevitable that our views harden. Laurin's aforementioned research found that people reconciled their views with their reality most when they felt those circumstances were inevitable. For example, those who were told they probably couldn't leave the country during one study were far more likely to rationalize whatever policies that country had.[20] In fact, human beings often react negatively to any attempts to control or persuade them, experiencing the aforementioned phenomenon of 'reactance'. It's only if changes seem inevitable that our beliefs tend to shift. What this means, politically, is that a great deal hinges on whether people see their lot as inevitable and unchangeable.

The scope of our political imagination matters a great deal, and our hope for a different outcome.

And that's not all. If we're cognitively overloaded, research suggests, we're probably more likely to adjust to the world we're already in, but if someone draws our attention to the way we might be being manipulated, we may become less likely to reconcile our views with the existing world.[21] In short, our experiences and actions change our minds, and the less mental bandwidth we have to give to reflection, the more likely we are to align our views with our actions uncritically. Surely many overly busy people, without time or a particular reason to stop and question things, assume that the world has to be the way it is and align their beliefs with the status quo. But with time and a different understanding of their circumstances they might do differently. So while it may be depressing that our beliefs are so strongly shaped by circumstance and even by oppression, this is not inevitable, especially if we can discover that there might be another possibility for how to live.

The idea that action is a fundamental part of reasoning challenges cultural notions of what reasoning is. In the supposed divide between jocks and nerds, between doers and dreamers, between 'theory' and 'practice' or 'book smart' and 'street smart', lies the cultural assumption that thought and action are different, even opposing, activities. But when it comes to politics, taking action is a crucial part of thinking.

If there are not enough opportunities for people to act differently in the world, it is very likely they will end up justifying the world as it is. And addressing this is particularly important today, when the emergence of new technologies has made organizing protests superficially easier: 'getting involved' in a social movement requires less of us when things can be organized online. The trouble is that when it is easier for people to join movements it also becomes psychologically easier for people to leave them.

One of the reasons why action is so central to political thinking is that it is only in trying to change the world that we discover how it works. When I ask activists and organizers how they became involved in politics, they often tell me that their journey began when they tried to improve one relatively small thing about their life, and in doing so discovered that the entire system was profoundly dysfunctional. Americans tend to learn about this when they first encounter a difficulty getting health insurance to cover a relatively basic medical treatment. One activist told me they learned about the power and danger of corporations when they were fired after trying to unionize. Another organizer, Louis Ramirez, began work in flood-affected areas in the UK. He wondered if homeowners were going to be ready to organize politically to challenge the government on climate action. Some were, but, interestingly, they were most upset not about the flooding itself or even about the threat to their homes and house prices.[22] No, what they were most angry about was the fact that the government was ineffective and unresponsive, and that insurance companies could abandon them without consequences. They learned, in a sense, how things work precisely when they sought help and found it wanting.

Of course, one can be radicalized by the action-possibilities implied by positive experiences too. Rosa Parks first got to ride racially integrated public transit on a federal Air Force Base – Maxwell Air Force Base – during her time working there in World War Two. She told her biographer, 'You might just say Maxwell opened my eyes up. It was an alternative reality to the ugly policies of Jim Crow.'[23] Seeing that something is possible in one place often makes us realize just how unjust it is that it isn't happening elsewhere.

Effective organizing involves providing experiences and actions for people and then giving them space and tools to make sense of what they are doing. Food co-operatives, for example, can do this. I was lucky enough to visit one in Gospel Oak, London, when writing this book. It is part of a larger network called Cooperation Town, and it is not the sort that some readers may already be familiar with, where upper-middle-class people club together to buy especially fresh or organic groceries. Rather, the co-ops in this network are for anyone, usually working-class people, to have the opportunity to collectively purchase less expensive food. The one I visited was housed in a community centre, where small children played with the delivery trolleys as their parents collected the weekly groceries.

I spoke to Shiri Shalmy, who works for Cooperation Town and is also a co-op member herself.[24] She's found that members of the co-op come to think about their neighbours and the economy differently. Food co-ops are, in a way, very simple: once people join, they take turns purchasing the food in bulk for the group for that week, bargaining with local stores and distributing to their neighbours. The result, especially when donations of food are included, means that many people can get their groceries for as little as £3 a week. In the process of buying and distributing, members gain new knowledge and organizing skills. For not only does organizing a food co-op look a lot like, well, organizing people for political action, but along the way many members witness first hand how broken the food system is. As they bargain with local stores for batch prices, buyers learn how much food is wasted because supermarkets are overstocked with excess produce, which is generally thrown out, all to ensure complete and constant availability of every fruit or vegetable.

They also know not just one another's fridge contents but their families, hopes and worries. And they look out for each other. I learned that when an older woman in the food co-op fell, hurt herself and couldn't get up, and her family didn't know what to do, it was other members of the food co-op who noticed the woman's husband was coming by himself and asked gently but persistently until they discovered the issue and sprang into action to get her medical care. People look after one another in practical ways, which builds commitment to everyone's well-being. And this, Shalmy notes, means 'when they come to demolish the [housing] estate, we're already organized.' Indeed, when members have faced eviction, their fellow co-op members have shown up to guard the home and prevent it.

Shalmy notes that, in a lot of traditional models, getting people to care about political issues happens at a point of conflict: when the landlord raises the rent, when the employer cuts hours and so on. It is only then that people who may otherwise have been disengaged, overwhelmed or unmotivated join struggles and dive into political action. Cooperation Town, and projects like it, are powerful because they rely not on a point of conflict but on fulfilling basic human needs. 'It's an easy point of entry for getting people into organizing,' says Shiri. For it to be relevant, 'you just need to eat and have neighbours.'

None of this requires arguments, in either sense of the word. Instead, people begin to think about how they should have cheaper food, or about how supermarkets shouldn't be allowed to mandate overproduction, or why evictions are wrong as they encounter these issues in the world. Indeed, none of this involves much abstract discussion and yet, along the way, members of food co-ops tend to change their views on how the economy functions and what they'd like to do about it.

The fact that action changes beliefs points to another core concept: affordances. Affordances are the action-possibilities that a particular tool or technology permits or suggests; they are what a given situation or technology 'affords' their user. A motorcycle affords one the opportunity to go fast and travel alone; a car affords one the possibility to do the same, but with more people. This concept is often used in studies of technology; consider, for example, how the kind of conversation it's possible to have on a landline is totally different from the various ways of communicating made possible on Instagram.

Indeed, the affordances of technologies are at the heart of much of the way we think: psychological research suggests that many of our basic units of cognition are concerned with these action-possibilities. In theories of cognitive science, for example, we can see that even at the most basic level of bodily movement and perception, action and thinking are tied. Theories of embodied cognition show that the body is the locus of thinking for much of what we do (for example, it is the seat of our emotional reactions, and these then form our judgements). This idea fits into theories of 'extended cognition', which show that our thinking happens not only in our brain and our body but also through the tools we use in the world around us. Our phones are a primary example. When I want to remember a thought I've had, I can scribble it in the 'notes' function on my phone, which is painfully omnipresent in my life, usually at my literal fingertips. When I can't remember something, I no longer rack my brain: I simply pick up my phone and search for it. But it's not just our immediate technological devices that shape the way we think. Even structures such as the law organize our thinking for us. Look at how much we think in terms of 'I have the right to' or 'she is entitled to'. We think through our bodies, yes, but also through our social structures. We think, in other words, in terms of the things we could do. As the philosopher Thomas Metzinger notes in a study focusing on the brain and consciousness, this is apparent in the way that those with brain damage (from, say, a stroke) often experience 'alien hand syndrome', where their hand or hands begin, with no conscious prompting, to grasp at and even interact in complex ways with anything in the immediate vicinity – scribbling on notepads, picking and pulling at clothes, grabbing onto other random objects in the vicinity and sometimes even clutching at their own throat. Is this a case of some kind of horrible devilish possession?[25] No. Instead, as Metzinger notes, the behaviour of this hand is

> driven by visually perceived objects in your immediate vicinity that give rise to what psychologists and philosophers call affordances. There is good evidence that the brain portrays visual objects not only as such but also in terms of possible movements: is this something I could grasp? Is this something I could unbutton? Is this something I could eat or drink?[26]

Our brain is busy calculating the affordances available to us all the time.

We don't, of course, consciously notice exactly how our brain is doing this. Metzinger suggests that for most of us, most of the time, a larger set of psychological structures (including our sense of self and our sense of the world around us) suppresses our conscious recognition of the affordances around us, allowing us to focus only on those that appear sensible (say, moving towards the one thing we actually need). This is a great thing, as otherwise we'd be consciously cycling through and considering all sorts of unnecessary actions. Yet while we might not be consciously experiencing, much less acting upon, all these affordances, they are still at work in the way we navigate the world.

Indeed, the fact that most of us can easily type without thinking about the physical movements of our hands shows how well our brain operates in terms of implicit movement-based affordances. We may consciously think in terms of the words and sentences we want to see on the page (as I am doing while writing this now), but amazingly, beneath the level of our conscious perception, our body speaks the language of movements and actions.

Why might our brain think in this way? The 'predictive processing' strand of neuroscience suggests that most of our brain power is used to generate a predictive model of the world around us. This allows us to act quickly enough to avoid suspected danger and seize opportunities that become available to us. And if these ideas about affordances are correct, then the predictive modelling that the mind is engaged in is not primarily modelling of the world itself (for example, 'there's a chair there') but rather the modelling of actions available to us (for example, 'sitting could happen there soon'). This is, after all, more efficient: the brain can skip the chair itself and go right to engaging in sitting-thoughts, and therefore sitting itself. (If that seems a bit abstract, consider the way our brain goes about helping us balance on one leg or even drive. Often we are not thinking deeply about the distance to the floor or the shape of the road; rather, we are bodily adjusting, moment by moment, in one direction or the other based on the feedback we receive.) Interestingly, research shows that this kind of affordance-based thinking seems to be at play when we interact with each other too: our brains spend time predicting not only our own possible actions but also other people's, which is useful to us as social animals. We adjust to their moods, behaviours and actions in real time, without consciously thinking about it.[27]

All of this means, in short, that our beliefs are shaped not only by our daily actions, but also by our unconscious evaluation of the actions available to us. And this fundamental role of action-possibilities in thought probably affects our political beliefs as well.

Today technology has radically altered the way we understand our own capacities and possibilities for action. We can now (as tech companies love to point out) do amazing things: communicate across the globe, represent ourselves with avatars, access information in an instant. We can also curate a world of people who largely agree with us. We can block or stalk our exes. We can fall into rabbit holes and join new subcultures. But none of these options occurs naturally or by chance; they are painstakingly designed by people who understand just how powerfully our brains are influenced by the action-possibilities available to us. Trust me, I work for technology companies to earn my living, and I cannot overemphasize how much time and money are spent testing where buttons should go and how to keep people's attention. Those who design software and web interfaces know that you can get people to do things by making them seem easy to try out. They do not waste time explaining why features of a product are good but instead demonstrate how and where to swipe, click and type. So, although those who worry about politics rarely think about the power of affordances, those who engineer human behaviour (often very successfully and not necessarily for good) know just how powerful these possibilities for action can be when it comes to changing what people think.

The way that affordances structure our thinking is even clearer when it comes to speech. Studies on persuasion show that a focus on possibilities for action helps people convince one another more easily. The 'Elaboration Likelihood Model' of persuasion is one of the better-researched models of whether, and under what circumstances, people change their views or decide to take a particular action. It suggests that people need to feel both a sense of personal relevance and a sense of their 'self-efficacy': that is, they need to feel that they can do something about the matter at hand before they are likely to consider changing their mind.[28] Telling a person about an issue, then, is only one piece of the puzzle when it comes to convincing them; another key piece is to allow the person to feel that they are in a position to do something about it. Being shown that there are actions we can take is more likely to capture our attention and even imagination. It is, of course, also rational only to go to the trouble of changing your beliefs about something if doing so will realistically allow you to help.

In this context, it's not hard to imagine that part of what has made capitalist and neoliberal ideologies so appealing, at least to some, is that they suggest a series of future possible actions that one can start immediately. *You can work hard, become an entrepreneur!* Or, of course, other ideologies might promise one a future as a successful political party member, virtuous trad-wife or whatever else. Naturally these ideologies often obscure the true power dynamics at hand for those who follow these paths (being a Deliveroo driver might mean long nights and no savings; being a wife in a patriarchal marriage involves gruelling labour and limited independence), but on the surface at least these ideas appear to show real and clear possibilities for agency.

If action-possibilities are part of what our brains look for when they consider arguments, it's remarkable how little this has been exploited by political messaging. Short of a few key but vague slogans on both right and left (think of

'Make America Great Again' and 'Yes We Can'), most day-to-day political rhetoric doesn't focus on action-possibilities. It rarely suggests to people that they personally have the right competencies to do something meaningful about the issues at hand. We're living through a particularly pessimistic time, of course, with plague and war and many increasingly authoritarian governments, so perhaps it's understandable that there isn't a lot of inspiring rhetoric about the possibilities for change. Nevertheless, this disregard for listeners' agency may be contributing to our political malaise, and not just fuelled by it. Our brain's attachment to action-possibilities helps explain why being unable to imagine any useful course of action constrains our thinking so powerfully. Our brain's orientation towards action-possibilities suggests we should be sceptical of accounts of the future that are too gloomy or closed off (which come as much from the left as the right, in many cases). Our world is certainly dark, but seeing it as unchangeable may keep people paralysed. The cultural theorist Mark Fisher coined the term 'Capitalist Realism' to describe the world we live in today, where there is 'the widespread sense that not only is capitalism the only viable political and economic system, but also that it is now impossible even to imagine a coherent alternative to it'.[29] His suggestion was that the foreclosing of any other, future world is itself a powerful ideological mechanism, one that prevents people from acting meaningfully. It is an idea that becomes true the more people believe it.

This research has also left me sceptical about political arguments that rely on abstract ideas, as abstraction can be disengaging and even counterproductive. Abstract arguments about 'truths' (Exactly how much privilege does a particular person have? What is gender? Is progressive taxation 'fair'? Who would we like to be able to immigrate to our country?) are dead ends, not only because people are unlikely to come to an agreement but also because these questions frame the issues badly, as if each were a complex maths problem with a right answer. It is more psychologically productive to ask if we want to create a world where certain actions are possible: where people can work a bit less, choose and change their gender expression, afford university or move countries easily.

More generally, this action orientation of our minds helps explain many frustrating aspects of the way people think about politics. It's galling, at times, how bad people are at dealing with ambiguity, but it makes sense when we realize that our own actions trap us in this position, to a degree: we want to feel moral clarity about our actions, as otherwise we feel guilt or shame, and ambiguities threaten this. No wonder we even frequently misremember our actions in the past in order to maintain our sense that we've been good ... Of course, it is important not to jump too quickly from a psychological finding to a political consequence. I am enthusiastic about research involving action and affordances, but much more is needed for researchers and citizens alike to understand how it all informs the way we think about the world. More research is needed, but the research that exists so far suggests a focus on action-possibilities might well offer a more constructive approach to politics.[30]

If thinking about actions is powerful, getting people involved is all the more so. Indeed, this knowledge is already regularly weaponized, often by groups outside of politics. Consider the hazing involved in fraternities and sororities, where those being inducted are asked to do extreme or embarrassing things to join the group. Studies that replicate some of these conditions (as much as research ethics committees will allow) show that the more embarrassing an induction is, the more people who undergo it feel committed to the group. For example, women who had to talk about sexually explicit things as part of the induction to a discussion group found the group more interesting than those who did not, even once the groups went on to identical readings thereafter. To reconcile their dissonance about having done something fairly embarrassing to join the group, they valued the group more highly than they would otherwise have done. (So they could say to themselves, 'Yes, that was embarrassing, but it makes sense I did that – it's such a good group!'[31]) To reconcile discomfort about how much we've put in up front to join a group or commit to a course of action, we adjust our sense of how much that choice means to us. Here, as elsewhere, our actions change our minds – and, generally, we don't notice it happening.

There's a particularly neat and instructive model that describes how people become believers in cults: this is called the 'behaviour, belonging, belief' model, proposed by Douglas A. Marshall.[32] In short, Marshall theorized that joining members must first engage in the same behaviours as the group, then they feel they belong, and only after passing these thresholds might those who join a cult really come to believe in its ideas. This happens for a number of reasons, including 'the misattribution of behavior, the justification of behavior, and self-perception'. But, of course, what works in cults also works out in the world. In all likelihood, whenever we commit ourselves to new actions we extend ourselves towards new beliefs, especially if these actions lie outside our comfort zone.

In this way, I would suggest, we can think of protest as a recruitment session. Newcomers commit themselves to new actions, whether it's holding a banner, shouting, blocking roads or whatever else. This may or may not convince other people, but it is very likely to make them feel more like they belong to the group and agree with it. These days, when I see protests, I mostly consider them to be gateway drugs and recruitment opportunities, rather than a way to directly pressure governments or convince the wider public. This is an uncomfortable truth in some ways. It makes me wonder how to invite people to join protests, given their true nature. It also makes me think social movements should spend time trying to stymie protests organized by their opponents.

To think effectively about politics, then, is not only to think about action; it is also, by necessity, to take action. Good political reasoning cannot happen simply by reading and debating, because there are some things we can only learn through our attempts to change the world. Certain kinds of knowledge are better achieved through action than reflection – even if it's highly undervalued in our current media and educational systems. Rather than focusing so closely on debate and discourse, on tweets and op-eds, on coming up with better arguments, we'd do better to organize even the smallest of political actions. To change people's views on the importance of climate change, for example, it may be more effective to provide incentives for them to install a solar panel on their roof than argue with anyone about climate change. Having done something towards the cause of decarbonizing, they are far more likely to be receptive to environmentalism as a whole.

Some scholarly literature calls this the 'gateway/getaway' debate: researchers have sought to test whether 'lifestyle' expressions of politics serve as replacements for more direct political engagement or whether they are in fact gateways to further political engagement. In other words, if you recycle, are you more likely to go to the climate protest, or do you feel you've done your bit? For the most part, the literature seems to suggest that lifestyle actions are gateways, not getaways: recyclers soon become more active in environmental movements (for example).[33] When we think of this in light of cognitive dissonance theory, these kinds of 'small' actions are probably valuable for organising because they enable people to change their minds: when we act in a way that's consistent with a new possible belief (especially if these small actions are fun or successful), we are more likely to entertain that belief.

And what cognitive science shows from one angle, social science can demonstrate from another.[34] Social theorists have written about how our society affects the way we think about the world. The sociologist Pierre Bourdieu describes the importance of habitus, 'a subjective but not individual system of internalized structures, schemes of perception, conception, and action common to all members of the same group or class'.* Our habitus describe the way we have learned to adapt to the possibilities and limits of our social position. It explains why members of the same social class might all internalize the same way of speaking, dressing and talking, or for that matter engage in similar hobbies, well-being habits or social experiences: it allows them to reap the benefits or opportunities of their particular social world. There is a reason that my university-educated friends and I wear some items of clothing but not others, ask fellow guests 'What do you do?' at dinner parties, throw said dinner parties and do more yoga than drugs; it fits with our class position, with the lifestyle of young professionals and the benefits we can access

---

*You may have noticed by now that this book involves intellectual history, interdisciplinary social science, political theory and cognitive science, as well as experience and learning design, a discipline that itself involves a lot of cognitive science. There are downsides to this eclectic approach, certainly, but when it comes to understanding complex human phenomena there are upsides too. Ideas like this – that action in the world is a form, even an inextricable part, of thinking well about politics – can be understood in a more complete way only by combining these many different disciplines. It is possible to 'triangulate', as interdisciplinary researchers put it, between multiple datasets, methods and theories to understand the same human phenomenon, and in so doing achieve a more accurate and complete picture.

through that class position. All of us, in fact, are responding to the affordances of our particular social position, and these affordances end up changing our values.

Similarly, political theorists, especially left or Marxian ones, tend to emphasize the importance of praxis, or the application of one's theory in the real world, arguing, in part, that only in trying to change things can we discover how they work. But thinking 'outside' the abstractions of the brain is nevertheless relatively rare in the broad field of political and social theory. I suspect this is because so many political and social theorists have prided themselves on their removal of the world, in line with the sterile model of rationality outlined by David Graeber, a model where to think is to be apart from the world and control it. Thinking through the world (instead of merely about it) is messier; in many ways it asks more of us, and ultimately it leaves us rather vulnerable. For it means the world changes us and our ideas, and not just the other way around.

This idea – that our lived experience is what shapes our ideas, more than the strength of the ideas themselves – is tough to accept at first if you're someone like me, who has spent most of her life in academia and related professions. There's an implicit myth in education that ideas on their own, if they carry truth, have power over the mind. But even I have to acknowledge, when I think about it closely, that it's actually changes in my life that have most profoundly affected the way that I think. The same is true when I consider others, even anecdotally. Most of the time, when people end up thinking about things in new ways, it's because something has changed – perhaps they've moved away, become a parent or quit the booze. They didn't usually just wake up out of the blue and change their life from scratch because of a really good book. Even when really good books are involved, this is usually because that book chimed with the actions and experiences currently happening in their lives. In fact, I am making a bet that if this book has any power for you, dear reader, it is because your daily life in the twenty-first century meaningfully demonstrates parts of what I have to say and gives you action-based reasons to want to change the way you think about politics. Only then can my book be of any help.

Modern-day protest movements thus face a peculiar dilemma: as I mentioned earlier, less is required of those who join the movements because of new technologies that make reaching people easier. This means people may put less effort into their activism and ultimately become less invested in the movement than if more had been asked of them, so that they leave the movement more easily.

Zeynep Tufekci spent years following big social change movements – living with Zapatistas, camping in Turkey's Gezi Park protests, visiting Occupy's Manhattan encampments and helping activists coordinate the protests in Tahrir Square. Huge crowds joined these protests, drawn to demonstrations against income inequality and a lack of meaningful democracy. They had found the movement via social media networks and interpersonal networks. When these movements exploded onto the scene, activists were incredibly hopeful. Watching protesters clash with police in 2012, I distinctly recall my best friend musing that maybe, finally, real change, history itself, was happening. And indeed, there was something that felt era-defining about these protests. Like many previous uprisings, those within them often described them as some of the best days of their lives – even when they were being beaten and teargassed by police. The encampments appeared as a slice of a future, a better world occupying the present moment. The libraries these encampments built were just one small example of the larger way that many of these movements created within them a model of the society they hoped to prefigure: where food and medicine and knowledge itself were free, where there was abundance of the crucial things, and where anyone could give and be involved in an important way. Mandy Henk, an access services librarian who worked on one of these People's Libraries, described their purpose as to 'engage in direct action to build a new and better world, one based on old principles embedded deeply in the American psyche but lately forgotten'. The libraries, she suggested, represented 'the idea of a Commons, of shared resources, of equal access – access mediated not by a market, but granted as a fundamental right that all people share by virtue of being part of the human family'.[35] The libraries and the encampments were a place for people to try out in miniature the ideas they would later take with them for life.

But they were less effective at changing the outside world. In fact, almost as quickly as they rose, the movements began to fall apart. Occupy Wall Street's physical occupation lasted just 59 days. The movements involved in the Arab Spring were also relatively short, and often, even when they succeeded in removing someone in power, led to other oppressive regimes. And of course, many protests seemed to be completely ineffective. Although she was enthusiastic about many of these movements during their peaks, Tufekci nevertheless writes that years of organizing has changed her mind about just how effective protests really were. During the protests against the Iraq war, she and fellow anti-war activists noticed a frightening groupthink among right-wing politicians and mainstream media pundits alike. But those protesting against the war had their own faulty groupthink too: they thought that surely, if enough people gathered in protest, it would change the course of history. There was, Tufekci acknowledges, probably some form of hopeful bias at work: 'I really, really wanted our demonstrations – against the invasion of Iraq, against deepening inequality, against the authoritarians in the Middle East, in support of human rights and environmentalism – to achieve more of their goals.'[36]

Yes, Tufekci writes, these protests mattered in some ways, highlighting issues and challenging legitimacy – but perhaps less than one might hope. There were many reasons for this – not least the constant government brutality – but perhaps one reason is simply that, in a strange way, organizing these protests was too easy. These protests were called 'networked' protests because they were organized through people's networks, and specifically through their 'weak ties' – not just close friends but friends of friends, their colleagues, their more distant acquaintances. This kind of organizing was made possible by social media, which affords incredibly easy mass communication, often in a non-hierarchical manner. But these exact same affordances have a downside too: people don't have to get deeply involved to join in, which means they don't necessarily create the long-term structures that can continue to be powerful even after police clear out a particular occupation. If less time and energy are required to make sure people show up, and that means fewer contact hours, fewer people doing the hard work of recruiting and far fewer people changing their beliefs.

There were a number of crucial downsides to this type of quickly organized mass protest. Governments are well aware of how easy it is to organize a protest compared with what it used to take; one million people protesting no longer sends such a strong 'signal' that people are discontented. The risk is that the whole protest itself can be, in some way, hollow. It can become a kind of 'folk politics', to use a term from theorists Nick Srnicek and Alex Williams, who argue that many protests simply serve as a place for a self-righteous outpouring of sentiment (and some strategic photos to post on one's social media). Then it's back to our normal lives. 'This is politics transmitted into pastime – politics-as-drug-experience, perhaps – rather than anything capable of transforming society,' they suggest.[37] Those involved tend to boil down complex issues to overly simple soundbites, and many do not have a sense of what it would mean to push on real, structural levers of power the way, say, strikes or years of organizing do.

Indeed, not only may networked protests fail to build both the long-term commitment and the internal capacity that previous movements did, but we may be living through a period where fewer and fewer people have been involved in the kinds of committed actions that are more likely to change the way they see the world or deepen their political engagement. As public policy professor Alasdair Roberts notes, this has been compounded by the erosion of organized labour.[38] Today's unions are weak compared to the way they were in earlier eras, when unions helped organize anti-war campaigns or were an ally in the struggle for Civil Rights.[39] As a result, Roberts suggests, there may be fewer robust and effective movements and, downstream of this, fewer protests than there otherwise would be. For example, during the financial crises around 2008, there were higher rates of protest in Europe than in the UK and the US, and this may have been because there are higher rates of organizing within the workforce in Europe. Indeed, those who study 'associative democracy' suggest that trade unions help citizens develop the skills (of speaking out, negotiating and treating others as equals) that not only help them engage in other democratic processes such as voting and protest but also make them far more likely to vote and demonstrate.[40] In the US, unions have also been at the forefront of legal struggles to expand voting rights, and there is even evidence that unions get higher numbers of non-members out on the streets for protests too.[41] As trade union membership has fallen, voting rates have also declined, often in a somewhat causal manner. Social movements could similarly provide support for these activities, but to do so they might have to ask more from members in a formal way, as trade unions generally do.

All this, in turn, points towards an apparent paradox. The easier it is in theory to recruit someone to a movement – for example, by simply sending them an invitation on social media – the harder it may be to have them commit to and join a movement in the long run. For if we judge by the psychological and social science research on how action changes one's mind, then the less work it is to join a movement, the less likely it is that involvement will change the minds and lives of those within it. Those who want to change the world may be hamstrung by the ease with which they can mobilize short-term anger and the technologies that have made it relatively easy to get people to show up once or twice. What is often required, instead, is a longer-term, deeper investment, which often begins by asking more, rather than less, of those who join. If this is not possible straight away, it might mean asking people to engage in a 'gateway' action ('Would you be willing to man the food booth at our meeting?'). Movements can then build up from there.

Without this kind of long-term network- and capacity-building, even very large protest movements today often quickly flame up and then burn out, without having a lasting effect on public opinion. Right-wingers like to speak about 'paid protest' and 'astroturfing', implying that protests are in some sense fake and do not represent the concerns of real people. Beneath the impulse to dismiss their opponents, they may be responding to a vague discomfort or surprise arising from the fact that protests can arise very suddenly and even unexpectedly these days and disperse just as easily. But this is almost certainly not due to a great many paid protesters, not least because these do not generally fit in the budgets of movements. Rather, today protests can be very swiftly assembled and just as easily disassembled, and along the way little internal capacity and few long-term relationships are built. Today's protests simply require, and therefore usually involve, less work and care, and so far less is built along the way.

But of course, that does not mean that protests can never work well again. In fact, we already have examples of how they can work well from past movements, when organizing was harder but also required much more of its participants. In a particularly amusing part of her book, Tufekci notes that the civil rights movement tended to plan their demonstrations down to the last detail, including the condiments in the sandwiches. For the 1963 March on Washington, they decided against mayonnaise as they thought it would spoil in the heat.[42]

There's a funny paradox, then, for the organizer of a protest. Considering what protests actually do, a truly honest organizer might feel obliged to give a more realistic pitch to those interested in joining a movement, something like:

> Hey, you should come to the protest with me! It will have no discernible long-term impact on the state of the world, but it will radically transform your understanding of everyone around you, remake your circle of friends and make you more likely to have a serious break-up while earning peanuts!

It's not exactly catchy.

Yet although it's not catchy, it underscores the important point: protests are effective for recruitment and retention, not for persuasion of anyone who doesn't join, and not for persuading the government. That doesn't mean they don't 'work', so much as it means they work for this very specific thing. It means activists should use protests precisely this way (and, cynically, that they also benefit from disrupting the protests of their opponents).

What I've outlined in this chapter also suggests that we should not underestimate the importance of 'gateway' actions; small actions that lead people to re-align their views. Indeed, more broadly, this research shows that when it comes to politics, thinking happens through doing. If we are to connect all this research about action, affordances and political reasoning, what emerges is a picture of political reasoning where action is one of the most important parts of thinking well about politics, and helping others do the same.

What does all this suggest about our wider political world? Simply put: if you want to change people's minds, you must change their lives.

When it comes to politics, we've probably placed too much societal emphasis on words and too little on action. Many people would say that democracy is about whether people can make up their own minds and then vote. But this is, in fact, a fairly passive idea of political involvement. It would look a bit silly in other contexts: would we say that abstract thinking and making decisions are the main part of being a friend, or being in a family? Probably not; on this smaller level, most of us understand loving and thinking and doing are all intertwined, and that one has to be actively involved to have any clue about how to act wisely. Despite this, our collective common sense of what politics is has, I'd suggest, become hollowed out. It involves too little of what truly changes people, their priorities and their actions.

A broader and more solid definition of democracy includes not just voting and freedom of speech but also a wide variety of other important measures, including protections for the rights of minorities, protections for dissent, equality before the law in practice and not just on paper, meaningful and realistic opportunities for people to be involved in the shaping of their political world, and (some, including myself, would argue) relatively egalitarian power structures throughout society, including in the economy. I'm not going to provide a singular definition for democracy in this book, because it's more fruitful and interesting to consider what we might collectively want it to be. But these are some key features to consider.

To return to our society's current, often-superficial understanding of democracy: the changing technological affordances of our times may well have contributed to this superficial understanding by making it too easy to mobilize people to engage in temporary demonstrations and speech acts, without building longer-term networks of action and care. As a result, some of the power of social movements, especially those that rely on demonstrations alone, may be diminished, and older tactics may no longer make as much sense.

Our current political culture has, I'd suggest, romanticized and glamorized the wrong things: the big speeches at the giant protests, but not the women (and it was mostly women) carefully planning the sandwiches. And we have turned our collective attention this way at our peril. It would be more productive now to think about politics in terms of taking action and becoming stewards of one another's transformation through action. Of course, this is difficult, because doing is difficult or, at least, generally more difficult than talking. But taking action together can also be joyful, compelling, and can even change the way people think about the world, far more than debates or mere exposure to ideas. It can also connect us to other people in profound ways, and this changes our thinking too. Which brings me to another underestimated aspect of thinking well about politics: our relationships with others. Let's turn to that now.

4

Think with Your Friends

After the end of the Second World War, the US decided to desegregate its military.[1] This raised a question for social science researchers: what would happen when two groups of people with high levels of distrust (some of whom might even hate each other) worked together in close proximity and defended one another's lives?[*] An influential economist named Gordon Allport measured how integrating the military led to lower levels of prejudice, though only in a very specific set of circumstances. From this he eventually developed the 'Social Contact Hypothesis', also called 'social contact theory', which he described in his 1954 book *The Nature of Prejudice*.[2] There he outlined the key conditions under which he believed prejudice could be reduced.

Building on this over the next 70 years or so, social contact theorists found four key factors that predict whether prejudice will be reduced when groups mix. These factors were: (1) members of the different groups making contact should have equal status in the environment they are in; (2) they should

---

[*] To be clear, the most concerning hatred here was doubtless on the part of the white folks.

meet in situations where co-operation is regularly required and where they have goals in common; (3) close relationships should be possible; and (4) contact between groups should be legitimized through institutional support.

Allport found numerous examples where managed contact reduced anti-Black, anti-Semitic, anti-Catholic and sexist prejudice. Theorists after him, with some variance and occasional doubt, similarly found meaningful contact to reduce prejudice with groups as diverse as Muslims, the elderly, gay men and, amazingly, in a particularly curious study, 'social robots'. (Yes, if you're sceptical of robots, once you feel warmly towards your own Alexa or therapy bot, you'll apparently begin to think differently of the lot of them. Perhaps this is one of the few cases where we might be suspicious of the effects of this prejudice-reducing propensity of long-term meaningful contact.[3])

These four factors create a noticeably high bar. Clearly, it's not enough for people just to live on the same block. These conditions are also probably not met by (say) children attending the same school. It's also not enough for an institution to integrate in a manner that means the lowest-ranking workers in a company are disproportionately people of colour – this does not send the message of equality or encourage people to actively collaborate.

Under the wrong conditions, people may superficially like members of another group without changing their overall views. They may think, 'Well, he's all right, but he's not like the rest of them.' There seems to be something about these four factors – perhaps the institutional support, perhaps the equal status, perhaps the long-term collaboration with shared goals – that means that people do not just conclude the person they've met is 'not like the rest of them' but rather that 'the rest of them' are all right too. As for which of the four factors plays the biggest role, I hope more studies are run soon: it doesn't appear to be clear. But it is no surprise that working towards shared goals is one of them, given all the findings described in the last chapter about the way our actions change our minds. I suspect social contact theory describes the shape of a relationship where two people can grapple together with the challenges of the outside world as equals and, in so doing, think better together. These are the conditions, research suggests, that we need in order to overcome our prejudices and other faulty forms of thought – but they are not easy to achieve.

They are rarely, if ever, met by online spaces such as Twitter, even though social media platforms may appear to be places where people can encounter others very different from themselves as equals. On the internet we may be equals in a superficial way, each with our own account and so on, but of course in practice some people have more followers than others or more money to verify and promote themselves. Moreover, it is rare for those on the internet to be required to co-operate in a long-term way, or to have goals in common. And most social media platforms spend relatively little time legitimizing connections across groups in the same way that universities, for example, can do more easily. Social contact theory may help explain why the internet has not done great amounts to lower prejudice, as optimists once hoped it would. I am personally not overly optimistic about technology as a solution to social problems. It is, however, an interesting thought experiment to consider what kind of social media platform could meet more of the criteria required to reduce prejudice.

Being exposed to people who are different from ourselves, when they are positioned as our equals, collaborators, legitimate allies and yes, our friends, reduces prejudice. This is – to use a word that rarely comes up in political theory – cute. Touching, even. Research shows that it is meaningful friendships, in particular, that allow people to lose their prejudices and change their minds. As one researcher, Miles Hewstone, put it, 'cross-group friendships are perhaps the most effective form of intergroup contact, and have widespread effects and implications.'[4]

But, although it is touching, these findings challenge our common-sense notion that friendship should be outside of, or above, political concerns. This romantic idea of friendship lingers, even amid major societal rifts. It implies friendship might be something that transcends politics, rather than influencing it. I notice this when I hear people boast of their ability to have friendships across party lines. Perhaps the most famous example in American public life is that of the Supreme Court justices Antonin Scalia (a very conservative judge) and Ruth Bader Ginsburg (a very liberal judge). The two connected over their love of opera, and their relationship became an example of the idealized friendship that transcends even the most hotly contested ideological differences. Scalia's son even wrote a passionate op-ed instructing Americans to learn to have friendships of this type just before Donald Trump was elected for the first time.[5] Of course, after Trump was elected for the first time, many Americans found this ideal of friendship regardless of politics (which perhaps never fully made sense, since presumably we would want our friends to share *some* of our values and beliefs) less tenable. One poll found that 13 per cent of Americans had ended a friendship or close relationship because of that election.[6] Many more may well over the next four years. But as with 'the marketplace of ideas' and 'debate', these implicit ideals about friendship may obscure our understanding of what friendship actually means when it comes to politics.

Instead, research suggests that our social connections, and particularly our friendships, are the foundation for quite a lot of what we come to believe about the world, especially when it comes to prejudice against groups but also in other areas (more on the latter shortly). Perhaps one of the most famous studies in social contact theory showed that having just one gay or lesbian friend changed people's minds on homosexuality and gay marriage. As the researcher who conducted the study, Daniel DellaPosta, put it, it is really friendship, even more distant forms of friendship, that turned the dial on some seismic changes in American public opinion:

> If you take the next level to mere acquaintanceship – someone whose name you know, someone who, if you saw them on the street, you might stop and chat with them for a moment – the 'contact effect' sets in ... when you suddenly have to interact with someone from an 'out group' as an individual, it forces you to reconsider your biases.[7]

Exposure at a personal level, as in social contact theory, seems to reduce our sense that those different from us are a threat.

In the US, the change in views about gay rights is probably the fastest-recorded shift in political views on any civil rights issue.[8] Social scientists and psychologists theorize that this might be because someone's sexuality is not necessarily observable – and so one comes to see someone as a peer and friend first, and is left to then wrestle with one's views about their sexuality later.[9] To return to cognitive dissonance, the psychological phenomenon explored in earlier chapters, someone with homophobic views has their sense of self disrupted when they discover that someone they like and respect is gay. In order to maintain a consistent worldview, they generally need to decide either they no longer like that person or that gay people are all right after all (though of course, some people do mental gymnastics to decide that 'just this one is all right' or 'hate the sin, love the sinner'). On the whole, it seems, many people abandoned their homophobia rather than the people they loved.

Indeed, one particularly interesting finding is that 'in general, categories must be salient during contact' for the prejudice-reducing effect to work, meaning that it is important that people's characteristics, such as their sexuality or race, are eventually relevant and noticed during encounters in order for prejudice to be reduced. In other words, we have to go through the process of effectively thinking and noticing that 'Joe is in category x of people I don't like', then 'but now I do like Joe' and finally 'I suppose maybe I can like category x people'. It is not useful, in this sense, to be 'colourblind'. Rather, we lose our prejudices and change our minds precisely when we engage with and notice those differences in our friendships.

Sure, you might say – by now wise to the endless complexity of social sciences – it might seem that change in views on civil rights is impressive, but perhaps it's really that those who are already more open-minded to begin with are also those who end up with friends who are different from them. In that case, it's not that contact causes a change in beliefs, it's just that both are enabled by open-mindedness … right? This is a sensible, cautious thought but, interestingly, studies that compare those who choose who they interact with against those who cannot do so (because, say, they are assigned to interact with them) find that both routes work fairly well. It is true, however, that there is a virtuous spiral. Once you become less prejudiced against a group, you hang out with them more, and then become less prejudiced still.[10] It is the contact itself that seems to do the work, and to create the eventual empathy, liking and trust that come from it.

Friendship is thus not 'above' politics – it is a fundamental part of it, a key way we learn what other people's lives are really like, and so develop our understanding of the shared world.

In one way, all this simply makes sense. Aren't our friends our closest, clearest windows into the innermost lives of, well, anyone other than ourselves? It is from my friends who grew up poor that I learned the most about the constant everyday cognitive, emotional, material burdens of poverty. It is from my friends of colour that I learned the most about the sometimes subtle yet consistent racial ignorance, discrimination and aggression that lace even my supposedly progressive social world. It was certainly not the job of these friends to educate me, nor did they always seek to do so directly. But it is nevertheless through them that I came to understand better, and even to imagine (in a very secondhand way), what it might be like to be materially without, or to be talked over constantly, looked down on or otherwise disrespected. I now find myself wondering whether asking people to come to meetings in person is really fair and affordable for everyone, or whether I am overly impressed by the eloquence of people of colour when I should instead expect it. It is through the eyes of my friends that I find I most critically judge formal policies and even entire social worlds (for example, professional environments, meet-ups, implicit expectations that may or may not work for, say, parents or low-income people). With my friends in mind, I find myself wondering, 'Would this work well for them?' I am describing not merely an intellectual realization or a cognitive shift here but a shift in my world of concerns. No matter how much I may have theoretically cared about these issues before I met these friends and came to love them, I notice and care more about these issues now, in the sense that they somehow feel more 'real' to me.

Some people find it enraging to think we empathize only once we know someone in a group personally, which is, frankly, fair. I too sometimes find it frustrating to observe this phenomenon where people change their views when things get personal, as in the clichéd example of men who suddenly are able to care about women's issues once they have a daughter. I readily accept this point: we should be able to care and have solidarity for groups of people different from ourselves without meeting a likeable member of that group. That would be better for everyone, more just. And we should strive to care about groups even if we do not have friends in them, to see all forms of suffering, oppression and difficulty as relevant to us on the basis of our shared humanity. We would be wise to cherish the phrase of Roman playwright Terence that 'nothing human is foreign to me'. But, for the most part, apparently, this is just not how people come to think and feel about political issues. We are a profoundly social species, moved to both emotional depths and new activities, experiences and thoughts in large part through our relationships with others. This must factor into our calculus of how to make the political world more navigable and thinkable for us all. And perhaps it is also sometimes OK, and even profound and helpful, to learn to see things through the eyes of our friends. While debate and exposure to ideas do relatively little, our relationships with other people have a profound impact on what we believe and how we think, including our social and political views.

Indeed, much of political reasoning is, in practice, necessarily *interdependent* rather than *independent*. This may sound unusual, because 'thinking for oneself' has become a common way of describing someone who can think well. And yet when people radically change the way they think about political issues, it is in many ways unavoidably the result of their social relationships.

When people radically change their political views (for better or worse), they often do so because of the relationships and friends they have. For this reason, it is not so much ideas or arguments that change our political worldview as other people. And for the most part, it is specifically the people we like, respect and even love who can change our minds. Of course, there are better and worse ways for people to influence our views. Thinking well doesn't mean blindly following a herd, caving to peer pressure or assuming the people we love are always right. But it still means relying on other people, especially when it comes to matters of politics. Rather than imagining that the ideal form of political thinking comes from somehow abstracting ourselves from our relationships, then, we might re-imagine thinking well about politics as judicious interdependence, as a matter of relying on others wisely, thinking together carefully and even choosing our friends well.

So our friends and contacts reduce the prejudice we might have against specific groups of people. But is it also logical to assume that contact with other people will change our beliefs? The answer, based on available evidence anyway, is yes, probably, but not always in the way one might suppose.

The most common, folk-psychological assumption about how our friends influence our political views suggests that friendships act like a gravitational force, where we move towards each other gradually, owing to exposure or even peer pressure. (This explains why parents worry about what their children might learn at university: it's not so much about the professors, in many cases, as the 'wrong crowd'.) There is plausibly some truth in this gravitational model of belief change but, on the whole, the evidence that our friends directly change our views is not that strong. To the degree that it is possible to study the effect friends have on one another, research suggests something far more interesting: friends change our minds, but mostly by engaging us in the world, or helping us think more deeply.

One way to measure this is to look at groups of students arbitrarily assigned to live and/or study together in university systems. One study, conducted in Brazil in 2017, found that, once a lot of factors were controlled for, friends had only a very small effect on one another's political views. But they had a huge impact on each other's political engagement – being around politically interested people made less political people more interested in politics. In other words, if you are a relatively liberal student and you make friends with a relatively conservative student, his views will not change yours very much. But if he is deeply involved in politics and talking about it all the time, you are more likely to engage deeply too, ultimately clarifying your own beliefs in the process. This clarification process probably explained the slight apparent move towards the centre by students who spent time discussing politics extensively: it was not so much that their deep beliefs changed, as that they acquired a clearer sense of what their positions really were. In short, then, the evidence suggests our friends are not going to persuade us to prefer progressive or regressive tax policy just by talking to us. But they can inspire us to care more about politics in general, if they care a lot about it. They do also seem to help us figure out what our views actually are. And they are great motivators to political action.

The authors of this study note that their findings are, arguably, beautiful, because they suggest that even 18-year-olds do not engage in groupthink. Rather, friendships encourage us to think more deeply, and understand our own position more clearly, and to engage with politics more broadly. We think, in other words, through our friendships, but this does not make us sheep.*

This research provides more reason to doubt the metaphor of the marketplace of ideas (as it shows that mere exposure to ideas, even our friends' ideas, has little direct effect). But it also provides good reason to think that having robust social networks and many friends can help us come to care about politics more, and perhaps even a little differently, with greater clarity. And that, I must agree, is beautiful.[11]

All this talk about friends engaging us politically may well remind you of the role of protests as recruitment in the last chapter. And indeed, friends are the best predictors for what political groups people join, and for the actions they take (which, of course, can have a profound effect on their views). Those who study both political movements and cults find conversion to and membership of these groups are largely a matter of one's social networks. Even groups that are relatively mainstream tend to rely on what sociologist Mark Granovetter first termed 'strong ties': the influence of very close friends, family members and so on.[12] Interestingly, however, the

---

*This idea fits into theories of 'extended cognition', which show that our thinking happens not only in our brain and our body but also through the tools we use in the world around us. Our phones are a primary example. When I want to remember a thought I've had, I can scribble it in the 'notes' function on my phone, which is painfully omnipresent in my life, usually at my literal fingertips. When I can't remember something, I no longer rack my brain: I simply pick up my phone and search for it. But it's not just our immediate technological devices that shape the way we think. Even structures such as the law organize our thinking for us. Look at how much we think in terms of 'I have the right to' or 'she is entitled to'. We think through our bodies, and technologies, yes, but also through our social structures, especially our friends. C. F. S. Campos, S. Hargreaves Heap and F. Leite Lopez de Leon (2017), 'The Political Influence of Peer Groups: Experimental Evidence in the Classroom', *Oxford Economic Papers*, 69(4): 963–85.

opposite is (probably mostly) true when it comes to things wildly outside of the mainstream, such as cults that believe in aliens. In that case, recruitment may be more likely to happen via 'weak ties' (distant friends, acquaintances, friends of friends and so on), possibly because people who have friends and are strongly embedded in social networks tend not to join alien cults at all.[13] Cults aside, the evidence suggests, the stronger the ties, the more likely it is that a person can get us to join their movement, whether religious or political – unless, interestingly, both people are relatively poor, in which case strong ties appear as ineffective as everything else, probably because people who are relatively poor lack the time and means to engage in committed social action at all.[14]

Researchers studying how to get people to shift their climate-friendly behaviours (such as taking up cycling or installing a heat pump in their house) found that social influence from friends had greater effect than education, feedback, commitment, appeals or even financial incentives.[15] In fact, studies show that the best predictor of whether someone joins a cause is whether their friends do so.[16] One researcher, Jacquelien van Stekelenburg, is wonderfully direct about this, noting: '[F]riends made the difference. If their friends were going [to the protest], they were going as well. Apparently, it was people's friends who kept them to their promises.'[17] Friends seem to be the strong link that keep people involved in social movements in the long run too. One group of researchers found that when activists take time out of activism to tend to their family or career, they will still come back to the movement if their activist network stays intact.[18] People also tend to leave movements when their friends leave, often creating a negative bandwagon effect.[19] In short, friends make the decisive difference in whether we care about, show up and return to movements. This is all, again, probably not friends strong-arming or brainwashing each other, but rather them engaging one another further in areas everyone already cares about.

It's also pretty clear that people can get their friends to vote – because recently people have been making that happen via something called 'relational organizing'. One example is the work done by the team at the New Data Project, a group largely made up of ex-Obama staff, who created an app called Vote with Me. Their efforts were aimed at getting voters to turn out in the US midterm elections, where turnout is notoriously poor. In the US, people's phone numbers, party registrations, records of when they did and didn't vote and voting districts are all public information. (How they voted is not.) So the app could take this data, link it to the contacts in your phone, and tell you which people that you personally knew were voting in marginal districts. You could filter for those who were likely to vote for the party of your choice (although the app was largely used by progressive organizations). The app also gave people special prompts to send to friends, to more distant contacts that one hadn't spoken to in a while and to colleagues. From the perspective of increasing turnout, anyway, it worked beautifully. There was a 2.4 per cent increase in voting, compared with the roughly 0.8 per cent shift generally associated with door-knocking and the approximately 0.2 per cent change associated with phone-banking. Compared with other types of 'transactional canvassing' (as relational organizers like to call it), this technique worked much better for changing people's political behaviour. The useful insight, of course, is that strangers matter little, compared with friends. It is our social world that changes our behaviour most of all.[20]

In short: friends don't convert each other to new positions out of the blue. And they don't usually have to anyway, because we tend to interact more with people who already agree with us. But friends can not only make us less prejudiced; they can also help us figure out our own beliefs and mobilize us to go out in the world and act on them. And that, of course, as we learned in the last chapter, changes and deepens our beliefs as well.

How far can our friendship really extend? I have suggested it is a romantic fantasy to imagine that it is easy or even a good thing to have friends who are utterly opposed in their political views. But that does not mean we cannot have any differences at all. To limit who we are friends with to only those who agree with us suggests a narrowing of the windows we have onto the world, as well as the winnowing down of our own interpersonal political influence. The phrase 'It's not my job to educate you' has become a common phrase in leftish politics lately for good reason, as many exhausted people, often minorities on one axis or another, decide they would really rather not spend time trying to convince people, even indirectly, to see them as equals. And they are right that people who are particularly oppressed or traumatized by an issue should not feel they have to do the work of educating others about it. But the psychology and sociology of political belief change have led me to feel that it is at least somewhat on all of us to educate one another, that this is part of the work of being a citizen, a political agent, even just a human being, in this world. In particular, all this research suggests that it is of vital importance that we build a world where it is at least possible for people regularly to end up in the kinds of scenarios that Gordon Allport and fellow contact theorists suggest change people's minds: in scenarios where we have to collaborate, be positioned as equals, have deep conversations, share experiences and, yes, become friends with people who are not like us.

Why do friends matter so much? I'm going to suggest there are at least two important things that friends do (besides taking us along to protests and puncturing our prejudices), based on the scattered available research. First, our friends widen our field of concerns; and second, they provide us with the kind of space and time and relationship required to truly listen to the experiences of other people and grapple with our own ambivalence.

First, then: the widening of our field of concerns. This has to do with what some psychologists call our 'affective context': our field of immediate concerns. Our affective context is the set of things that seem to matter to us in our real life, the realm of things that feel real and important to us. In the abstract, of course, we nearly all care about what happens to orphaned children in another country or bird habitats nearby, but in truth our affective context is mostly about things that our brain needs to spend immediate energy on, things like our next pay cheque or the people we see day to day. For those who design learning experiences (long a part of my professional life), this is most obvious in that if you teach using things in people's 'affective context', they learn much more quickly than if you teach with abstract examples (however theoretically interesting those abstract examples might be).[21]

Our friends can change what we care about because we care about them. And if our friends care a lot about politics, then politics itself can become part of our affective context, something that we care about because our friends engage with us on it and because thinking about political issues has become part of our daily actions too.

Our friends may even show us who we can love and care about by example. Social contact theorists have found that 'indirect friendship' can also weaken our prejudices; so to know that your friend is friends with an out-group member is almost as good for reducing prejudice as knowing an out-group member yourself.[22] (For example, if you are prejudiced against people from the Middle East, it might be just as powerful for you to have a friend who has a Middle Eastern friend as to have one yourself!) It's as though our friends form an unofficial advisory group for us, advising even just by their examples. The way they live their lives gestures to us about who we can also trust.

There have always been debates about what motivates people when it comes to politics. Some argue that people are primarily motivated by material self-interest. But theories about self-interest have trouble explaining 'champagne socialists' (richer left-wing people) and poor people who support conservative fiscal policies. Other theorists have suggested that status is what motivates people. But what does status truly provide? In most cases the answer is: relationships. Indeed, the sociologist Martijn van Zomeren has argued that relationships are our primary motivation, which means that humans are *relational actors*, not rational actors. Many of the actions we might ponder day to day – from our plans for the weekend to our goals for the next few years – are really ways to gain or retain relationships. Even things that are ostensibly about professional life, hobbies, health or personal appearance can generally be boiled down to a desire to be lovable or desirable or connected to or have more time with other people. (This is actually quite the thought experiment, I find, and something worth pondering when it comes to one's own life.) Van Zomeren notes that relationships tend to trump even societal pressures, and that 'this is why a son who has committed a crime remains a son; and why Romeo and Juliet defied cultural norms in order to be together'.[23]

It can be helpful to think about our friends as those we are tethered to, and in some sense must respond to. Van Zomeren, notably, quotes Antoine de Saint-Exupéry, who wrote, 'man is a knot into which relationships are tied.' He suggests that we can understand what human beings really are by thinking about them as a sort of spider, a 'spider that can feel any movement in its web so that it can respond to it ... most people, most of the time, are moved and motivated by feeling any movement in the social relationships in their social network.'[24] Indeed, I would argue that not only are we a spider sitting on a web of social connections but also, like a spider, we think through that web, defining what we think in and through the relationships we have with people and the relationships those people have, reacting to people, learning from them, emulating them, distinguishing ourselves from them.

Now on to the second way our friends change our minds: by introducing new thoughts in an open-ended way, and sitting with us as we grapple with our own ambivalence.

One model for this might lie in 'deep canvassing', one of the few interventions in recent years that has proved strikingly effective on people's beliefs, even though it happens between strangers. I became familiar with this technique during my years studying cognitive dissonance theory, because it is a technique that uses insights into cognitive dissonance, and which has been shown to be especially effective at changing minds on political issues. Deep canvassing is called 'deep' because it requires more time and effort than normal political canvassing. In 'normal' canvassing, those campaigning for a particular candidate or issue might knock on the door of someone's house, ask them who they are voting for and, if they seem to be on the fence, give them a few reasons to come to their side. Often the data they gather is the most important resource – I have done this kind of canvassing, and it is well known that a lot of the value is having a list of people who say they will vote for your candidate. Then, on the day of the election, the canvassers go around again and make sure those people have actually voted, driving them to the polls if they would like. In other words, even the most enthusiastic 'regular' canvassers know their main job is turnout, not persuasion (and social science findings back this up).[25]

In contrast, deep canvassers are doing something slightly different. Rather than spend about ten minutes on the doorstep with someone, they tend to take up to 30 minutes, sometimes more. The technique starts by asking the person to rate where they stand on the issue on a scale of 1 to 10. (As people tend not to rate themselves either a 1 or a 10, they therefore have to begin to reckon with their own ambivalence when engaging in this exercise.) The deep canvasser then asks the person they are canvassing why they aren't at a 'zero' or 'ten' in their beliefs (which lets the person articulate their view in a way that allows for ambiguity) and listens in the least judgemental way possible (this may take some training). Then the person shares their own experiences, which often contradict the views of the person being canvassed. (For example, deep canvassing has been influential in changing public bathroom legislation in Massachusetts, and many of the canvassers were trans or queer themselves. So the canvasser might listen to someone's views on why people should go to the bathroom of their assigned sex, and then share their own experience of how difficult this makes their life.) Finally, the deep canvasser simply asks what the person's views on the topic are now that the conversation has occurred. Most of the time, the person's views have moved. And more strikingly, they often have moved a lot, in a permanent way.

In fact, deep canvassing is shockingly effective for an intervention of relatively short duration. As my friend, journalist David McRaney puts it,

> the overall shift [researchers David] Broockman and [Joshua] Kalla measured in [one deep canvassing study about trans rights] in Miami was greater than 'the opinion change that occurred from 1998 to 2012 towards gay men and lesbians in the United States' ... a mind change of much less than that could easily rewrite laws, win a swing state, or turn the tide of an election ... This was one conversation with people who mostly had limited experience with the technique ... about ten minutes each. Had the canvassers been experts, had they continued having conversations over several weeks, had those conversations been longer, the evidence suggests the impact would have been enormous.[26]

Remarkably, these changes also appeared to remain in place many months later, when researchers returned, and to be effective across the political spectrum.[27] Just as interestingly, those whose views had changed were no longer as susceptible to attack ads on the minority groups they had discussed (so attack ads on transgender rights, for example). In other words, what seemed to have occurred was a relatively permanent, relatively significant, relatively unchangeable shift in beliefs for people across the political spectrum. While most instances of deep canvassing work on questions of prejudice, deep canvassing also appears to have been successful when it comes to climate issues.[28]

I had the pleasure of interviewing one of the aforementioned researchers studying deep canvassing, Joshua Kalla, about this technique. Kalla told me that it's still not 100 per cent clear to researchers why deep canvassing works as well as it does. He and other researchers are still testing it out in different ways to isolate different variables in the process and see which have an effect. However, based on the research that has already been done, he suggests that three things in particular seem to have the ability to change people's minds:

1. Staying non-judgemental during the conversation. This seems to decrease 'reactance', the phenomenon I mentioned in earlier chapters, where people strongly resist what they perceive to be any attempts at manipulation. This also sets the stage for the person to take in new 'information' or ideas without immediately arguing back against it and reinforcing existing views. Once trust is built (through non-judgemental listening), we are ready to take in new points of view, and at least integrate them into our understanding of the world.
2. 'Narrative exchange', or the exchanging of stories. Those studying deep canvassing tried different scripts, and they found that the most important part is the canvasser telling a story about their own life experience. Analogies don't work so well, but what does is a story told by the canvasser about their own lived experience with that issue. Kalla told me that he thinks this is effective because, in short, when someone tells you their experience, you can't tell them that it didn't happen (or at least, people are very unlikely to).
3. Finally, Kalla thinks it is probably important that the canvasser then asks about the person's views again. This, he suspects, helps the person being canvassed recognize that they've actually made a shift.[29]

I am fascinated by deep canvassing, though not because I think it is a silver bullet for political problems (after all, it's time-intensive, exhausting and potentially just as useful for those I disagree with). Rather, I think it's important because if research on it continues to show these kinds of results and insights, it points to the specific aspects of communicating with another person that shape the way we think about politics. It suggests that what changes people's minds on political issues is: (1) getting the sense from another person that it is OK to be ambivalent and shift our view, that we won't be judged for either of those things; (2) hearing stories from someone else that show the issues in another light, especially if the two people have a strong rapport; and (3) discussion that helps the person verbalize their thoughts and see that they've changed their mind.

In other words, what happens as a curious experiment in deep canvassing is very plausibly what happens all the time between friends, and may be why friends tend to help us elaborate our thinking and shift our views. Deep canvassing experiments have thus far occurred with strangers, but it's interesting to consider what kinds of even stronger effects they might have if they happened between trusted friends. In fact, conversations like this are probably happening between friends all the time, and this, I am willing to theorize, is part of the political power of friendships. Even without a specific framework of speech between friends, it's likely that part of what makes our friendships such a strong driver of changes in political understanding is this kind of non-judgemental listening and learning about the life of someone else. During this period we are refining our thinking against their reality, testing out our ideas to see how they work. If we're lucky (and we are not all this lucky, and not all friendships are like this), our friends are also people with whom we don't always have to get it right; we can say something a bit off, and they can challenge us; we can disagree or end up cranky with each other and try again another time. This, too, I suspect, is part of the core of good thinking on any issue. But we're unlikely to manage it except with people who really care about us.

'Don't talk about politics' is a common rule of thumb when it comes to polite etiquette, at least where I grew up, in the US. Politics is usually listed alongside religion, money and sex as something not to be discussed in polite company, as it ruins social gatherings and friendships. My own suggestion in this book is not quite that censorious. I don't think we should never discuss politics, and I even believe we should sometimes do so, at the cost of a bit of awkwardness. But my suggestion is that if we want to build a world that would actually enable all of us to think better about politics, we'd have to start somewhere else: with creating new social ties and forms of belonging, new friendships, new possibilities in our social world. One of the key challenges for our current political age is to create a world that is full of the kinds of experiences and environments where we are likely to make and keep friends, and have these kind of belief-shifting 'deep' conversations regularly.

Deep canvassing isn't a realistic option for most political change. But imagine if our lives were structured so we had conversations like that all the time anyway. Imagine if our friends were more deeply tied into our lives – if we more commonly organized our children's schools together, sat down to dinner together, created local policies together? In researching this book, I spoke to dozens of activists and organizers. I was particularly struck by someone working with a renters' union in Washington, DC. She noted that residents in the buildings she worked in would be likely to see electoral canvassing as fairly transactional. This was not how people became politically involved or came to see issues differently. Instead, over the years, people in her group had learned that, no matter how much you might wish to organize people politically or convince them of your point of view, the way people are moved about political issues is actually through relationships. For example, one building's leaders wanted more police to come onto the property because there was poor security, a lot of break-ins, some shootings, car theft and so on. This troubled the left-wing housing organizers, as they were staunch police abolitionists, but they got nowhere on this front for some time. Then the apartment building had a Thanksgiving turkey giveaway, and management called the police on the tenants, who were incensed that police would come out for that but not for an actual crime. It was at that point, when they already had a strong relationship with the housing activists, when something crucial had happened in their world, that the tenants and the housing organizers could finally begin to consider who the police really served, and what another vision of a safe housing block would look like. But both, notably, were necessary: the long, slow build of a relationship and the particular event.[30] There is no substitute for being there for people, over and over again. Which is, of course, what friends do. We should talk about politics, but the key challenge is not the conversation but the relationship, not the arguments we have but the actions we end up taking together.

In contrast to what I have described above, Western culture still, on the whole, lauds the idea of 'independent thinking' and often equates it with good thinking, especially when it comes to politics. And notably, this idea of independent thinking has a history. As modern democratic movements took hold in the West, many feared the passions (often violent) of the crowds that came with them. Perhaps most famously, the French polymath Gustave Le Bon wrote a book outlining the dangers of the psychology of the crowd, which he saw as highly suggestible and manipulable. Le Bon had watched members of the Paris Commune burn down large sections of Paris, including the Palais des Tuileries and the library of the Louvre, and this had a profound effect on his thinking, which became fiercely conservative, and indeed arguably reactionary in many respects.[31] His writings on the crowd became enormously influential with a variety of audiences. Hitler and Mussolini liked the book because it suggested that strong leaders could take hold of the passions of the crowd.[32] The book also influenced the work of Sigmund Freud, as well as Freud's nephew Edward Bernays, considered the father of public relations. Even the American president Theodore Roosevelt was drawn to Le Bon's work.[33] In all these cases, Le Bon's analysis was considered important because it showed that most people were highly manipulable, especially when relating to others. Much of political theory has carried this assumption too. As theorist Fredric Jameson puts it, 'This loss of self in the crowd ... has been the central indictment proposed by counterrevolutionary ideology since its invention, knowing its high points in the grisliest mob scenes of the French Revolution.'[34] Perhaps it is in part because of the fear of crowds that a variety of political theorists, from Marcus Aurelius to John Stuart Mill, have insisted that good thinking is fundamentally independent thinking, set apart from others. These theorists (perhaps understandably) feared the inability of people to resist the influence of others, whether those are often oppressive institutions such as the Church or state or simply the peer pressure of those around us.

To be honest, I get it. Big crowds can be terrifying. A descendant of Holocaust survivors, I always think of the crowds that followed Hitler. But, while the crowd may often be dangerous, it does not follow that good thinking is done alone.

There are ways of thinking with others that do not follow the logic of the feared (mindless) crowd.

In my own research into the psychological pressures that are part of persuasion I have come to believe that today we face another kind of political danger, one where people are thinking badly not because they are caught up in vociferous conformity but, rather, precisely because they are all convinced they are thinking 'for themselves'. This is perhaps exemplified by the phrase 'Do your own research!' which is often used by conspiracy theorists. The desire to do one's one research is probably part of a drive towards autonomy that is observable over and over again in human beings, one that is in fact a common theme in cognitive science research. Psychological phenomena such as cognitive dissonance and reactance occur in part due to subjects' desire to see themselves as having agency: that is, not being manipulated by anyone else, choosing actions for themselves, and thinking well of themselves and their actions. While this sounds good, the pressure to feel this way can have the perverse effect of making one defend against any sense that one might have been wrong.

Today I'd suggest, based on both the way we see people defend their beliefs and the psychological research to hand, that it's more likely that we'll remain closed-minded, convinced that we're thinking independently, than get drawn into a bloodthirsty crowd. In other words, what left-wing theorists have sometimes termed 'false consciousness' may no longer look like mindlessly obeying norms and power structures. Given new technologies that allow for echo chambers, disinformation, a weakening trust in institutions and a cultural ethos that emphasizes the self (in everything from our social media profiles to the concept of 'self-care'), today faulty political consciousness may look like exactly the opposite of the historical fears about people being swept up in a mob. Faulty political consciousness today is perhaps more likely to look like someone who is insistent that they are an individual, an independent thinker: yes, doing their own research. The person we should most fear will convince us of something wrong is ourselves.

The alternative, I'd like to suggest, to both the harmful crowd and the harmful individualist is the person who thinks in an interdependent way, relying on but not solely reliant on a select group they can trust – working and therefore thinking with their allies. As I have shown, our friends exert influence not by brainwashing us or corralling us into their way of thinking, but by helping us become less prejudiced and more politically active and thoughtful.

Nearly all good reasoning involves other people. The philosopher Elijah Millgram has argued that this is in fact especially so today, owing to a key feature of the modern world: increasing hyper-specialization. He points out that early humans were, at least compared with humans today, largely unspecialized in their knowledge, such that all members of a small group would know the basics of how to hunt, gather food and so on. (Of course, this may be a romanticization of early societies, but it is probably true that none of them had a job title like 'Domestic Commodities Logistics Account Executive, MENA Region'.) In any case, Millgram argues, the amount of information and expertise available to the human species has skyrocketed as a result of modern scientific knowledge, as well as a highly specialized labour market, such that all knowledge now relies on trust between a long, interconnected chain of experts:

> We are, all of us, playing a variant of the children's game of telephone, in which, at each stage, a player receives a handful of premises that he is not equipped to properly understand, reassess, or reason with; his move is to

deploy those premises to produce a conclusion in his own area of expertise; he then dumbs it down, stripping out the hedges, qualifications and so on needed to make intelligent use of it, and makes it available to a different player (one who is not equipped to properly understand, reassess and reason with it), for that next player's turn.[35]

Much of the time this game of telephone in modern societies seems to work remarkably well; most of us happily get on planes, drive on the highway and buy packaged food without worrying too much, trusting the expertise of everyone from regulators to corporations. It's worth marvelling at the amount of trust that is happening all the time in our modern world. Even something as common as getting on a subway car is in fact a massive feat of trust. And Millgram's point is that it is an act of trust in the people who engineered the subway, in their expertise. But as a political theorist I notice other acts of trust necessary to that experience: in the driver, in the news reporter who told me the city was safe that day, even in my fellow passengers, that might help me in case of any emergency. This is a more general social trust which, yes, is fraying but is still a requirement in modern life. We are constantly in the hands of others. And, I would argue, this is not true only when it comes to technology but also when it comes to understanding our political world. We cannot know how sexist our world is without listening to women, or how racist the world is without talking to people of colour. Many conceptions of a good thinker suggest they are a person who knows a lot, or who can argue well. But much of thinking well is actually about relating to and trusting other people wisely.

It's rare that political theorists and philosophers have given much attention to this aspect of thinking. One exception, however, is the connection between certain feminist theorists and the work of 'consciousness-raising' groups. These groups were particularly popular in the 1970s in feminist and gay liberation circles, and they generally involved women taking turns giving examples from their own lives of areas where they had experienced oppression. For example, women might end up each bringing examples of poor treatment from men at work. Often these groups allowed women to slowly identify or even develop new ideas or concepts to elucidate their experiences – so that women in consciousness-raising groups coined the term 'sexual harassment', for example, a term that did not exist before this movement.[36]

Consciousness-raising groups have fallen out of vogue today, which is unfortunate because, like deep canvassing, they offer a format to convey some of the benefits of friendship through a wider and more egalitarian practice. For, although I have been talking up friendship and its political possibilities, it's worth saying that friendship, however important, remains a flawed institution for political change. It is exclusive, after all, and rather unequal too: some of us are frankly more popular than others. This can happen for quite arbitrary reasons, and sometimes even for reasons that are sad or cruel. Plus, as so many social scientists note, we tend to pick friends like ourselves, who are likely to already agree with us.[37] I hope that something like consciousness-raising groups can become a practice once again, so we can learn to listen deeply to people who are not yet our friends, and engage with them in the way that friendship and long-form relationships allow us to do.

When it comes to politics, it's the relationship, not the conversation. (And it's certainly not the lone argument, however sharp that argument may be in theory.) Given all the evidence in this chapter, if we were to consider the skills and virtues of a person who is 'good at' politics, in the sense of either helping others reason well or building political power and consensus, they look, interestingly, much like a good friend. A good friend can be critical of others, they probably have firm boundaries, they might even have some enemies, but they also have a key set of emotional and relational skills with which they navigate the world, in addition to a set of intellectual insights. And this set of skills and relationships is as central to their thinking as anything else. This friend is not engaged in a sort of crossword puzzle of checking all one's facts or looking at 'both sides' of an argument in forensic detail, and they are not only engaged in what is usually considered to be 'critical thinking'. They are attentive to the truth, but they are also good at discerning who they can trust, good at retaining the relationships they need to engage in a form of reasoning that is necessarily interdependent and communal.

The idea of political virtues as adjacent to the virtues involved in friendship is ancient: Aristotle opined on the virtues involved in friendship and their similarity to the virtues involved in good political life. (Aristotle argued, in fact, that friends are people who share their intellect when it comes to both practical and intellectual concerns, and that there was such a thing as 'political friendship', the kind of friendship all citizens should arguably engage in when it came to the running of their homeland.[38]) Other theorists throughout history have also theorized friendship as a set of virtues. And even today, modern academic theorists such as José Medina have argued that there are 'epistemic virtues' in politics; Medina's include humility, curiosity, diligence and open-mindedness.[39] In both the most ancient and modern cases there are, interestingly, overlaps between what makes a good friend and what makes a good thinker. So while the prevalent emphasis on 'independent thinking' I've described may neglect the important social skills at work in thinking well about politics, there is an interesting, quieter tradition in

Western political theory to draw on for those of us who want to understand the deep connection between being a good friend and being a good citizen or political thinker. And we should.

This chapter and the last also illustrate large parts of why 'critical thinking' and arguments on their own are so ineffective. Compared to all the weight of our own actions and our strongest relationships, it would truly be surprising if an argument here or there could change some of our most fundamental beliefs.

To think better about politics, then, (and help others to do so too) one might focus not on only arguments or intellectual exchange but on the practices that help people be and acquire better political 'friends', on the structures that let them actively explore the world around them. I'll also look at what doesn't help with any of this, and what is counterproductive. Which means (and you may have been wondering when I'd get to this): it's time to consider Twitter.

5

Take Back Twitter
(and Other Infrastructure)

A few years ago, in the fall of 2022, after several threatened lawsuits and a strange stunt involving a sink, the richest man in the world, the billionaire Elon Musk, bought Twitter for $44 billion.[1] He claimed he did so because 'it is important to the future of civilization to have a common digital town square, where a wide range of beliefs can be debated in a healthy manner, without resorting to violence.'[2] He claimed, in other words, that he was there to save debate, the marketplace of ideas and democracy itself.

Whatever we might think of his claims (and I suspect readers will have plenty of thoughts), things almost immediately went preposterously wrong. In those first weeks, after Musk laid off thousands of employees, he also instituted harsher workplace policies, and many more employees quit. Soon about 80 per cent of Twitter's employees were no longer working at the company.[3] Payroll, security failures and a lack of crucial staff led to issues with its servers and code that threatened to shut down the platform permanently.[4]

Meanwhile, in this newly purchased supposed marketplace of ideas, Musk himself swiftly tweeted an anti-LGBTQ conspiracy theory, then deleted it.[5] People started to use the new blue check verification system to impersonate people, especially Musk himself, often causing widespread misinformation.[6] Someone impersonated the drug company Eli Lilly and claimed it was offering free insulin (which it usually sells at extortionate rates), causing a massive fall in the company's stock price.[7] Employees criticized Musk publicly on his own platform, and he fired them.[8] Uses of hate slurs rose dramatically.[9] Advertisers, concerned about Musk's position as a 'free speech absolutist' (his preferred term), fled the platform, and revenue shrank by as much as 80 per cent.[10] Ever the diplomat, Musk simply told advertisers concerned about his endorsement of an anti-Semitic conspiracy theory to 'Go fuck yourself.'[11]

And then, of course, with X in tow, Musk began to bestow favours, time and attention on President Donald Trump, then out of office. Trump had been banned from Twitter after the storming of the US Capitol building, owing to fears he would continue to use his account to deny the 2020 election result and encourage violence. Yet Musk put out a poll asking if Trump should be reinstated, and 'Yes' won by a narrow margin. 'Vox Populi, Vox Dei,' Musk declared, and Trump was back.[12] Trump previously loved Twitter so much that, when he was banned, he funded the creation of an entirely different site, Truth Social. From there he insisted that he had no use for Twitter. But such is the power of Twitter/X's huge platform that Trump was willing to return, despite his protests to the contrary. Upon being reinstated Trump tweeted a photo of his recent mug shot from a Georgia jail and the words 'Election interference. Never surrender!' Plus a link to his fundraiser, of course.[13]

Meanwhile, members of Twitter's Trust and Safety council resigned, and then it was shut down.[14] A few weeks later, under pressure from the board of his other company, Tesla, and under fire for banning the mention of competitors and suspending the accounts of journalists who appeared to criticize him, Musk put things to a vote, using a poll on Twitter asking if he should step down as CEO and promising to abide by the results of the poll.[15] Twitter users voted 'Yes'. And this time the vox populi did not get what it wanted; supposed democracy defender Musk did not step down, claiming he would do it later and then suggesting the vote was rigged by bots.[16]

With Trump and others reinstated, and journalists banned, X limped along, having lost most of its share value, only intermittently profitable at best, with perhaps less meaningful moderation than ever before.[17] But although it may not exactly have been doing well as a business, it remained a central part of how Musk sought to reach Trump and the American people.[18] In February 2023 Musk noticed that his tweet about the Superbowl had done much worse than President Biden's on the same topic. He called a 2.30 a.m. emergency meeting of X engineers (and indeed any employees who could code) to change the algorithm and expand his reach.[19] The engineers designed a new algorithm that inflated Musk's tweets' reach by a factor of 1,000. Musk's tweets are now wildly overrepresented to basically all Twitter users, so that using Twitter often feels as if the worst guy at the party had trapped everyone else in a one-sided, unending conversation. Six months after that, X allowed political ads back on the site after banning them in 2019. This meant that, if X was meant to be a marketplace of ideas, users were being exposed mostly to those ideas that had money behind them.[20]

By the time the next American presidential election came around, Musk had also become increasingly obsessed with X personally, and not just professionally. One journalist noted that during some weeks 'there was [only] one 90-minute period – between 3.00 and 4.29 a.m. local time – when he never posted. Every other half-hour period, night or day, he [had] sent at least one tweet [during the course of that week].'[21] Because Musk is chronically online, speaks English and sleeps odd hours, he has ended up taking in a great deal of British content (since Britain is five to eight hours ahead), which made him strangely and deeply invested in British culture wars even as the US election loomed: 'His shortest overnight break [was] ... him logging off after retweeting a meme comparing London's Metropolitan police force to the Nazi SS, before bounding back online four and a half hours later to retweet a crypto influencer complaining about jail terms for Britons attending protests.' The algorithm of his own platform shaped his brain. And perhaps not for the best. X's own AI, Grok, flagged Musk as perhaps the biggest spreader of misinformation on the site.[22] As went Musk, so went the platform. Studies from the University of Wisconsin and Cambridge University show that X has become increasingly right-wing, with right-wing ideas reaching more people and other, (somewhat) left-wing accounts, including Biden's White House, reaching fewer.[23]

Of course, Musk didn't stop with spreading misinformation on his own platform. He began a 'secret lobbying campaign' to convince Trump to pick J. D. Vance, a venture capitalist with ties to Silicon Valley, as his running mate.[24] He founded several special PACs, or political action committees, to get Trump elected. He created a giveaway for registered voters in swing states, helped fund false, contradictory, misleading ads to misrepresent on everything from Israel–Palestine to abortion to election fraud, and even funded text messages and advertisements that were deceptive and superficially appeared to be sent by Kamala Harris's campaign.[25]

For all the reasons outlined in previous chapters, I am not suggesting that buying Twitter did all that much to sway the election by itself, especially not in the sense of *changing minds*. The best data available so far suggests Twitter has not changed any previous election results, although it probably did sway a small number of independent voters to vote *against* Trump in 2016 and 2020.[26] This should not be surprising, because digital infrastructure like this is unlikely to have enough influence on people's real-life relationships or daily actions to change their minds, though some people do occasionally change their politics when using it heavily.

It's more likely that Twitter was useful for two reasons: first, Trump liked Twitter, so Musk could regulate X to suit Trump and try to win favour this way. And second, as with the *Requerimiento*, Twitter provides a sort of illusion of public discourse and support that make both Musk and Trump appear more legitimate, especially to their supporters. It gave them a crowd to cheer for them, and offered a decoy, false form of democracy for people to focus on.

On election night, Trump and Musk celebrated together.[27] And Musk, who has $3 billion in contracts with the US federal government, was set up to head a newly created 'government efficiency' commission aimed at shrinking (and outsourcing) the federal government. This positioned him to regulate the regulators who investigate his companies (there are at least 20 recent investigations or reviews).[28] Should he not have a falling out with Trump (and he may well have by the time this book is published), he may be able to take apart the federal government and all it funds, from academic and medical research to environmental regulation. If he does not, other wealthy men (or, occasionally, women) hungry for unregulated markets and bits of our infrastructure surely will.

Through all this, Musk's wealth continued to grow. In the month after Trump's election in November 2024, Musk's personal wealth grew by about 70 per cent.[29] If his wealth keeps growing at the same rate as the last few years, he will be a trillionaire in three years' time.[30] Of course, other billionaires want in on the same astronomical wealth and power. So this term they've got in line: for the first time Mark Zuckerberg and Jeff Bezos have praised Trump and his victory, and donated to his inaugural fund.[31]

Many of the people who were upset or outraged by the changes to Twitter tried, and sometimes struggled, to explain why. It was, strangely, as if they didn't quite have the language for it. For example, in March 2023 Musk announced that soon 'only verified accounts will be eligible to be in For You recommendations … Voting in polls will require verification for the same reasons.'[32] In response, Luke Zaleski, the legal affairs editor at Condé Nast, wrote a popular rejoinder tweet: 'Just a reminder to everyone – Elon is a rightwing media mogul with massive conflicts of interests in various fields that require governmental oversight and regulation – who's openly and not so openly – utilizing his giant personal social-media platform to serve his own political purposes.'[33] Absolutely. But our capitalist society generally allows wealthy people to buy companies and do things for political gain. The thing that made people especially upset in this case, I'd suggest, is that the company Musk owns is a vehicle for the public to engage in activities that are central to civic life. As an unknown tweeter, Avi Bueno, put it (his account later disappeared), 'We should probably have a serious discussion about the ease with which a billionaire haphazardly purchased & immediately destroyed a company that ... facilitated essential communication for hundreds of millions.'[34]

The missing word here is 'infrastructure': 'we' let Musk buy a crucial piece of digital infrastructure. (More on infrastructure in a moment.) Musk purchasing the platform was painful to many people not only because it changed their digital habits but also because they sensed, without necessarily being able to express it, that he had captured a piece of potential democratic infrastructure and turned it into something far worse. Although most probably didn't think about Twitter as 'infrastructure', many already grasped that there was something about its function that was potentially more socially and politically important than, say, Netflix. The frequent fury over being charged for premium use emerges from people's intuitive sense that something like Twitter should be an important, free service (not owned by a belligerent, radicalized billionaire). It probably also emerges from the sense that, while Twitter was of course coded by a specific company, like so many platforms, what really made it successful was the free labour of millions of us – writing, tweeting, connecting, sharing.

Twitter may well also have become so popular in part because of our cultural fascination with debate and the marketplace of ideas, as it appeared to provide all this instantaneously. More than this, many commentators (perhaps extra-keen on the platform as the perfect vehicle for social commentary) had long believed that Twitter might play a central role in certain kinds of political and social change. As the journalist Vincent Bevins notes, around the time of the Occupy Protests and the Arab Spring,

> Andrew Sullivan, for *The Atlantic*, published a piece titled 'The Revolution Will be Twittered.' In the *New York Times*, Nicholas Kristof claimed that 'in the

quintessential 21st-century conflict ... on the one side are government thugs firing bullets ... on the other side are young protestors firing 'tweets'; ... Mark Pfeifle, a former deputy national security advisor in the George W. Bush Administration, tried to give the Nobel Prize to Twitter.[35]

I suspect Twitter will not be winning that prize now. But once upon a time many idealized it as the platform that would lead to all their favoured democratic uprisings and/or enact the ideal of democracy itself. Many activists, commentators and even everyday citizens saw Twitter as the incarnation of democracy-as-discourse. In practice, as Bevins notes, Twitter was a weak point for movements in many ways, not only because it meant that protests were only loosely organized, or because activists often thought they were doing more than they were, but also because governments used social media platforms to find and arrest dissidents.

Indeed, infrastructure is always contested in this way: used by both the powerful and the masses in competing ways to gain power, used for and against democratic life. At one end of things, users might feel they are engaged in democratic life, but at the other end, the platforms and governments involved in digital communication are often pulling their own strings, sometimes with greater effect. For example, Meta – Facebook, Instagram and WhatsApp's parent company – offers 'Free Basics' internet access to low-income people in many parts of the world, accessible, of course, largely through their apps. What this means in practice is that many people get free data to access the internet, but only very specific parts of the internet that Meta permits (much is censored), and often only the sites of third-party providers who are collaborating with or favoured by Meta: a violation of the principle of 'net neutrality'.[36] If you are poor, Meta will let you have the infrastructure of the internet, but only in part and on their terms. Similarly, TikTok has now been caught up in a cold war between the US and China.[37] So while these platforms seem frivolous on the surface to many (all the weird dancing videos! All the incomprehensible disputes and subtweets!), they are the centre of conflicts between the most powerful states on earth because of their central, infrastructural role in public life.

And in truth, as upsetting as the takeover of Twitter was in some ways, the most remarkable thing about it was that it wasn't remotely an anomaly. Nothing about a billionaire owning an important piece of communications infrastructure (or using it to try to influence democratic elections) is unusual. Fifteen or so billionaires own a huge percentage of America's news channels, and six corporations alone control much of it.[38] Rupert Murdoch owns Fox News and the *Wall Street Journal*. Jeff Bezos owns the *Washington Post*. Michael Bloomberg owns, well, Bloomberg. Donald and Samuel Newhouse own the media company that in turn owns *Wired*, *Vanity Fair*, *The New Yorker* and *Vogue*. In 2016 the Cox Media Group division owned seven daily newspapers, 59 radio stations, more than a dozen non-daily publications and 14 broadcast television stations. And so on.

Twitter's takeover felt upsetting because it felt like a piece of infrastructure for democracy. And it felt extra upsetting because it already *felt* like it belonged to all of us: so many users helped make it the place it was. It was Twitter users' labour, interests and relationships that made the site work. It felt wrong for a collective conversation about the future of the world to be purchasable, weaponizable. But from the perspective of capitalism, the only unusual thing about the Twitter acquisition was that people could see it happening and understand its impact on their life straight away. The world was treated to a real-time demonstration of what happens when our public discourse infrastructure is owned by someone with his own particularly obvious, slightly bizarre and constantly live-tweeted agenda.

In previous chapters I argued that both a 'marketplace of ideas' and 'debate' are poor frameworks for democratic thinking. Instead, I suggested, people require very specific kinds of social ties and daily activity to think well. In this chapter I'm going to sketch out what that implies about what we need in order to live in a democracy. My suggestion is that we need infrastructure to think well when it comes to politics: democratic infrastructure of several very specific kinds. Twitter's purchase was upsetting because it seemed like the takeover of some of this democratic infrastructure. But, in truth, Twitter often functioned as anti-democratic infrastructure, even before Musk took it over. Which is to say: it worked against many of the features that tend to define democracy that I have listed in earlier chapters: protections for minority groups and people's ability to see one another as equals, for example. And compared with real-life relationships and changes in people's lives, it could only ever have done so much. Platforms like Twitter are simply better set up to polarize and agitate than to facilitate deep reasoning, and this will probably be true so long as they exist with a profit motive, owned by capitalists.

In this way, Twitter/X provides an example of a key reason that the myth of democracy as a 'marketplace of ideas' is so dangerous. A piece of communications infrastructure like Twitter can often only offer weak support to democratic life, while it can all too easily be misappropriated to anti-democratic ends. When this happens, its relationship to the myth of a marketplace of ideas means that X can provide a façade for highly undemocratic forms of life. The powerful and wealthy can capture infrastructure and make it antidemocratic. They can use instruments like Twitter not only to limit our understanding of democracy to mere idea exposure and voting but also to provide a veil of democratic legitimacy for their schemes and rally those who are already on their side.

What this means for all of us is that we need to build a much wider variety of infrastructures for democracy, on- and offline. And we need to, either literally or metaphorically, take back Twitter and other platforms, which is to say, we need to either turn them back into democratic infrastructures by owning and running them collectively or abandon them and shut them down.

Understood broadly, infrastructure is the physical and organizational stuff that enables our regular action-possibilities. It is what underlies markets, making them possible in the first place. You cannot get to the grocery store without roads, for example, or go online shopping without wifi access or mobile data. We just cannot function, individually or collectively, without it. Our basic human needs (air, water, food, shelter) are either literally provided for or else heavily influenced by infrastructure, nearly all the time. The scholar Susan Leigh Star put it beautifully when she wrote that infrastructure is 'transparent to use, in the sense that it does not have to be re-invented each time or assembled for each task, but invisibly supports those tasks'.[39] We don't notice that we rely on infrastructure too often, but that is precisely because we rely on it so thoroughly and continuously.

In fact, mostly we notice infrastructure and its importance only when it breaks. Which is part of what happened when it came to Twitter. Prior to Musk's takeover, a lot of people had come to rely on Twitter not only for news and a certain kind of viral light-hearted silliness but also for communicating in vital ways about political issues, or to find and build communities. In addition, writers, journalists, artists, scientists, activists and government leaders who had come to rely in very significant ways on Twitter, in order to communicate with their followers or the public at large, lost out overnight as their followers left the platform and Musk changed the algorithm to give visibility and priority to those who paid for the service. Those who stayed soon found their experience dimmed: more bugs, fewer people and less relevant timelines with a suspicious quantity of Musk's own tweets.[40] Musk had sort of broken his own favourite toy, which would be funny if it hadn't broken so much for so many other people.[41] Whole digital communities were being displaced, especially vulnerable ones. Communities built over long periods of time, from activist groups to Black Twitter (a group who used Twitter to discuss issues of interest to the Black community, push for social change and share information, especially about police violence), suddenly found themselves struggling to know how to organize or reconnect if they wanted to leave the platform. If they stayed, their experience was more fragmented and the environment more hostile.[42]

Infrastructure is a relatively modern term, which probably originated around the 1800s in France.[43] There has, of course, been infrastructure underlying societies for much longer: the Romans were notable champions of infrastructure in their time. But it's fair to say that, the more technologically advanced our societies have become, the more we rely on infrastructure. More of us use roads, public water supplies and wifi than ever before, and more of us too are educated in a school system or read the news – two other services that, I will argue, also function as societal infrastructure, even if they are less commonly understood this way.

Infrastructure is never 'neutral'.[44] It nearly always automatically empowers some and disempowers others. Public transport radically alters the values of all the houses around it, for example. Like wifi and public transport, Twitter doesn't just enable a marketplace; it creates it a new one – and alters the apparent value of the ideas within it through its design.[45]

Infrastructures are enabling systems: they create affordances, they encourage certain kinds of actions and interactions. Roads take us places, schools teach us to be able to do things, the internet gives us digital action-possibilities and so on. Infrastructure shapes not only our action-possibilities but also our thought-possibilities. We think in terms of what we have read and heard, which reaches us via not only our social network but also the technologies and structures that enable it. We tend to form our views through our relationships with others, and we often meet the people we do because of the infrastructure that surrounds us, from roads to schools to the social infrastructure of coffee shops. Infrastructure frequently determines, prior to any 'debate' or 'marketplace', what it might be possible for us to believe. One of Musk's first priorities was to change the algorithm so that users increasingly saw tweets only from those with blue checks – that is, from those willing to pay for a subscription.[46] Later on, he prevented the sharing or retweeting of Substack links and other platforms' links, limiting the easy movement of users towards competitors.[47] That too is the power of infrastructure: it can trap people and block knowledge, or movement.

Given what I have laid out in previous chapters about what actually changes people's minds, if we care about building and living in a world where people can rethink their views, or where the world itself can change, then we must attend to what kinds of infrastructure enable us to have, or disable us from having, strong, varied relationships, and what infrastructure allows us to try new ways of living. We need, in short, to build back three specific types of infrastructure if we want a more democratic life:

1. We need to build better forms of the infrastructure we already associate with public, interdependent thinking. This involves the type of infrastructure we commonly think of as attached to public discourse, such as the media and education and social media platforms. Making better infrastructure for public discourse might mean seizing the means of social media production (or regulating the hell out of it, or building a clone website via an anarchist collective or ... depending on your preferred political position: in this chapter I haven't come to some kind of preferred strategy for change, focusing instead on why infrastructure is so central to the problems we face and why some infrastructure helps democracy and other infrastructure hinders it). It certainly means remaking the media and communications systems and education systems and internet platforms, and maybe even governmental processes, attending to the infrastructure that we use to find and consider ideas about our social and political world, and democratizing the ownership of this infrastructure and its design.

2. We need to build better forms of 'social infrastructure'. A good deal of the infrastructure that supports us in considering new ideas doesn't appear as directly related to 'discourse' but nevertheless allows us to belong with new kinds of people and thus be open to new ways of thinking. This is especially true of 'social infrastructure', 'the crucial organisations, places and spaces that enable communities to create social connections – to form and sustain relationships that help them to thrive'.[48]

Bringing social infrastructure into our understanding of democratic infrastructure means understanding democracy in a much broader way, so that its vital infrastructure is not just media and education but also more integrated neighbourhoods, institutions, online platforms and more. We need to build more opportunities to bring people together who otherwise wouldn't mix, so they can have relationships that ultimately enable them to think about politics differently. The next chapter discusses this further.

And finally –

3. We need to build infrastructure that indirectly supports public discourse by expanding people's action-possibilities. Because people's political views are so much about what they do, we also need infrastructure that helps people access a much wider variety of life experiences. This means thinking about the material conditions of people's lives not only as a matter of inequality or injustice but also as the conditions for them to think. Building people new possibilities for action, and through these new possibilities to think differently as well, means considering changes to things that don't usually fit into our definition of infrastructure but which change how people think, according to sociological research. Policies that make it easier to switch jobs, move locations, live in different configurations, start a business or become a parent all give people opportunities to think differently. We might think about how to create easy and cheap ways for people to (say) put a solar panel on their roof, host a refugee, feed a neighbour or start a social enterprise – not just because these are good things to do but also because they enable us to think differently. Of course, there are plenty of actions that might pull people towards far right or reactionary positions too. But my suspicion is that, right now, our fragmented, underfunded lifestyles at a minimum keep people trapped in hopelessness about a better world and often make them conservative or reactionary anyhow – so a key step for a better world is to increase people's mobility and social connections, and try to provide progressive and radical ways of living along the way.

Only if we improve all three of the aforementioned kinds of infrastructure can we have public discourse that is actually useful, liberating and productive, the collective reasoning that is the infrastructure for a better society.

Why think about all this as *infrastructure*?

Thinking about political reasoning in terms of infrastructure affords us a new way of understanding the problems of our current political moment, one that we might not be able to arrive at by thinking about ideas as commodities in a marketplace or debate. I want to acknowledge, however, that reading the word 'infrastructure' may feel like a bit of a let-down. Except by a small minority of nerds (the policy wonks in my hometown, Washington, DC, for example), infrastructure is not generally considered a sexy topic. Sewage management and highway construction plans easily come to mind. It also sounds like a very slow solution in an age of urgent crises. Still, in its expanded sense, infrastructure refers to so much of what determines the quality of our collective life. And there are things we simply can't attain without it. It's increasingly clear that many of our twenty-first-century crises (even those that are not primarily about 'democracy') are related to infrastructure. In the UK, a cross-party group of MPs and activists has begun to argue for childcare to be considered as infrastructure because, after all, the economy actively functions much worse, or sometimes not at all, without it.[49] The COVID-19 pandemic has (probably) helped many of us see the value of infrastructure in its broad sense. The idea that people and services are 'essential' is the recognition that some jobs are part of the collective infrastructure. We are likely to need a lot of new infrastructure, both physical and organizational, to adapt to future challenges such as climate change, migration, an ageing population and so on. So we face an opportunity now to think about how we could build that type of infrastructure so that it also helps us reason well as a society.

Thinking about the public sphere in terms of its infrastructure is a fast lane to thinking in a way that avoids the trap of moralizing and individualizing about what are really structural, collective problems. It is easy to think of the social problems displayed in discourse as lots of individually problematic people who have plugged their ears, devolved into screaming matches or fallen for 'biased' media content. (And of course, many of these individuals do hold morally objectionable beliefs and biases.) But it is more helpful to consider these problems the way city planners do when it comes to traffic jams. After all, there's no point in moralizing about a traffic jam. (Although notice how people frequently do, becoming enraged with the person right in front of them as though the traffic were their personal fault!) We may want to yell at the guy ahead of us when we encounter traffic, and blame it on him, but the odds are that we also are the guy ahead of someone, and didn't choose to be there.

An individual who happens to believe something we see as wrong or harmful may simply be stuck in an unfortunate 'point' in the system, like a driver in a particularly gnarly bit of traffic. And if there is an intersection that tends to be clogged every evening around 6 p.m., it tells us something more profound about the layout of the roads, not to mention the enforcement of workplace policies. Generally the area in question needs more lanes, or more public transit options, or both. These (literally!) infrastructural solutions are far more effective than telling a bunch of miserable commuters that they should have taken the overcrowded bus or left home sooner.

Thinking in terms of infrastructure also helps account for, and work around, human error, exhaustion and laziness. That's because good infrastructure makes something feel easy, natural, like the obvious best choice. The road curves before the school, and you automatically slow down. Right now, however, much of our digital environment is engineered in ways that *discourage* thinking well about politics. We live in a golden age of 'user experience design', where many thousands of designers are focused on building easy-to-use platforms, but nearly always in the service of an addictive experience, rather than anything else. The problem is not this or that 'driver' on the highway of the internet but the way it is designed, and the way it will probably always be designed when profit is the motive and one must maximize likes, clicks and shares.

Thinking in terms of infrastructure also points to thinking about how we can fix problems upstream and at scale. You can treat illness or simply build good sewage systems and ventilation; you can fight reactionary and bad ideas individually or you can, probably with greater ease and fewer resources, go upstream and create a world where people can try out new ways of living and form meaningful diverse connections.

Infrastructure-based approaches move us away from an inaccurate and unhelpfully romantic vision of what politics is (thinking as though it were a matter of a few key moral moments where everything changes). It helps us see the structures on which power really rests.

Thinking about infrastructure can also help us recognize when the privatization of infrastructure is creating a negative cycle. For private infrastructures create a negative cycle, pulling more and more resources out of public use: those who can afford to pay for better get it elsewhere and become less interested in supporting what is already free and available. This is why paywalls are not just annoying but a spiralling threat, because they not only gate information and ideas so that only those who pay can access them but they do so in a way that, over time, leads to more and more privatized thought and conversations, as the market turns towards only what those who can pay are looking for. The privatization of infrastructure means some of us are simply cut out. It is an exclusionary political vision. And this spiralling process, in which the wealthy receive better services, the owners of private infrastructures profit and everyone else can go to hell, is exactly why Musk and others like privatizing infrastructure.

This way in which private infrastructures more or less inevitably drain the resources of public ones means that society always allows for private infrastructure, from education to media, at the risk of general societal decline, greater polarization and widening inequality. (I am not entirely comfortable with this idea myself, having no certainty that the state, the most common creator of public infrastructure, is likely to always acts in our best interests. But the logic holds.) At minimum, clearly, the reach of private infrastructures and people's ability to opt out of paying for it must be limited if we want public infrastructure to exist.

This is likely to become all the more apparent as we go on allowing platform monopolies, such as X, to be managed by private actors. Platform monopolies function in many ways like other monopolies, in that they become more or less the only game in town, simply because everyone is already using them, and the value of the platform is about the number of users.[50] Sure, any given person can in theory turn to a competitor like Threads or Bluesky, but the truth is that, as of the time of writing anyway, most people haven't done so – Bluesky still has only a small fraction of the users that Twitter has. There have been various exoduses from Twitter each time Musk does something particularly egregious, but the difficulty is that this often leads to fracturing of community as people go in different directions.

Thinking in terms of infrastructure is also a meaningful approach because infrastructure is something that can be part of demands by a social movement, or created by progressive collective projects. It's not easy to build, but it is attainable and even popular. And while infrastructure will never be neutral, it is possible to create infrastructure that is more egalitarian and less harmful.

There are, of course, some problems with focusing on infrastructure, in both its limited and its expanded sense. Public infrastructure is expensive and hard to fund. The US, in particular, has an almost comical problem with outdated infrastructure, one that even a recent $1 trillion spending bill cannot fully ameliorate. And it's not just state-run infrastructures that face serious problems. Open-source infrastructures, such as some of the information structures of the internet, may not be owned by the state but they then face a significant collective action problem in terms of who wants to actually maintain them. In fact, even public infrastructures often suffer from the 'tragedy of the commons', where no one wants to spend their own resources to maintain something that everyone enjoys, and so common resources are maintained poorly. In many places people start to defund infrastructure when racial integration happens, or when migrants move in.

Getting it right is difficult. But doing without it is much worse. To consider the public sphere in terms of infrastructure is to use an admittedly imperfect, non-exhaustive alternative framework. But that framework illuminates the issue of public discourse in new and helpful ways.

Let's return to the three types of infrastructure that might support a democratic public sphere, and start with improving the infrastructure that obviously relates to the public sphere.

We need to build better forms of the infrastructure we already associate with public, interdependent thinking.

Societies rely on infrastructure to move people and goods around, to keep water clean and food in good supply. But of course they also rely on infrastructure to direct the flow of ideas, views, information and our very own thoughts. Most people intuit that there is some kind of infrastructure for public life; it is part of why most people agree that everyone should go to school and receive a basic education. It is also part of why most people think free and fair media are important (and very few people believe we have them).[51] If we consider infrastructure to be what structures and underpins crucial social processes, the nature of schools and media outlets as infrastructure becomes apparent. Our society needs some kind of media apparatus for many other aspects of our society to function: it is a crucial part of our infrastructure. People now tend to access a lot of their media coverage via social media.[52] And it seems likely that the trend of getting one's news curated through one's newsfeed will only continue.[53] If we consider this behaviour, then social media, especially their news distribution function, are an extension of this news infrastructure.

The question with internet infrastructure has long been how much the internet should be treated as infrastructure and how much it should be treated as a commodity, as the means to other vital social ends, or rather something to be gatekept and milked for profit. Consider, for example, the older debate over 'net neutrality', occurring in large part in the early 2000s, as service providers such as Comcast and AT&T discovered that they could block the work of small content creators or make certain websites run more slowly, all in order to favour their own or sibling providers.[54] Without regulation, internet providers can also create a slower, worse kind of internet for the mere workers of the world, and give superfast internet to those who agree to pay a small fortune. Now we face the same question about platforms.

In many cases when it comes to infrastructure, state-run or collectively funded systems, especially if administered well and not for profit, are far more efficient and better coordinated than what markets can provide. (British people reading this in the year of its release, 2025, have just lived through a period where this became especially obvious with regard to their national rail system, which was privatized and soon became so absurdly expensive that it was often cheaper to fly to another country than to take the train from London to Manchester.[55]) This is likely to be especially true for anything that is a natural monopoly, such as railways, or indeed anything that is any kind of monopoly, such as media platforms, because in both cases the potential positive effects of market competition are weakened or non-existent. In cases like this, it then becomes possible to radically rethink access to important services. Taxes allow for a pricing structure that ensures that those who can pay more do so, and that those who cannot pay less. One can thus generally skip the paywall and its attendant problems. There is guaranteed income for the entire project (as opposed to the month-to-month funding of so many subscription ventures), so grander undertakings become possible. You don't have to spend as much time providing perks to keep people from unsubscribing. As parts of our democratic infrastructure become private, they often have to juggle the demands of capitalism and the demands of democracy, and the profit motive pretty much wins, every time, by necessity. So when I suggest we need 'better' forms of these vital bits of democratic infrastructure, I mean not just better designed but better owned. Better owned than being owned by Musk, but also better owned than being owned by any one person or even a combination of profit-driven entities. Better owned, and therefore better motivated, better designed to enable everyone to think.

Now to the less obvious form of infrastructure that nevertheless profoundly affects our democracy: social infrastructure.

2. *We need to build better forms of 'social infrastructure'.*

In addition to more obvious forms of infrastructure for public reasoning, such as schools and media, there are also less obvious structures that support people's ability to consider political issues, often because they help us mix with new kinds of people. As you'll recall from previous chapters, our beliefs are strongly influenced by the groups we are part of and the behaviours we engage in. Infrastructure that helps us belong to new and/or more varied groups allows us to change our beliefs.

In recent years sociologists and other researchers have begun to appreciate the importance of what they term *social infrastructure*. The sociologist Eric Klinenberg defines social infrastructure very broadly, so that it is essentially what helps people know their neighbours and interact with them regularly in a meaningful way.[56] Social infrastructure, he argues, 'influences seemingly mundane but actually consequential patterns, from the way we move about our cities and suburbs to the opportunities we have to casually interact with strangers, friends, and neighbors ... while social infrastructure alone isn't sufficient to unite polarized societies, protect vulnerable communities, or connect alienated individuals, we can't address those challenges without it'.[57] Klinenberg emphasizes the importance of libraries, schools, playgrounds, parks, fields and churches: places where people can go just to be for long periods of time, generally without paying anything. The value of these spaces is that they tend to broaden people's sense of who they belong with and who is part of their web of concerns. They tend to allow for the kinds of deeper, open-ended conversations that help people overcome suspicion of one another and be open to new points of view. And in some cases they may get people involved in new activities, whether that's football games with people of different ethnicities and cultures, activism or simply a new style of parenting alongside other parents. Religious institutions and their spaces can be, for better or worse, part of the political infrastructure, and so can schools, universities and even public transport, because their locations and design all influence who we are aware of and feel connected to. There's evidence to show that social infrastructure, by facilitating friendships and relationships between diverse people, reduces people's dislike of those different from them, and also leads to greater civic engagement, community problem-solving, better relief in disasters and better public health outcomes.[58] This is, in part, because social infrastructure leads to the generation of 'weak ties', which are, as mentioned in earlier chapters, our relationships with people we know not well but loosely, second-degree connections and so on. And these connections have a vital role to play in our understanding of our community and of those different from us.

Klinenberg argues that social spaces like this are the gravitational pull away from our worst tendencies, and the antidote to the increasing privatization of infrastructure by rich people. (Think about private security for wealthy neighbourhoods, or the buses that take employees to Silicon Valley.) Indeed, as discussed in earlier chapters, there's a good deal of evidence to suggest that moving to a new, more diverse social context and forming long-term relationships of equals with people different to yourself has a great impact on how you think. Specifically, people who go to diverse schools or universities, or who serve in the military with people of other racial or ethnic groups, come to be more tolerant. This integration itself supports us in being able to reason in new (and often better!) ways.[59] Integrated neighbourhood and housing options appear to have a similar effect.[60] Ideally, the way our society is set up should widen the circle of humans we are concerned about and provide us with opportunities to broaden, sharpen and nuance our thinking, to see our personal lives in a political light and to take steps towards political action. But at the moment little incentivizes this. In fact, in many areas we are increasingly segregated.

And online infrastructures, for reasons outlined in previous chapters, don't seem to provide the social benefits of social infrastructure in the same way. One way to think about this is that digital infrastructure's affordances better polarize than persuade. Sure, the internet was originally imagined by many early idealists as a network of networks, a portal for anyone to communicate freely with anyone else. It was supposed to change our beliefs and let us think freely. But it generally doesn't, probably because it is now largely driven by profit motives and also because, while it sometimes changes our belonging, it rarely changes our offline behaviour.

Part of the propaganda of modern social media firms is that they offer important public infrastructure (even if they don't use this word): as Musk put it, 'the digital town square'. But in truth we may need real town squares, real actual physical places where it is free and easy to be together. This is because the kind of mixing we do on the internet is probably not nearly as important as the kind we can do in real life. Most of our internet life does not involve the same kinds of behaviours (deep friendships, exposure to others we can come to like, new actions to try out) that in turn influence our commitments and beliefs about the world. If belonging and behaviour determine our beliefs to a strong degree, real-life spaces are likely to have more power than online ones, because they are more likely to restructure our daily lives and actions and relationships.[61]

Which brings me to a final point about what 'democratic infrastructure' should mean, a point that is perhaps the least obvious one I could make: if we want people to be able to think freely, we need more infrastructure of any kind that increases people's action-possibilities in their lives.

3. We need to build infrastructure that indirectly supports public discourse by expanding people's action-possibilities.

This expanded sense of infrastructure is unusual but not unheard of; as some scholars put it, it's possible to think about infrastructure 'not just as a "thing", a "system", or an "output", but as a complex social and technological process that enables – or disables – particular kinds of action'.[62] Since our actions structure much of our thought, one of the best ways to allow people to think more broadly is to provide opportunities to try out new ways of living.

Again, recall that, owing to cognitive dissonance discomfort, people are most likely to engage with new ideas if they are regularly given new, relatively approachable options for how to live these ideas in their lives. This allows them to shift their actions in line with new ideas, rather than facing painful dissonance and reverting to whatever ideas align with their existing patterns of action. For example, it's not much use giving people reasons to worry about the climate crisis if we don't also provide them with options for acting on it – because it will be difficult for them to change their views and priorities unless they can also change their actions. It's probably more effective to give people options for getting to work without their car than to tell them their cars are bad: effective not only in terms of reducing emissions but also in terms of giving them the possibility of changing their mind at all.

To use the term from previous chapters, part of doing politics better is to create more affordances, more realistic possibilities for action for other people. Providing economic security and reducing inequality is one key way of doing this, because impoverished people trust others less and, as I have shown in previous chapters, are more socially isolated and less likely to try new ways of living. We could even (controversially) instate a public service requirement, where citizens are called up not only for jury duty but also to (say) build more housing, care for the elderly, plant trees or serve in their local government.[63] The broader idea, in any case, is to give people new ways to live out their lives, even in miniature and trial form, new opportunities to plausibly change their lives. Only then could they plausibly change their views.

Another particularly important economic factor in this area is time – and, specifically, time that is structured by geography and infrastructure in a way that might actually lead us to become active in our communities. But it's not just about time; it's also about what we can realistically do with that limited patch of free time each day. Technically speaking, Americans (to use just one example) have on average about five hours of leisure time a day – and even more strikingly, they seem to actually be happier when they have even less than this.[64] Perhaps this is because many of these hours are spent on screens and these screens do not really facilitate belonging or new actions out in the world. This time is spent on screens in part because our lives are not set up for us to use this free time in other ways. We are mostly not near convenient, fun community hubs; we do not know our neighbours; we cannot afford to go to places that are near us; and so on. It is easy to scroll and hard to get around our towns and expensive to be in public places. This inevitably leads to greater solitude and inaction, both of which are antithetical to democratic life.

People's views tend to narrow or harden as they get older, and this too, I'd like to suggest, based on the research provided over the last few chapters, is deeply tied to how they also have a narrower social world and set of action-possibilities. As people 'settle down', they often narrow their social circles, focus on their careers and have less varied life experiences, and this may also narrow their views about what is politically possible or desirable. It's possible to imagine, however, that we could build a world where people could change their careers and living situations more easily, where there was free lifelong adult education and more opportunities for public service, so we might all keep refining our thinking our whole lives long. We could also design the world so people meet the right people to speak to about important issues (say, doctors when it comes to COVID, or people of colour when it comes to racism), which then allows them to be capable of changing their mind or responding to evidence.[65] Or we might design systems to make the effects of particular problems (such as climate change) more obvious.[66] We should rethink everything from work schedules to the neighbourhoods we live in to the transit systems and public spaces to enable people to spend time doing new and interesting things – spending time physically with others, in particular. The point, in short, is that we need to talk less about politics (in the sense of arguing with people) and instead build a world where those people are likely to encounter more and thus change their minds. This kind of work of organizing and building social networks and changing the world is in many ways more a form of reasoning than anything that just happens with words.[67]

This way of thinking about things is speculative, both in the particular philosophical sense of attempting to bridge philosophical gaps and/or evaluate how we should reason and in the practical sense of guessing about the outcomes of possible futures. That's both unavoidable and productive. We need to be able to imagine new futures rather than stay locked in the often destructive and unproductive societal course we're already on.

The three types of infrastructure I've laid out above are key to what it might take to have a democracy, one where we can do so much more than argue with one another. One where we can also live as equals and come to understand the world differently by living in the world differently. But, as I said, infrastructure is never neutral, and that can cut both ways. There is always the dark twin to all of this infrastructure. There are forms of infrastructure that appear on their surface to be all about democracy – but which, in their core functions, actually work to undermine it. And Twitter, especially in the hands of profit-makers, especially in the hands of Elon Musk, is one such form of infrastructure.

Of course there were aspects of Twitter, for some time, that served democratic functions: there was free access to information, some ability to communicate with like-minded others and organize, etc. But, as I have described elsewhere in this book, democracy is about so much more than voting and discourse. It is about seeing others as equals, about protection for minorities, about living in egalitarian ways, about realistic access to new possibilities for how to live your life. Twitter not only could not provide most of this but actively inhibited it in many cases, both before and especially after Musk took the helm. Even as it felt democratic to chime in with one's own hot take or vote in Musk's polls, in practice the platform skewed our views in lots of ways, brought Donald Trump to the forefront of American politics and provided endless distraction from other ways of being involved in public life.

The problem, as some researchers have outlined in great detail, is that in practice places like Twitter do not function as sites for clear-minded individuals to develop coherent worldviews. Instead, what people often bring to social media are their fears, their anger, their other easily electrified emotions. And, with its algorithm and profit motive, with its formatting for virality, short-form-only content and image-based content, sites like Twitter/X are perfectly designed to hit those nerves for people over and over again. People can easily simply get 'turned on' by this network effect over and over. Thus what we see on Twitter and similar platforms is often not individuals considering ideas but networks having powerful emotional group reactions and individuals patchworking together a series of stated beliefs to justify those emotions. (Remember how this happens during cognitive dissonance.) It is the bad crowd Gustave Le Bon imagined, in a way – but dispersed all around the world.

In fact, I'd suggest that 'discourse' disconnected from action and relationships always tends this way: towards highly reactive and often reactionary networks of poorly thinking people. After all, relationships and actions require us to in some way try to live out ideas, and often in the process abandon non-functional ones, refine ideas or work through contradictions. In contrast, online platforms make discourse particularly likely to be disconnected from any actions in our daily life, or from any long-form, meaningful relationships with other human beings. An online platform like X has the tendency to become anti-democratic infrastructure, since it lacks both the key features that allow people to genuinely consider new ideas and the features required for people to lose their prejudices against others or to begin to see one another as equals. Of course, platforms like this are especially likely to become anti-democratic when run by incredibly wealthy men seeking ever more power. But they also have built-in functions that make this more likely, unless, of course, we take control of them and steer them in the other direction.

We may feel we are participating in a marketplace of ideas, but online we are often just having fears and anxieties stoked without recourse to any of the kinds of relationships or interactions that might help us judge the reality of the outside world. People who are online (especially, research shows, those who end up becoming part of the far right) are especially susceptible to 'perceptions of imperilment', things that feel like threats, such as a news report that claims, rightly or wrongly, that a migrant committed a crime.[68] Once this sort of claim goes out into a network, the network responds and reproduces it widely, and as it does so, it grows and strengthens. Remember the 'contagious media' mentioned in earlier chapters? As I've suggested in previous chapters, the subjects engaged in this network response may well feel and claim that they are 'thinking independently' or 'thinking for themselves', but this is the problem; they are thinking on their own in the sense of without an extended, embedded real-life social network, while still being influenced by the online world. And this leads them down a rabbit hole. (Indeed, when I present this idea in lectures, people often come up afterwards to tell me this has indeed happened, in exactly this way, to their elderly relatives. Or, less commonly, to their teenage children, or sometimes just to an adult they know.)

There is nothing particularly democratic about this, nothing that really allows for any of the other criteria I've listed for democracy. That is why researchers in this area have posited that it is 'the structures [that] need to be targeted' at this point in the twenty-first century, rather than specific leaders in far right groups, or even ideas. That is why we have to take back the infrastructure that is creating this anti-democratic effect. Doing so may be part of grappling with what the liberal theorist Karl Popper termed 'the paradox of tolerance'. Popper suggested that, in tolerant liberal societies, intolerant forces are often tolerated and then slowly take over, ending the tolerant liberal environments that supported them in the first place. His suggestion was that there is always a case to be intolerant of intolerance in order to preserve democracy. It is possible we must also do this at the platform and infrastructural level, and attempt to remove or take over platforms that tend towards intolerance, rather than targeting ideas or people individually.[69]

All this also underscores, once again, why it is so important that we turn away from the image of democracy mostly as discourse, from the myths of the marketplace of ideas and debate as the centre of what it means to think well about politics. For authoritarians and manipulators and far-right-wingers will always be able to give us fake and unhelpful and even very harmful versions of discourse. Today they do not ask for blind obedience as authoritarians once did; they are good at making us feel like we are choosing them for ourselves, all while the discourse they feed us serves only as distraction.

Nothing is entirely new about this problem, not really. Certainly nothing is new about a powerful man using the pretence and rhetoric of democracy and discourse to get power over others. There is a long history of supposedly democratic spaces, procedures and infrastructures being repurposed towards anti-democratic ends, especially in the United States. Remember the *Requerimiento* described in the first chapter, and how the pretence of dialogue and a legal system was used to justify the conquest and slaughter of millions? Or consider when President Andrew Jackson used the language of democracy to advocate for extending the vote to all white male citizens, while at the same time administering the genocidal displacement of thousands of native people. Or perhaps think of the way that, in towns across the United States, over decades, so many men gathered folks together in a town square for discussion and consensus and then started lynchings – approximately 5,000 of them, to be exact (and nearly 4,000 of these of Black people, of course).[70] Or perhaps think of how, in the US Congress, during the era of the House Un-American Activities Committee, various politicians similarly conducted witch-hunts and investigated, terrorized and blacklisted anyone who might dissent from the ruling ideology. Sure, many of these places and spaces seemed to have the trappings of democratic life (the crowd, the citizens, the testimony, the hearings, the laws and the procedure), but what they were up to was profoundly anti-democratic, in the sense that it made minorities and those who dissent unsafe.

All these men (and they were mostly men) used the language of democracy to turn what could have been democratic infrastructure into anti-democratic infrastructure, into a weapon aimed at minorities and those who live and think differently. Twitter, with its re-platformed white supremacists and banned journalists, simply follows in a long historical line of anti-democratic infrastructures whitewashed in the rhetoric of democracy. Indeed, those in both the US and other countries often fetishize democracy and use the language of democracy precisely when their politicians and even their everyday citizens are at their most racist, xenophobic or even fascist. The myth of a functional marketplace of ideas and the myth that debate leads to just and reasonable outcomes are both used all the time to make undemocratic forms of life appear democratic. These myths provide the pretence that all is well precisely when countries are experiencing what the nineteenth-century writer and political scientist Alexis de Tocqueville (who conducted a massive proto-ethnographic study of American democracy) termed the 'tyranny of the majority'. (And sometimes the tyranny is not even from the majority, just a powerful, anxious, paranoid minority.)

Without the right infrastructure and, for that matter, a suitable economic system, all talking about politics becomes blind chatter, and any given forum for discussion is likely to serve as a piece of anti-democratic infrastructure, granting power to those at the top and making it more difficult for everyone else to think differently or well about politics.

When it came to X, Elon Musk has constantly sought to make the platform appear democratic even as he implements solutions that actually make it less possible for minority voices to be heard or for people to dissent. One of his first ideas was that 'Twitter will start incorporating mute & block signals from Blue Verified (not Legacy Blue) as downvotes.'[71] What this meant was that users who paid $8 a month might have the power to police the site. Many who were willing to pay were fans of the new management, leading to a funky ideological shift where Elon Musk fans made up an increasing percentage of verified users. Indeed even before Musk owned it, Twitter never really worked like an idealized 'fair' marketplace for ideas, owing to similar infrastructural effects. In the pre-Musk day Twitter's design gave a few very loud voices airtime, amplified the most controversial opinions and rewarded people for posting frequently rather than thoughtfully.[72] In 2021 Twitter's own 'Responsible Machine Learning Initiative' admitted that its algorithm prioritized images of white people and amplified right-leaning content over left.[73] The infrastructure was also badly maintained: Twitter's permanent data was nearly lost in an accident, and it had such an unusually high rate of security incidents that the company had to report these to the government almost weekly.[74] What seems like a marketplace of ideas on the surface is very often something else, something shaky, vulnerable and reactionary, even before particularly loud and irritating billionaires run it.

And while we should care about the bad and manipulative features of Twitter, it's important to acknowledge that it is dangerous simply because it is a stand-in for a more meaningful form of democratic life. It is a massive time-suck. It is entertainment in place of relationship. It functions so as to polarize and mislead people, especially now that Musk runs it, and it also serves to suck up time and energy that could be spent elsewhere. It provides an illusion, at least for some, that democratic life is still happening. After all, there's fact-checking. (With AI!) Musk has people vote on things. (Even if he doesn't honour their votes!) Everyone is allowed on the platform. (Even the fascists!)

In the US, however, in part because of Musk, a great deal of infrastructure (not just democratic infrastructure but infrastructure more broadly) is about to be dismantled as Musk (or anyone who might replace him, should he fall out of favour) runs the 'Department of Government Efficiency' and takes apart or privatizes government functions.[75] (At time of writing, Musk has office space in the White House.) When it comes to problems of infrastructure, residents of the United States now have more to worry about than a powerful but flailing social media site. The same logic of increasingly for-pay infrastructure and power in the hands of a few will now guide the takeover of many of our major institutions. For the next four years, at least, much work will have to be done simply to protect what little public infrastructure already exists, or to build local replacements, governmental or otherwise.

How, then, might we build democratic infrastructure in this perilous, authoritarian, highly digital age, where so many of our interactions transcend borders?

If Twitter was a railway company, it could be nationalized (in theory, if a progressive government existed). There are many instances in history where services were first private companies and then nationalized, often in ways that mean we now can hardly imagine them as private commodities. The London Tube (Underground/Subway) was once a series of separate, private railway lines but was nationalized after the Second World War, along with all the UK's railways.[76] While some smaller parts of the service have been delegated to private companies (for example, some buses), it remains to this day a piece of public infrastructure. Perhaps more to the point, most Londoners would be confused by the idea that it *could* be private, never mind run by several private companies, line by line. It simply makes more sense as a joined-up public good. In fact, at the time of writing, nationalization of a large number of goods and services is increasingly popular. Polls show that in the UK, for example, where the population has just undergone decades of privatization, leading to incredibly expensive train tickets and beaches with sewage on them, most Britons now believe that infrastructure should be largely or entirely nationalized.[77] The majority of British people are now in favour of the nationalizing of water, trains, gas, electricity and the postal service.

But, of course, with major multinational communications companies it is harder to manage this. (Would there be a Twitter for each country? How would that work?) We are dealing, both when it comes to platforms and when it comes to the public sphere itself, with twentieth-century assumptions about what infrastructure looks like, but the problems and technologies we face are decisively twenty-first-century.

When it comes to the nitty-gritty details of a future with better infrastructure, I'm tempted at first glance to leave calculations in the hands of the ever clever minds of policy wonks the world over.[78] It's also tempting to simply point to the many competitors to Twitter already popping up. Perhaps we're looking for a platform that does what Twitter did so imperfectly, just much better: a digital arena for public life that makes communication between individuals and groups free, well framed, fact-checked and varied, no matter how noisy and hateful the world may be. And sure, there are currently new platforms growing and emerging, but we could build beyond them, especially in user-owned and publicly owned ways, and theorists and think tanks are already thinking about how to do this democratically – for example, by boosting the posts that spur collaborative conversations, making platforms inter-operable and thus more competitive when it comes to features, creating exits into community ownership and more.[79]

Indeed social movements or groups might build various forms of infrastructure and then pressure states to fund or adopt it. In fact, there is a long history of social movements creating infrastructure and governments adopting it to avoid the pressures that infrastructure otherwise creates on them. For example, the Black Panthers provided free school lunches, and the government then stepped in to do the same.[80] Of course, this can have a problematic depoliticizing effect also, but the larger point remains true: social movements can create infrastructure and then sometimes get others to sustain it. They can enact political change through this kind of provision.

Details along these lines might be sorted through by wonks and activists and experimenters. But the broader political goal needs to be clear: it must by necessity be about the ownership of these platforms, and their profit motive. As we adjust to the multiple intersecting crises of the twenty-first century, and as we necessarily revamp many aspects of our infrastructure to handle climate change, COVID and more, we will also necessarily have to revisit what is publicly owned (or collectively owned) and privately owned. Yes, building political momentum to regulate things differently, acquire public funding and reorganize society is hard. Creating grassroots infrastructures such as mutual aid groups and food cooperatives is also difficult. But sometimes the one big demand is the only way through. After all, what is the alternative? To continue with the ownership of public life as it is now can only lead somewhere dark, alienated and possibly authoritarian. It is wise to be risk-averse and avoid too much meddling with systems that serve us well; it is foolish not to be willing to uproot a system that is not working well at all.

It matters profoundly who owns infrastructure – more than what regulations we put in place, more than what policies each platform has, more even, given platform dynamics, than what competitors exist. When it comes to this and all questions of power, it matters more who owns the house we live in than exactly how we arrange the furniture. It matters that corporations can own our democratic infrastructure; it matters, especially, that the wealthy can buy their regulators. As long as both are true, regulations will always be somewhat like a decorative collar on a charging bull.

Infrastructure is power, whoever holds it. That is why Musk and Trump head straight for the infrastructure when they get into power, and why they take over the communications infrastructure and turn it anti-democratic. The enormous power of infrastructure is probably what attracts so many people to technology companies, in fact: an intuitive sense that certain large platform technologies are infrastructure, and therefore sites for a kind of power outside of the state. This is part of the appeal and mythology of Silicon Valley, of companies and technologies that can 'change the world'. It is certainly interesting and arguably telling that Elon Musk's big dreams are about wielding this kind of infrastructural power, about large, albeit unrealistic and private, forms of infrastructure, such as the 'hyperloop', a yet unproven idea for high-speed transit involving capsules in an underground tube. Indeed, he was one of a number who sought to take some of the most spectacular achievements and functions of state infrastructure (for example, the space race) and turn them into corporate luxuries for the few. Where robber barons like Andrew Carnegie used to build libraries for the public, increasing public and social infrastructure, today they buy up our national space programmes and satellites, and plan their private escapes to space. And they also tell us that our collective future lies not with politics but with technology, which is a very clever way of distracting us from their corporate takeovers and capture of the state. But, in truth, Carnegie built libraries the same way Zuckerberg offers free internet: to capture the public's imagination. Carnegie too was interested in the capture of the state and the oppression of workers. There has never been a time without men like Musk and Trump – we're just living through a resurgence of these men, at a time of polycrisis.

If we want to take the same power back from Musk and those like him, we need to avoid the discourse games they play, and the allure of engaging in their *faux* marketplaces of ideas, and focus on taking back the infrastructure itself. Indeed, the question of ownership and profit is really lurking in almost every other conversation one might have about technologies like this. Many like to blame 'the algorithm' for various problems they encounter on the internet. It is indeed frightening how algorithms structure the information architecture we encounter in a near-weaponized fashion, preceding our possibilities for thought. You think you are looking at the internet, but, as the architect Eyal Weizman puts it, it is actually looking back at you, tracking everything you do and adjusting so that you see a very specific image of the world.[81] Whatever critical thinking you may do occurs only 'on top' of the information and ideas you algorithmically encounter, and this remains significantly true even as you 'do your own research' and poke around the internet here and there. But this is not an issue of design error, or even so much about human dopamine addiction and frailty, though those are part of the story. It's because of how these platforms are (quite simply) businesses, committed to maximizing shareholder value over any other kind of good. Private infrastructure in the twenty-first century has the capacity to cause a number of democratic crises: everything from bad algorithms to underfunded public infrastructure and poor regulation as the rich opt out and take things over. It is vital for democracies that this privatization cycle, especially the privatization of democratic infrastructure, is fought at the political level; it is our public wealth, not our private wealth, that carries our liberation.

For this reason, X/Twitter provides a useful case study of why, if we want democratic life to function at all, we might have to accept that platforms, especially platforms for communication and discourse, cannot be controlled by billionaires and, perhaps, that they cannot be driven by the profit motive at all. Some forms of infrastructure are too important for this. For while some used to fantasize that Twitter might take down authoritarian regimes, it is now arguably part of one.

But that's just X. The larger question is: what would we need in order to have a world where everyone can think about politics well, not just talk at each other about it? One big piece of the puzzle is to not just build better digital infrastructure but also to own what exists and control it democratically (whether through the state or otherwise). But we also need to consider infrastructure that is not digital. In grandiose fashion Elon Musk imagines Twitter as 'a collective, cybernetic superintelligence'. But building collective intelligence involves much more than social media. Our worldviews rest on a wider set of behaviours, patterns and institutions. They reflect who owns the press, how we run schools, how (and how much) we mix with those unlike us in real life and whether we have enough time to have long conversations with others. The real issue we're facing extends beyond Twitter, beyond all the obvious things we call infrastructure, even beyond media and education, into creating opportunities for people to live differently, engage in new behaviours and belong in new places. (And also in preventing the hollowing out of the structures that already do this but which are under threat.) Only when we have a society where that is likely are we also going to be able to think better, to consider more options for understanding the world and think them through together deeply.

The temptation is to focus on the dramatic figures, on Trump, on Musk. But it's not really about them, comic and frightening though they are in turns. It is the system that brought them there; it is about the economy where the three wealthiest Americans own more than the bottom 50 per cent of the country.[82] And there are many ways to try to change that system, but when it comes to helping people think differently and engage in the form of life we might meaningfully call democracy, I hope we now turn our attention to democratic infrastructure. We need to own it collectively; we need to build new collective forms of it. We need to take it out of the hands of billionaires and the far right. The quality of this infrastructure will determine the quality of the thinking we are able to undertake.

In preparing for this book I read a great many definitions of infrastructure. One I liked best was from the CEO of the Vancouver Airport Authority, who defined infrastructure as 'the stuff you build for the future you want'.[83] Do we want a future where we are stuck now, tweaking the words we use but never really reaching one another? Or do we want a future where people have real options for how to live their lives and, as a result, sometimes change their minds? Without the kinds of change I have described above and describe in the next chapter – changes to social mobility, an easier time switching where we belong, more social spaces, more opportunities to change our life, including education, media and more – we do not have a public infrastructure that is capable of allowing us to navigate, or even really survive, the twenty-first century. But we could, with great pains, build one.

6

Fight Social Atrophy

In the months before I wrote this book, I finished my PhD. During that last, difficult stretch I largely stayed at home, straining at my computer screen, surrounded by my cats and aided by the occasional cup of tea delivered by a tiptoeing partner. To say it was 'stressful' makes it sound far too exciting. It was like being encased by an inescapable fog, weighed down by the foreboding sense that I wasn't working enough. This was bad enough, but by the time I submitted, I discovered something else had happened to me, something curious and coldly alarming: I no longer wanted to see my friends.

I did, of course, want to see my friends in the abstract. I still loved them. But in practice, when I thought about leaving the house or even writing back to them, I felt exhausted, unmotivated. If someone else cancelled, I was secretly a little relieved. People felt like hard work, even people I loved.

Until then, I'd been one of those irritatingly over-energetic extroverts, the kind that throws several big parties a year and has her calendar full of carefully pencilled meet-ups weeks in advance. But here I was, at home. And I wanted to stay there. It wasn't just me, I noticed. Many of my friends were also struggling to show up for each other. They would stay vague about plans, then bail at the last minute. Or they would forget to write back to people they adored. Everyone seemed to be throwing fewer gatherings and meeting up less. I found I worried more about how social interactions had gone or would go, concerned people didn't really like me. I watched as friend circles shrank and, more alarmingly, fractured altogether, with or without conflict. Many of my friends told me they felt others were not really there for them, even though they themselves had, until recently, barely left the house. It was as if we were all tired, wary snails, who had collectively pulled into our shells.

It was right around this time that I learned the term 'social atrophy'.

'Social atrophy' refers to the weakening, through disuse, of the neural networks that help us navigate the social world. Studies show human beings lose cognitive functioning and undergo a variety of other 'non-adaptive' changes when socially isolated, especially during chronic isolation. They become worse at emotional regulation, reasoning and memory. As with muscle atrophy, social atrophy can become profound, dangerous, especially because it often worsens over time, alienating us from other people, affecting our judgement, making us withdrawn and even paranoid. And, unfortunately, it's relatively common, something that should concern us all.

You may already be familiar with a wealth of data showing that long-term lack of desired social contact leads to negative health outcomes, from suicide to high blood pressure to poor immune systems to early death.[1] Researchers suggest that being chronically lonely has the same kind of effect on health and lifespan as smoking 15 cigarettes a day.[2] The link between social isolation and dementia is also very strong.

This shouldn't really surprise us because, as researchers in social psychology and evolutionary psychology love to restate, we are profoundly social animals, and have evolved to live in groups. For humans, interpersonal rejection and conflict feel like pain, and we get all the good hormones and endorphins when we're together.[3] No wonder being alone is so bad for us. Still, the studies on this topic never quite fail to amaze me. The 'Harvard Happiness Study' (as it is colloquially called) followed a number of Harvard graduates throughout their lives (as well as an otherwise similar cohort of poorer men). It found that close relationships were the single best predictor of happiness – more important than IQ, cholesterol or wealth. Close relationships kept these men in better physical and mental health, and even slowed ageing.[4]

When it comes to cognitive ability in particular, there's an oddly simple reason why social interactions have such a large effect: our brain's most complex everyday task is relating to other people, and doing this rigorously exercises our brain. In contrast, when human brains do not regularly use the parts devoted to navigating social interactions, those parts quickly wither, or get reappropriated by other systems in the brain. People with reduced social contact have 'smaller volumes in the temporal lobe, occipital lobe, cingulum, hippocampus, and amygdala'.[5] What this means, as one team of researchers put it, is that 'lonely individuals [are] more anxious, angry, and negative, and less positive, optimistic, comfortable, and secure than [socially] embedded individuals'.[6] This is true both when one compares groups of lonely and non-lonely people and when one compares the same person before and after a shift in their level of 'loneliness'.[7] It seems to hold even when studies control for people's intelligence, social-economic status and beauty; anyone who becomes more isolated, in short, quickly experiences a decline in their well-being, suggesting fairly direct causation between social isolation and these changes in the brain.

Perhaps the most extreme examples are the many older people whose dementia suddenly progressed much more rapidly during the start of the COVID-19 pandemic.[8] (This was true regardless of whether they contracted COVID-19, which carries its own cognitive risks.) But the effects can also be seen in teenagers during the early pandemic, whose brains aged more rapidly in unhealthy ways (girls appear to be harder hit).[9] And our increasing estrangement from one another in Western societies precedes the pandemic and has outlived the social distancing measures: in many countries, including the US, people are measurably more alone (spending more time alone, and having considerably fewer friends) than generations before.[10] We've become estranged from one another over decades, as we increasingly have weaker communities, fewer places to go to meet people and less of a habit of living either communally or socially.

There is something uniquely destructive about the long-term effects of this estrangement from others. Loneliness (as the issue is often termed) causes a change in personality that other forms of suffering do not. 'I accounted for the fact that loneliness is often accompanied by negative emotions', one researcher, Dr Mohsen Joshanloo, noted; 'surprisingly, even after controlling for negative affect, many of the associations between personality traits and loneliness remained significant. This suggests that loneliness affects our personality in ways that go beyond just feeling bad. There's something unique about the experience of loneliness that has lasting consequences.'[11] Being chronically isolated causes a certain kind of, well, brain damage.

This damage, this atrophy, leads not only to a significant decline in well-being and a shift in personality but also to a decline in social ability. As some of the researchers noted, lonely people (no matter how beautiful or intelligent!) ceased to reach out to others or even recognize when there were opportunities to do so; they 'made less use of social capital, expected negative outcomes, were less likely to reach out or to seek help from others, and were more likely to think they were already doing all they could do in their relationships'. Socially isolated people underestimate, in other words, the opportunities available for them to connect with others, and fail to see what they should be doing to build and maintain relationships. Moreover, social isolation appears to make people more emotionally volatile and easily upset, especially in social situations.[12] All of this suggests a negative cycle, where those who are isolated quickly lose the capacity and judgement involved in social interactions, withdraw and/or experience conflict and become more isolated, in an ever worsening cycle. The same researchers describe the life outcome for such people: 'complex yearnings for intimacy yet feelings of insecurity and mistrust, anger combined with anger suppression, punishing feelings of isolation coupled with a fear of negative evaluation by others, emotional dysphoria and withdrawal rather than active coping attempts'. Ouch.

The 'ouch' isn't just personal; it is political. Because political reasoning is a social, interdependent activity, social atrophy harms it immensely. And in both a literal and a metaphorical sense, our societies are probably more socially atrophied than they have been in about 60 years. That is, our brains have withered, and so has our social and political world.

These two 'levels' to the problem are profoundly related. Social atrophy and the atrophy of the public sphere are not only metaphorically similar; they are, in fact, directly and profoundly connected. Our social worlds have shrivelled, dangerously, and this has harmed our collective ability to reason about political questions and to do so together. Social atrophy provides a case study on how shrinking infrastructure, especially social infrastructure, affects everything from our neurons to our friendships to our capacity for political action.[13] There's no way around the most obvious solution; if the infrastructure we need in order to do better is lacking, we have to rebuild it.

If you're the sort that's interested in niche policy issues, or even if you're not, you may have heard that 'we' (implied: denizens of various Western countries) are in the grip of a 'loneliness epidemic'. In May 2023 the US Surgeon General declared a 'loneliness and isolation epidemic', while a few years before that the UK established a commission and a minister devoted to loneliness.[14] The World Health Organization has also set up a 'commission on social connection' to combat similar problems at the global scale.[15] And it is true that many people in modern societies report being lonely. In the US, for instance, the rate of self-reported loneliness seems to be about a third of people; the global rate is about one in four.[16]

Oddly, though, there is little evidence that people subjectively feel lonelier than they did in other recent periods of human history. As the researcher Esteban Ortiz-Ospina puts it, 'Despite the popularity of the claim, there is surprisingly no empirical support for the fact that loneliness is increasing, let alone spreading at epidemic rates.'[17] When one looks at rates across various Western countries, including Finland, Germany, the UK and Sweden, there is no evidence that people report feeling lonelier. Instead, if one looks closely at the data, it is not so much that people are feeling lonelier; it's just that they're increasingly alone.

How could humans be more alone than ever, yet not self-reportedly lonelier? There are, of course, many possible explanations, the most obvious of which is that being alone is not the same as feeling lonely. It is very possible to be happily without company (ask anyone with a toddler). But it is also plausible that many of these people are alone to an extent that is psychologically harmful but do not recognize this as the case. After all, feeling lonely is the reaction of the healthy mind to too much time alone; loneliness is an urge to nudge us back into the social world. However, research on social atrophy suggests people left alone for too long no longer recognize there are social opportunities to take advantage of. So if you're alone long enough, owing to social atrophy, you lose the urge to socialize and the feeling of loneliness altogether. Then you might no longer feel lonely, even though that would be the 'right' feeling to feel. Indeed, one of the most insidious and dangerous aspects of social atrophy is that those who are experiencing its harmful effects don't necessarily feel lonely, and thus don't take steps to rebuild their social world. This is why the word 'loneliness' not only doesn't capture the problem at hand but actually somewhat obscures it: the problem is often that people aren't feeling lonely when they should be.

It is isolation, then, rather than a felt sense of loneliness, that is rising, and which should perhaps most concern us (though it is also clear that those who report feeling lonely are also suffering in a real and important way). At the time of writing this book, people of all ages, ethnicities, education levels and genders have become more alone, spending less time with people outside their homes.[18] The American Time Use Survey, which tracks what Americans do hour by hour of their life, shows that all groups have radically reduced their face-to-face socialization time in the last few decades. Men have reduced their hours of face-to-face socializing by 30 per cent, unmarried people by 35 per cent, teenagers by 45 per cent.[19] The pandemic made all this more true, but the trends far pre-date this. Technology certainly contributes to this problem also, keeping people glued to screens rather than meeting in person, but the trend pre-dates any particular technological shift (and does not neatly correspond to the rise of either television or the internet). In fact, it's relatively clear that it's not just that people have moved their socializing online; instead, we're actually forming fewer meaningful friendships and relationships altogether. People's number of friends has dropped: the percentage of Americans who have five or more close friends has dropped about 25 per cent in the last 30 years or so. All around the world, people are living alone more frequently, which may also contribute to a decline in social hours.[20]

Even if people are not complaining of loneliness, an increasing lack of social contact shapes the way people see the world, often for the worse. One especially clear case of this is the corresponding ongoing crisis in 'social trust', a sociological construct that more or less measures how much people trust neighbours or strangers. While people in many countries still trust their friends and family (even if they see them less than they used to), they are now much less likely to say they trust strangers or neighbours, and also proportionately less likely to have spent any time with them recently.[21] This, in turn, correlates with whether they are engaged in politics. Those who trust their neighbours are most likely to vote and otherwise be civically engaged (and they also tend to be happier and in better health). Those who trust their neighbours least do exactly the opposite. Data such as this suggests that what is being measured when it comes to 'trust' or 'loneliness' isn't a passing feeling of disconnection but a profound alienation from others, one with political consequences.

This alienation both causes a number of political and social effects and is probably also caused by them.* First among these

---

*It is not by accident that I use the term 'alienation', which has long roots in left-wing political theory.

related variables is, quite simply, people's material positions and inequality. There is a striking class divide when it comes to isolation. Wealthier people and college educated people have more friends, are more likely to belong to organizations, have more people they can rely on in a crisis, and have more places nearby to gather, from coffee shops and bookstores to barbershops and public parks.[22] Interestingly, this class-(and especially education-) related gap in friendship is relatively recent; three decades ago, Americans with more formal education did not have any more friends than their less educated fellow citizens.

Moreover, the decline in social trust has a relatively straightforward, and probably causal, relationship with income inequality. Strikingly, economists suggest that in the US alone there are three factors – ever more unemployment experiences, ever less confidence in political institutions and a slight but systematic decrease in satisfaction with income – that can 'explain half of the 1973–2018 decline in [social and governmental] trust'.[23] Indeed, the pressure of financial precarity may by itself tear apart both families and the social fabric. As one researcher on the topic, Frank Infurna put it when explaining why middle-aged American people are more isolated than any group of Europeans, and British middle-aged people are the loneliest in Europe: 'Middle-aged adults reporting the lowest levels of loneliness live in countries with robust government-supported safety nets … generous family and work policies likely lessen midlife loneliness through reducing financial pressures and work-family conflict.'[24] Continental Europeans do better than Americans or British people because they have stronger economic social nets, and those with even stronger social nets do better still. That's why the middle-aged in Britain, Germany, Spain, Italy and Greece are somewhat lonely, and the middle-aged in the Netherlands, Denmark and Sweden less so.[25] It is difficult to get global data on social trust, social capital and social atrophy, but one study suggested that 38% of countries in the world were experiencing a negative trend and that 'the high number of negative developments reflects the decline of equality across the globe.'[26] All this suggests it's our economic environment that most profoundly shapes our social world when it comes to isolation. It is our economic system that determines how isolated we are, and that in turn determines our level of social trust.

Access to certain kinds of universal social services seems to specifically matter. Researchers have found that having healthcare through the Affordable Care Act ('Obamacare') when one gets ill protects against a worsening in social trust that will otherwise occur.[27] Some social scientists suggest that the US has particularly bad social trust precisely because it has few other programmes that are universal like this. More generally, the more unequal the country, the less social trust it has, and vice versa.[28] Relatedly, most of the most lonely countries are in the Middle East, South Asia and Africa, which are on average poorer or else very unequal. The more people have to compete for resources, the less they feel they can trust others.[29] Inequality also tends to lead to the corruption of other important institutions, such as the government, and it means we are less likely to see our neighbours as being 'like us'. Social atrophy happens in our brain, but it originates, in so many ways, with our economy and our government.

This would suggest that isolation and alienation strike the poor worst of all – and that's right. Most of the available research suggests that poorer people are lonelier, and wealthier people less so.[30] In the US in particular, this is strikingly true. The college educated are even much more likely to go on walks than the less educated, and far more likely to have conversations with their neighbours. Unsurprisingly, perhaps, they are also far more likely to trust their neighbours.[31] This class gap, when it comes to social isolation, is due not only to problems of social trust but also to the fact that wealthier people have the money to go out and do things, either meeting new people via activities and groups or else staying in touch with existing friends. A higher education level (and to some degree, the income, free time and wealth difference this generally entails) makes people much more likely to volunteer, participate in a group meeting, attend a community event, or host neighbours, family or friends. One might assume that the wealthiest capitalist countries, which are also often more individualistic, would have higher rates of loneliness, but this isn't the case.[32] The reason is probably relatively simple: whatever negative effects individualism may have, they appear to be cancelled out more or less entirely by the affordances for social interaction that money can buy. And if a country is rich but relatively equal, that's even better and more predictive of social interactions, because it means everyone else is available to socialize too. This is, I'd like to suggest, very good news. It means that the right economic and structural measures can overcome isolation, transcending other cultural and historical influences.

As my social world became less reliable, and as I researched social atrophy more, I was increasingly fascinated by one aspect of its effects in particular: the way it caused paranoia and suspicion of other people. The common way of phrasing this is that people who experience social atrophy tend to interpret neutral cues as negative.[33] (Is someone not texting you back? They probably hate you.) Perhaps because we don't have as much cognitive capacity directed to the social world, people's motivations are harder to parse and their behaviour more difficult to understand, and our brains tend to develop a negative default interpretation for ambiguities. For the person experiencing social atrophy, a joke that stings, a moment of friction or a lapse of attention can all be interpreted quickly as deep aggression, someone not liking you or a profound lack of care. While people do, of course, experience real instances of aggression or harm regardless of social atrophy, research suggests that, when we're socially atrophied, lots of signals that are in fact signs of something else (social awkwardness, or just that someone is bad at responding to text messages) are read as signs that something is profoundly 'off' or bad. And this, in turn, can make people wary or even aggressive in response to what they perceive as aggression, creating conflict where none originally existed. I noticed that, after the pandemic restrictions had been eased, people in my social world were just more on edge, more suspicious of each other, more easily hurt or put off by minor interactions. Friendships came apart more easily. It was painful to watch.

But, as with everything about social atrophy, it's not just about our individual lives but about our collective life. It is difficult to read about the paranoia-inducing effects of social atrophy and not see their tie to the massive declines in social trust. We may, in other words, distrust society more not only because it no longer provides everyone with what they need but also because, as we become more isolated, the suspicious and paranoia-inducing structures in our brains become more and more activated. A rise in income inequality and social atrophy and a decline in social trust have, I'd suggest, probably all contributed to the rise of polarization and xenophobia that has occurred over the last few decades, as well as an increase in right-wing and authoritarian beliefs. (Indeed, numerous psychological studies have shown that right-wing people are more likely to be sensitive to threats and suspicious of others and, interestingly, that being cynical about other people is a good predictor for someone moving to the right in their political beliefs over time.[34]) Given all this, debates, which often generate aggression and suspicion, may well aggravate these consequences of social atrophy and worsen our tendencies to be suspicious, shredding the social fabric as we consume it for entertainment.

It is also easy to see how social atrophy might be part of (perhaps both causing and caused by) the paranoid culture of the internet, a place laced with conspiracy theories where one is likely to be viewed and interpreted in the worst possible light. Indeed technology is another contributing factor, particularly the internet and mobile screens. Not only does screen time correlate with decreased hours socializing face to face, but when researchers pay people to deactivate their social media, those people then go and hang out more in person.[35] This suggests a causal relationship, where having the option of being on our phone provides a less challenging replacement for in-person social interaction. If we are already struggling with social atrophy, we might choose this sort of artificial or halfway-house fix for one of our deepest needs. Indeed, as I watch yet another influencer chat the world through the process of making a smoothie, I start to wonder whether 'influencers' are so popular because they provide a weak replacement for in-person friendship.

In any case, for a great many reasons, the online world is a poor substitute for many forms of social life. Influencers are, quite simply, not our friends. The way social interactions happen online tends to make fragmentation more likely. It is notoriously easy to hide behind a username while you bully someone; it is similarly very easy to interpret neutral cues as negative ones in the digital arena. People speak to one another more harshly and experience things more harshly.

Not only that, but online conversations allow us to disengage quickly, to mute and block. In comparison to real-life conversations, when you're online you can, in effect, avoid whatever is draining or scary, at least to a degree. But doing so might come at a cost. You might forget how to navigate such interactions, how to surf the discomfort that happens regularly whenever human beings meet in real life. This is part of the weakening of one's social 'muscles'. In many ways, then, technology is likely to be a significant factor contributing to social atrophy. But, interestingly, the trend seems to be larger than any specific technological shift, or indeed technology in general.[36]

The pandemic has, of course, probably also contributed to these profoundly tangled trends. Most people around the world were asked to 'socially distance', keeping apart from one another physically. Yet as the sociologist Eric Klinenberg notes, what was really needed was for people to be physically distanced but socially close.[37] Interestingly, during the early pandemic, there was only a small rise in reported loneliness around the world.[38] This may have been because, although people were kept apart, they turned to those in their bubbles and had more time for them. Or it may even be that having a shared condition (of living through the pandemic) led to people feeling solidarity with one another even when physically apart. Or it may be that loneliness really measures our sense of being left out, and fewer people felt socially left out when they knew no one else could leave their homes either. Or it may be that social atrophy prevented people from feeling lonely even when they were isolated. (You can perhaps see now the difficulty of measuring something like 'loneliness'.) It is probably most accurate to say that the pandemic exacerbated existing trends and also led to shifts in people's routines and belonging that might mean they were more alone even after social distancing ended.

As is so often the case, none of this data provides a single simple story of causation. The economy, the pandemic, the internet, the unravelling of the social fabric, the shrivelling of our social brains and the distrust that has seeped into our political life are probably all 'overdetermined', not to mention mutually reinforcing. Which means this is going to be a complex problem to solve.

On a lighter note, however, one thing does appear to be specifically caused by the pandemic: the amount of time we spend with our pets is up – the average female pet owner spends more time 'actively engaged' with her pets than in person with other people.[39] My cats, who faithfully kept me company through my PhD, approve of this shift. But (sorry, Val and Leo!) for sociopolitical reasons, I cannot.

I have suggested that social atrophy is a curious problem because, although it appears in the brain, it is in fact partially caused by our material world. Our social position is a great determiner of our level of isolation; women and low-income people seem, for example, to have suffered more from social anxiety during the ongoing pandemic.[40] But our isolation is not only affected by income inequality or by the pandemic or technology. There is another factor. One that isn't necessarily more important than these others but which presents what is arguably a more manageable, and less widely recognized challenge; something that can be created, demanded or built by social movements, policymakers and even the average person: social infrastructure. It may sound counterintuitive to say that building a great deal of infrastructure is a manageable challenge (who ever said restructuring the economy was easy?), but compared to other options, it is. Stopping people from using their cell phones so much or preventing pandemics altogether are both even more difficult. So we may need to focus on building infrastructure most of all. As described in the last chapter, social infrastructure is 'the crucial organizations, places and spaces that enable communities to create social connections – to form and sustain relationships that help them to thrive'.[41] It is what makes it possible, even easy, for us to spend time with those in our communities. It matters for lots of reasons: it makes places more resilient in disasters and reduces inequalities of all kinds, for example.[42] But, perhaps most clearly for our purposes, it is an antidote to social atrophy.

Social infrastructure, where it exists, provides a truly amazing number of benefits. It not only allows people to escape isolation but also appears to reduce some of the negative effects of inequality on long-term well-being. For example, even if someone individually has money, living in a poorer neighbourhood can in itself lead to isolation and loneliness.[43] (This is probably because other people in it cannot afford to go out and do things, and in poorer neighbourhoods, there are fewer activities around.) The inverse, happily, also follows, with significant caveats: *if* a neighbourhood with collective wealth uses that wealth to create social infrastructure that is accessible for everyone, even the poorer members of the community can benefit.

Social connection is, it turns out, a form of wealth that one inherits from one's neighbourhood, something one cannot gain in isolation; it is a kind of 'wealth' it is impossible to own alone.

Interestingly, there is also some evidence that creating third spaces (that is, spaces outside of both work and home) reduces inequality and segregation when it comes to housing markets. One study in the UK found that one of the best ways to build mixed-income neighbourhoods is to encourage higher-income single people to move (yes, this also causes gentrification, so it has rather mixed social effects).[44] One of the main 'pulls' for young people to move to neighbourhoods is 'sporting and cultural centres'. In other words, not only does creating third spaces, especially cheap and free ones, help people at all income levels to be less lonely but strategically building and funding third spaces could also help societies create more economically – and otherwise – diverse neighbourhoods. And it does appear that it is neighbourhoods and neighbours that make the difference: some studies suggest that people mostly socially interact with those that are physically near them (rather than going out of their way to see people slightly further off).[45] In the age of the internet, this is remarkable. In any case, it suggests that nearby physical social infrastructure matters and that, when it is built well, it allows for people of very different backgrounds to mix socially and reduces the effects of inequality. While some of this is, of course, speculative, it provides one promising avenue for addressing the grave state of so much of modern democratic life.

It's not just that social infrastructure allows people to mix; it also changes the basis on which they do it. These 'third places', a term coined by sociologist Ray Oldenburg, are spaces which are neither our spaces of employment nor the entirely private spaces of home but, rather, places 'providing the means for people to gather easily, inexpensively, regularly and pleasurably'.[46] One notable thing about third spaces, Oldenburg argues, is that they are neither spaces of hierarchy and restricted speech (as spaces of professionalism tend to be) nor spaces of exclusion (as the private home necessarily is). People in third places are, at least in theory, equals; they can say what they like, they can mix freely and, for the most part, anyone is allowed. Without such places, human beings are often stuck in their hierarchical and/or exclusive ways of relating to one another. Social contact theory, the theory that predicts when people mixing freely will lead to reduced prejudice, posits that reducing prejudice requires a space rather like this, where citizens are positioned as equals and can form true emotional connections. In short, we need third spaces to even begin to exist together in a meaningful way, and for our social and political life to function. (No wonder they're so central to the writings of Jürgen Habermas, the political theorist I mentioned in the first chapter of this book, who suggested they were central in the creation of the 'public sphere' in the first place.) Many of us, I think, already half-sense this when we enter such spaces. On optimistic days, when the sun is out and I'm getting my favourite latte, I sometimes wonder if part of people's love for their favourite cafés stems from a not quite elucidated sense of just how personally, socially and politically magical that meeting of strangers and acquaintances really is.

Today, however, the challenge is probably far greater than just bringing back affordable coffee shops (although sign me up for that campaign). Even those in literal coffee shops today are distracted, on their phone and less connected to their social world in every other respect. In a digital, socially fractured age, we're going to have to build differently, and even more thoroughly and intentionally than before.

In the US one of the foremost writers on this curious problem – that is, on the disconnection of citizens from one another – is the political scientist Robert Putnam, whose 1995 essay 'Bowling Alone: America's Declining Social Capital' became hugely influential overnight. In that essay and the book that followed it, Putnam described how, in contrast to historically high levels of civic group participation in the 1960s and 1970s, in recent decades there had been a vast decline in Americans belonging to membership organizations, from parent–teacher associations to bowling leagues.[47] This, in turn, Putnam argued, led to a decline in collective 'social capital'. The term, coined by Glenn Cartman Loury and others before Putnam, refers to the power and value of social bonds.[48] That value, in many ways, can be boiled down to a kind of social trust. As Putnam puts it in his most recent documentary, living in a society with relatively high social capital means that people are connected such that they can and do mutually rely on each other to build a shared future. It also means that 'if you cheat somebody, someone will hear about it'.[49] All this, in turn, means people tend to behave in more co-operative and upright ways. Societies with greater social capital engage in political life in a way that means there is less suspicion, less destruction and more concern for the good of the whole. Social capital often seems to have more of an effect on civic-mindedness than other frequently cited factors such as polarization or education. That is, it is more powerful in creating politically engaged members of democracies than other frequently mentioned solutions, like more education or 'teaching critical thinking' or getting people to feel empathy or meet in the middle on a particular issue.[50]

Since the success of 'Bowling Alone', Putnam has become a sort of celebrity. His work has appeared on countless TV shows and magazines, and even inspired Bill Clinton to invite Putnam to Camp David. It led to the creation of a task force group that included Putnam himself but also conservative politicians and a young community organizer named Barack Obama, who later awarded Putnam the National Humanities Medal.[51]

Putnam is a deeply earnest, even sentimental, man. In his recent documentary, he cries repeatedly about his duty to American democracy. (I first watched the documentary with a number of Europeans, who were somewhere between shocked and appalled to see this show of American patriotism in an academic.) So when Clinton first began to hold hearings on Putnam's book and tout his research, Putnam figured that surely Americans would turn towards each other now, that this problem would reverse. Unfortunately he was wrong. To this day social capital has continued to decline. Membership of groups is down. Membership of the PTA is down. Union membership is down. Dinner parties are down, which somehow particularly hurts my still extrovert heart. Thirty years since he published his piece on bowling alone, isolation and atomization are more striking than ever, in the US and elsewhere. And, of course, all this is especially bad because, as Putnam and his co-researchers note, joining even just one group is very good for us: it seems to increase one's educational attainment, improve one's social mobility, and cut one's risk of dying in a given year in half.[52]

Indeed, clubs are at the centre of Putnam's surprisingly moralistic and individualistic plea to fix the collective, political and social problem of social capital. As the title suggests, 'Bowling Alone' placed special emphasis on the fact that Americans had started doing alone the same activities they used to do in groups – such that, for example, while Americans were bowling more than ever, they now joined bowling leagues in far lower numbers. As a result, Putnam often argues that what Americans need to do is rejoin associations and clubs. He notes that Americans used to be ardent joiners of clubs, from religious organizations to unions, from explicitly political organizations such as the Japanese–Mexican Labor Association to plain old bowling clubs. There were also many organizations that served both social and explicitly political functions (consider the rise of Phillis Wheatley clubs across the US in the 1800s, where Black women met to both organize and socialize). Nearly anyone in society might be a member of not one but several clubs. Towns even used to have formal directories that helped you find and contact clubs you might wish to join.

I like associations and clubs too, in moderation, but I don't find this line of analysis so promising after a certain point. While I admire much about his work, Putnam has a tendency to suggest that what is needed is a moral change, or at least a moral change first. A plea for individual moral change is still the centre of his work. In his more recent book, *The Upswing: How We Came Together a Century Ago and How We Can Do It Again*, he and his co-author write, 'The Progressive Movement was, first and foremost, a moral awakening.'[53]

Yet while there are many factors that have led to a decline in social capital, a vast number of them are structural, and no amount of moralizing alone can help. As Putnam himself put it, what happened over time is that 'half of all the civic infrastructure in America had vanished'.[54] Today, more than half of all Americans have no or minimal access to 'civic infrastructure'. A fifth report no access at all to spaces where they could meet or talk to neighbours, just 18 per cent have good access. Once again, the college educated fare far better, and Black Americans fare far worse.[55] And this, of course, profoundly affects people's friendships. As one report puts it, 'The density of civic infrastructure and the robustness of American friendship networks correspond remarkably closely. Americans with less access to civic infrastructure – such as parks, coffee shops and libraries – have many fewer friends and report greater difficulty making social connections. Americans with no access to public or commercial places are more than three times more likely than those with the most access to report having no close friends.[56]

Social capital in the US has been declining ever since the late 1960s or early '70s, and this (it may not surprise anyone to realize) is precisely when the US, and many Western economies for that matter, experienced a massive slowdown in economic growth, one that no doubt turned many denizens of capitalism towards more individualistic endeavours (doing their side hustle, doing self-improvement, helping their children achieve at school) in order to survive. Shortly thereafter, in the 1980s and '90s, this slowdown in growth turned into an experiment with neoliberalism, which is to say a policy regime that privatizes public services, goods and land while practising austere public spending. Gone were funds for after-school activities where parents might meet other parents, or for parks or community centres or even sidewalks where people might come to know each other and inquire about the substance of each other's lives.[57] Indeed, these economic policies chipped away at not just social infrastructure but all infrastructure, and the social world itself. In those 60 years economic policies and measurable forms of individualism have grown together, hand in hand. In his latest book Putnam puts forward what he calls the 'I–we–I' curve, a graph that shows how by a plenitude of metrics Americans were highly individualistic in the 1890s or so but became much more communitarian over time until the 1960s, when they started to become more individualistic again, such that we find ourselves today in a period of intense individualism akin to that of the Gilded Age.[58] This is, no doubt, in part because neoliberalism tends to eat away at public goods, including the many parks, playgrounds and libraries that provide free third spaces for the community.

But it's not just our economic system that has impoverished us when it comes to social capital (though more on that in a minute). It's also that social capital is politically inconvenient for those in power, most of the time. In truth, it should not surprise us that Putnam's clarion call, boosted by the literal liberal presidents of the US, did not take effect, because politicians and governments have at best an uneasy relationship with social capital and the spaces that generate it. Public spaces are so politically powerful that governments have intentionally enclosed them to prevent or end protest, resistance and dissent. In the US, nearly all major cities had their relatively walkable, narrower streets replaced with broad avenues and shopping districts, in part because these are easier to police.[59]

Or, to travel further back in time, the Chartist movement in the UK was a powerful working-class movement in the 1830s and '40s. Its most notable demand was universal male suffrage, alongside other related democratic reforms. The Chartists regularly used public spaces to organize, grow the movement and gather millions of signatures to present to Parliament. Thousands of Chartists gathered at Kennington Common, a publicly owned open space, during the movement's peak; to prevent this happening again, the common was forcibly enclosed and refashioned as a highly landscaped, policed and gated public park, one where large gatherings of that type were no longer physically possible. The road to electoral democracy in Britain is, in effect, now landscaped over, paved with the gravestones of the very places that made such a movement possible in the first place.[60] And to go yet further back in the same country, in 1675 King Charles II attempted to close all the newfangled coffee houses in the country, conscious that these might be places where people not only met to discuss the latest literature or the prices of commodities but where they could also plot against him (as indeed, they did).[61]

Indeed, the histories of both Europe and the Middle East are absolutely filled with rulers surveilling coffee shops, shutting them down and even banning coffee itself precisely because they knew that gathering in this way provided a social infrastructure that allowed people to build civic power, often in resistance to their rulers. It wasn't just that coffee houses provided a place for people to gather and uncover mutual interests and concerns; it was also that something about them led people to learn a new kind of conversational style that wasn't possible in, say, houses of worship or even open marketplaces. (Which suggests, once again, that the logic of the marketplace has little in common with the logic of profound political conversations). This is, perhaps, why one sees such a wide range of fears about coffee houses: French authorities became convinced that coffee would cause people to stay awake all night, learn radical ideas and overthrow the government. (They weren't entirely wrong!) Meanwhile, the British worried that coffee would make men impotent and that coffee shops would make men effeminate.[62] This poses the interesting question of whether those important democratic skills gained in early coffee shops were, in fact, close to or even precisely the virtues women already had learned to cultivate in other areas of life: talking things through, being polite to anyone, seeking common ground, listening, compromise, relationship building, discursive care. Is there something about civic life that requires all of us to learn and embody these feminine-coded virtues? The version of me that has fruitlessly debated so many men in so many seminars is tempted to agree.

In any case, social infrastructure generates a form of social life that is powerful and often uncomfortable for those already in power. Sure, politicians may pay lip service to the ideals of public life or encourage you to 'join a club' (perhaps the tamest way to build social capital), but notice how nervous they tend to get around an encampment.

Indeed, governments and activists alike have long been aware that some environments are clearly easier to politically organize in. For example, on an architectural basis alone, it's no wonder that university campuses are ripe for political organizing. Sure, there are other reasons why protests frequently happen there; professors may on average be more 'woke', and youth are too. Plus, college students have more time. But university campuses (especially the 'college' campuses of the kind I experienced in the US, which are highly residential and walkable) also structurally support political life. On this kind of campus there is an abundance of indoor and outdoor public space, from gyms to laundromats to cafeterias and more. There are communal living areas where people can mix freely, often with people very different from themselves. There are numerous free events happening all the time. Environments with these features, even when not geared towards the youngest adults, lead to opportunities for political engagement. They provide the affordances, the opportunity for people to build relationships that are the underpinnings for any meaningful form of political thought and reasoning. And these are increasingly rare.

Because social trust and social ties are so strongly linked, all this means we are currently living through a particularly disempowering and inactive period in democracies. This may sound slightly strange given, say, the level of 'wokeness' on social media or the pressing political issues at hand (it's particularly likely to sound strange to you if you willingly picked up this book), but it's sadly true when we look at data from all around the world.[63] Particularly striking results can be found in a survey from the UK, the Hansard Society survey that measures political engagement. Before this survey was discontinued, political engagement had reached its lowest point ever in the UK. As mentioned earlier, in 2019 over half of all citizens said they had not done any of the 13 political activities listed on the sheet, and many more than ever before said they were not prepared to do any of them. Many reported that they felt no sense that their political actions matter at all. More than this: that year, the highest number of people ever said they were 'not at all' interested in politics or knew nothing about it. Thirty per cent said they never discussed it. A full third of the population said they did not want to be involved 'at all' in local decision-making, up ten points that year. In many places around the world this kind of disengagement has risen, along with the aforementioned decline in social trust.[64] What looked like a serious problem in 1995 looks ever more dire now, both in terms of how lonely and alienated we are from one another and in terms of what it means for anyone to be willing to think about politics at all.

We're also less likely to want to think about politics because more and more of us don't get out much or do things that stretch our experience of the world. At the same time as public spaces have become less accessible and open to public life, housing crises have also led to a shrinking in action-possibilities for many: precisely the opposite of what we would wish if we want to encourage political reasoning. This is a reverse of a trend that used to be familiar: during the rapid urbanization of the last century, people around the world moved to cities, often mixing with those very different from themselves. Today, through waves of suburbanization and rising inequality, the reverse trend is occurring: people are less likely to live in diverse neighbourhoods and are also less likely to be able to choose to move anywhere at all. In the

US, for example, people used to move from poor states to rich states, seeking opportunity. Now they're doing the opposite, moving to poorer areas to access cheap housing.[65] As Harvard economists Peter Ganong and Daniel Shoag write, the housing crisis causes 'segregation along economic dimensions, with limited access for most workers to America's most productive cities'.[66] People in my generation, the Millennials, are moving less, probably in part because they don't have any particularly exciting job opportunities to move for.[67] We're re-segregating along both class and racial lines. The social networks that could change our minds are now both less varied and less dense.[68]

The same economic trends (widening inequality, less physical proximity to the centres of metropolitan areas) mean that my generation are also less likely to switch jobs or start businesses.[69] This is remarkable given that Millennials are more likely to rent rather than own their homes, and less likely to marry or have children. (They should be free to move around regularly and try new things.) But it seems that economic opportunities are limited enough that, even with these other factors, Millennials are likely to move less than any of the previous generations, including their grandparents and great-grandparents. Here as earlier, material well-being erases the effects of culture, parenthood, marriage and more.[70] In any case, the result is that people move and mix less and take fewer risks in their lives. For structural reasons people are now less likely to mix with others in third spaces, move at all and/or move to a place with people different from themselves. They are likely to be less active in the public world than previous generations and in many ways less likely to try out new ways of living too. This harms their ability to reconsider political issues or add complexity to their existing views (cellphones and woke memes notwithstanding, for one's in-person social network and actions matter more). The economy has made it far more difficult for people to mix with others or try new ways of living, and this has limited our ability to think about our shared world.

Just as social atrophy is a negative cycle, so is the atrophy of social infrastructure, of all infrastructure. Once infrastructure begins to be privatized, as I mentioned in the last chapter, a negative cycle occurs. Those rich enough to opt out and rely on private services do so, which means they then no longer have an incentive to care about public funds for infrastructure at all. The wealthiest, ruling class then has even more motivation to cut public services and funding. Rich and poor increasingly live in different worlds, almost in different governmental systems. As writer and academic Sheila Liming notes, this happens in housing markets too:

> What we can't agree to share has to be bought and paid for on an individual basis. ... In other words, if you don't have a local park that your children can walk to, you wind up building a playset in your own backyard, one that you pay for yourself; there, your children can play, but they can't gain exposure to the kinds of social challenges that are the unique provenance of interactions between strangers. Meanwhile, your neighbors are also building playsets ... the need for yard space ... is suddenly greater. The average house size starts to metastisize; the market for housing grows more expensive, squeezing out low-wage earners.[71]

If low-wage earners send their children out onto the street to play (because they have no space for playsets and there are no parks nearby), this often makes the wealthier, usually whiter, people see the streets as dangerous, and they withdraw further into their enclosed private spaces. And so on. Which is a shame, because 'Third spaces exist to span the divide between rich and poor, between the backyard playset class and the playing-in-the-street class, and to make the experience of being around different kinds of people feel habitual, meaning both more likely and less threatening.' Of course, this negative spiral of increasing enclosure and distrust closely mirrors the effects of social atrophy, where the more isolated a person is, the more they lose the skills and motivation that would drag them out of isolation. Once the problem starts, it tends to simply get worse, as with the shrivelling of our brains.

Even those third spaces that involve some costs (coffee shops, bars) have become less affordable. As I write this, the number of pubs in the UK has shrunk by a quarter in the last 25 years.[72] While the number of coffee shops has gone up during this time period, coffee is often a takeaway. Indeed, a massive shift to a delivery economy, particularly for food, has meant that even restaurants are less likely to see sit-in guests. And this is a trend you can see playing out across many privately owned third spaces, which host fewer physical meetings than ever before.[73] More to the point, it is possible that even when people enter the coffee shop, they are in effect 'coffee-shopping alone' (as with bowling alone): that is, people are going to coffee shops but only to get coffee and sit alone, or speak to another person they already know very well. The rich coffee shop culture that Habermas imagined as a part of the creation of the public sphere is, I'd suggest, rare these days, even in our beloved local coffee spots.

In a world of incredible crises, it may sound rich to complain that our coffee shops are not happening enough. But it shouldn't, because coffee shops and public parks and even schools and libraries and sidewalks are where people tend to run into each other and end up forming the kind of relationships that lead them to political action about exactly these crises. This may seem an odd point at which to intervene in a series of interconnected political crises, but it shouldn't. For social infrastructure is something we can build collectively. It's not that there aren't other factors involved in the decline of civic life. I do not doubt that we are too much glued to screens, nor do I deny (of course!) that a lack of concern for other people is a moral problem; but it's not all that helpful to look at these problems that way. We are not going to manage to prise people away from their phones, and moralizing doesn't seem to help much either. What we need are material changes: either the creation of space or the providing of financial resources or related resources such as greater time. (And yes, really fun and meaningful clubs help too.)

To think about the political effects of decaying social infrastructure further, let's just for a moment try a slightly suspicion- and paranoia-inducing thought experiment (perhaps exacerbating the effects of our own social atrophy). Imagine there is a government that does not want its citizens to mobilize politically (Sound familiar...?). Might it not delight in, and even encourage or build, a world with less social infrastructure? I think it would, particularly where many people disagree with it, for a few reasons.

First, getting rid of social infrastructure is likely to reduce the number of friends people have. And, as we know, fewer friends means, in effect, less capacity for us to think politically. It also means less time spent in circumstances where people might have the kind of long-form conversations that do have the potential to change minds on political issues, which I described more in Chapter Four. Engaging in individual acts of explicit, short-term persuasion may make us feel virtuous, but it is so time-consuming that pursuing them is a bit like building sandcastles while the 'tide' of social networks, infrastructures and daily actions washes the effects of our conversations away. But social infrastructures might have a far more permanent effect, if they function in a way that brings groups together repeatedly, changing who they belong with and their daily actions, and creating the long-form social contact that seems to really matter. Joshua Kalla, one of the main researchers studying deep canvassing, reminded me during our conversation that there is evidence that once affective polarization is reduced (that is, once people dislike the people they disagree with less), people also hang out with each other more, and come to persuade and move each other towards their points of view, so there is a possible virtuous cycle that happens within social infrastructures. The more people use them, the more they are likely to interact in meaningful, long-form ways, and this in turn makes them less suspicious of one another, which also makes them more likely to interact.[74]

Social infrastructure is also frequently a gateway for people to try new ways of living, which in turn allows people to consider new ideas and take on new beliefs. Indeed, infrastructure more broadly allows people to try out new possibilities for action. Both allow citizens to move around, cheaply socialize and try out new ways of behaving, whether that's protesting, trying vegan food, going to church, experiencing democratic decision-making in a group household, joining the PTA or volunteering for older people. Some of these actions may seem trivial, but many seemingly trivial activities may lead to other activities, from direct political organizing to simply discovering that other people in your block are experiencing a similar social problem.

Getting rid of social infrastructure, in contrast, keeps people isolated from one another and suspicious of one another, which is beneficial to our imagined bad government, and to real ones. That is why those who study authoritarianism are increasingly concerned about what they call the 'shrinking space' problem, where in many countries (especially, but not only, those that are commonly seen as authoritarian) there are increasingly few truly public spaces where freedom of expression is possible.[75] Spaces may be heavily surveilled, heavily policed or closed down. Even in countries that we do not currently consider authoritarian, the privatization of space makes it less able to function as a political arena. Often these spaces are in fact part of a number of Privately Owned Public Spaces, or 'POPS', which means the owners can call the police on anyone they like, or close them down. Even in spaces that are technically legally public, hours are often reduced, hostile architecture is put into place to prevent loitering, and some spaces are plainly in states of disuse and decay. Governments are often apathetic at best about this problem, as they do not necessarily relish a politicized population. If you're a government that does not want political or social change, cutting infrastructure, and perhaps especially social infrastructure, is probably going to be beneficial for you, the government. Which, in turn, suggests that the rest of us should treasure it and fight for it.

The importance of social infrastructure for the possibility of social change becomes most obvious, I'd argue, when you look at the way some successful political movements tend to rely on, and even build, social infrastructure. The Civil Rights Movement, for example, was effective at recruiting and retaining people in part because it asked members for a lot in terms of actions. Members had to go to great lengths – enormous, terrifying lengths, in fact – for the movement. People could get beaten and put in jail for years. People risked being lynched. Some ultimately paid that price. And, while less striking in terms of risk, as I pointed out in previous chapters, people had to spend a great deal of time organizing every single week to create something like a million-man march. These types of actions are likely to have profound psychological effects, building greater commitment to a movement.

It wasn't only the actions that helped to keep people in the movement, however; it was also the community and relationships. The Black community involved in the Civil Rights Movement built relationships and spaces for relationships to form. Because they faced both legal discrimination and general estrangement and violence from white people, Black people, especially those in the south of the US, generally carefully relied only on businesses that reliably served them. There was, famously, a 'green book' (*The Negro Motorist Green Book*) which catalogued establishments where they would be safe and welcomed. These spaces where Black people could be together often became places for organizing at both the formal and the informal level.[76] It is perhaps a little tiring to hear a white woman expound on Black movements and social spaces, so please let me cut to the work of Joyce Balls-Berry, a public health professor who created public health interventions for Black men that took place in barbershops. She provides a brief but well-put history, in her own writing:

> The role of the Black barbershop is well documented in the history of the Civil Rights movement as a gathering place in which to plan strategy and promote unity. … These barbershops quickly became a gathering place where Black men could gather to socialize, play chess and checkers, and discuss politics. The rise of Jim Crow laws limited spaces where Blacks could gather, and the

barbershop filled this void, similar to Black churches but on a smaller scale. Many politically active barbers handpicked the reading materials, and the barbershop provided an opportunity for men to read Black newspapers and magazines. Barbers also conducted voter-registration campaigns. Civil rights activist Stokely Carmichael (aka Kwame Ture) attributed his early political education to his weekly visits to a barbershop in Harlem. Quincy T. Mills, a history professor at Vassar College and author of *Cutting along the Color Line*, describes the Black barbershops as 'private spaces in the public sphere for Black men'.[77]

This was a form of deeply embedded organizing, embedded in the sense that activists were building a very significant set of infrastructures that allowed people to belong together and to act. Churches and mosques too played important, in many ways similar, roles as centres for organizing. These places did not just distribute ideas and pamphlets but also provided a place for people to build relationships.

These spaces, and barbershops in particular, are sometimes referred to as the 'original Black Twitter'. But, of course, there is something about belonging to a community outside of social media that is perhaps more powerful even than Black Twitter could be. The result of having deeply embedded relationships in a community of activists, of course, is a much higher investment and a longer life to one's activism. When you were recruited, it was not as a fun hobby on the weekends or a badge on your social media. You were recruited into an entire community. It was not about one's personal brand but about belonging. (It was 'selfless and we-ful', as my Black sister put it when we watched documentary films about the Civil Rights Movement together.)

Today, of course, movements are not organized like this. Indeed, from the perspective of social movements organizing, I would argue that activists and citizens today are hamstrung when it comes to political change. We lack much of the infrastructure that reasoning well about politics requires. Many political movements are only loosely connected to each other and to their members, who may really merely be people on their mailing lists. There are exceptions, of course, but if the social-scientific data has anything to say, it is that they are exactly that: exceptions. In many cases, political spaces, communities and infrastructures have also been replaced by other forms of belonging, on- and offline, that are less politically promising and even reactionary. As one activist, the anarchist poet Jeff Shantz put it:

> By the time I went to work in the plant and became a member of the local [union] myself, most of these activities and spaces were things of the past. My fellow workers on the line were finding support and solidarity not within the shared spaces of the local, but often, instead, in born-again religions and reactionary clubs.
>
> Indeed this is perhaps one of the lessons to be learned from the successful organizing done by the Right in the 1980s and 1990s. In times of need and crisis, the evangelical churches provided institutional support and emotional defence against capitalist alienation.[78]

It is plausible that something like unions would need to be built up again in order to address some of the challenges of the twenty-first century. In the US and elsewhere union membership is down, and so is membership of political parties, with massive downstream consequences for both political organizing and the social fabric.[79] Indeed, without the structure of unions (which once conducted political education, organized people politically around a variety of issues and brought out the vote), far fewer people are actively political. Some have argued that, without its particularly robust and grassroots work, much political life has been outsourced to NGOs, who are 'advocates without members', leading to a further decline in active civic life.[80] Wherever people are, they are doing it alone. And since political reasoning has to do with action and belonging together, they are also reasoning less together about politics.

Another option besides union-building would be the return of the kind of high-intensity political party that, like a union, asks for dues and regular action from its members. But whatever the new formation of political life, if we are to rebuild our collective possibilities for political reasoning, we will need to create an infrastructure for the kind of strong ties and belonging, and possibilities for action, that are all too easily replaced by reactionary groups and conservative religious life.

It will certainly not be enough to demand infrastructure investment from governments (although we should do this – for example, in an age of Trump, we can instead focus on some local governments and states and pressure them for some forms of social infrastructure). Governments are generally undermotivated, at best, to create social infrastructure, both because of their neoliberal economic policies and their frequent authoritarian bents, which are likely to rise over the course of this century. Fortunately, there are many ways to create social infrastructure, and some people are already doing the work that is needed. The BBC podcast Now Here highlighted a number of examples of citizen-built social infrastructure, from the regeneration of miners' institutes (spaces that miners used to self-fund and which functioned as spaces to gather, learn and organize) to the creation of cheap laundromats where activities happen and resources are directed to people as they wash their clothes.[81] None of the examples suggest building social infrastructure is easy: it's all hard work. But it is also eminently possible, with and without the state. There is meaningful work to do in building it at the grassroots level, not just demanding it from governments (and having infrastructure that is not owned by governments is probably politically beneficial when governments become oppressive).

That said, lots of small grassroots movements on their own will probably not be enough either, because what's at stake here is really a question of whether we are going to allow capitalism to eat the society that produces it. To return to the terms of Jürgen Habermas, our theorist of coffee-shops-make-democracy-but-capitalism-can-destroy-it, are we collectively going to allow the 'system', especially a financialized model of capitalism, to alter our architecture, make going out totally unaffordable and ultimately keep us apart both physically and psychically? I hope not. To resist this will certainly take both the realization of core economic demands and a set of grassroots movements, together.

Ultimately, we are facing a choice about whether we allow capitalism to atrophy our social spaces, shrink our brains and make us more paranoid and withdrawn from each other. If we allow this atrophy to continue, it will be because we made a political choice to prioritize a certain kind of economy (one that also harms people and the planet) above the foundations of democratic life. Isolated people may well make productive workers. (After all, without social ties to tend to, what else do they have to do?) And they certainly make for more pliable political subjects. But I would rather have less productivity and more democracy. It's a choice we all make individually and collectively, including if we choose inaction.

All of what I have described thus far leads me to one of my most central frustrations about how people talk about and understand the public sphere. Across the political spectrum public commentators bemoan the state of political discourse: the polarization of opinions, the horrors of Twitter, the rise of conspiracies and so much more. I am horrified too. But many fewer writers and thinkers have considered whether it might simply be the case that we have slowly shrunk the infrastructure needed for meaningful political reasoning: whether, to put it bluntly, it is even really possible to have a certain kind of democratic life without a certain set of economic choices and infrastructures to underpin it. In other words, clearly a great many people care about what we might call the public sphere, or public life, or public reasoning. But it seems to me that many people who love the public sphere (including people who make their living as commentators) haven't fully thought through what it is or how it really works. They have let our most beautiful myths stand in for a thorough analysis of what is actually possible, just when we need something better than that.

If we had a better common conception of what political reasoning is (if we understood that it has more to do with belonging, social ties and actions, and less to do with 'debate' or mere exposure to ideas), then we would (I suspect) be less collectively confused or surprised by the increasing polarization and distrust that have led to the breakdown of public discourse. Our social infrastructure has been decimated by profit motives; our collective life has atrophied, and with it our brains. This is visible not only in the geography of public spaces but also in the MRI scans of our shrinking brains and even in the activities that people are increasingly not involved in. In the US, for example, data shows that volunteering and attendance at religious services are down. Community centres and youth sports use are down.[82] And everywhere these days, owing to remote working, many are not even getting something like community at work (always a tricky prospect at best, but some people do find their friends and organize there). The aspects of life that allow people to really see and care about each other, even to have the cognitive capacity to do so, have significantly atrophied away. We can also do better than frame this problem as a mere 'loneliness'. What we are facing is not merely a loneliness epidemic (not least because people do not in fact feel lonelier than they did in previous generations). It is a political problem, caused by capitalism as well as other factors including our collective political choices. And what is needed is more than joining a club.

We need to build social infrastructure, with and especially without the state. We need to build infrastructure for social movements. We need to stop framing problems (and letting governments and institutions frame problems) as 'loneliness', since what is really at stake is a collective problem about estrangement and alienation, not an individual problem or feeling. Once we look at things this way, a series of related issues come into sharper and more addressable focus. As we do all this, we need to create spaces that help reduce prejudice against minority groups and allow people to have long-form exchanges and meaningful relationships in the contexts where that is productive. And we need to see the social fabric as the canvas for the changes we want to see, even when this requires rupture, even when it requires repair.

You may be wondering, on a more personal note, if I ever recovered from my social atrophy. The answer is, 'only sort of, and with great effort'. Because I had read up on it extensively, and because what I had learned about the changes in my brain gave me the same horrifying feeling as watching a particularly gruesome horror film, I made an effort; I pushed myself to see my friends, to reconnect. And, of course, I was able to do that because I was fortunate: I had enough money for evenings out in London, and enough time. There was just enough money and infrastructure in my life for me not to lose my most important social ties.

But in truth, the answer is also only 'kind of'. I have my good friends still, but I have also let some weaker connections wither on the vine that perhaps I should have nurtured. More than this: it is harder for me to be open with others than it once was. I feel more easily judged and shunned in small interactions; I feel more exhausted returning messages. I feel, and sometimes really am, more distant from people. I notice more interactions where other people are wary of me, or where I feel wary of them, over issues as minor as the way I've phrased something in a casual conversation. And most people I talk to feel this way too. If anything, most people I know are experiencing more of this: more lost friendships, more lost trust, more inertia, such that they stay at home. My social world feels weaker, more fractious. I have found that the best thing I can do is schedule regular meet-ups and not bail, if I can help it. And that when I do this for groups of people, they are grateful. These individual steps won't fix the structural problem, of course, but they help me and my friends. I also find myself increasingly thinking about who in our world is particularly structurally isolated – especially those who are immunocompromised, disabled or parents of young children.

All this worries me, and not just as a matter of individual well-being but also because it seems likely to affect the way we all think about the world. It is so easy, in a state of social-atrophied alienation from others, to stop caring, or to care, but mostly in a paralysed and distant way. It is so easy in this state to throw in the towel, to see any form of difficult conversation, relationship maintenance or political mobilization as something done for people we don't even like or trust very much, as a Sisyphean struggle to manage relationships with tattered mental muscles. But it doesn't have to be this way, where communication and connection with others are an uphill battle. We could build another world, with a different set of infrastructures and a different economy, one that would allow us to be more connected day to day and more mentally and socially healthy (albeit perhaps less 'productive'). Many of the same economic changes that would allow us more time with others would also help in fighting climate change, authoritarianism and other key challenges of the twenty-first century. If we do manage to do this, we'll get the opportunity to discover what political reasoning could be, and how we might think about politics once we're less alone, once we're truly reasoning together.

7

Loving and Leaving the Liberal Ideal (or, To My Fellow Lovers of Ideas)

In July 2024, *The New York Times* sent David Brooks to interview Steve Bannon, Donald Trump's strategist and regular right-hand man, who was about to go to jail for contempt of Congress. Brooks kept suggesting that a guy like Bannon might benefit from chatting to his political enemies, as previous eras of Republicans, like Bill Buckley, seemed willing to do. Wouldn't that be a better strategy, Brooks asked?

> Brooks: I've found that most people are pretty reasonable. You can have a conversation, and you'll at least see where they're coming from.
> Bannon: I think you're dead [expletive] wrong.
> Brooks: That's where we disagree.
> Bannon: No, it's 100 per cent disagree. What are you talking about?... We're not looking to compromise. We're looking to win. Now, the biggest element that Buckley had that the book *Bowling Alone* had, and you talk about, is the atomization of our society. There's no civic bonding. There's no national cohesion. There's not even the Lions Club things

> that you used to have before. People tell me all the
> time: 'You changed my life. I ran for the board of
> supervisors, and now I'm on the board of supervisors.'
> They have friends that they never had met before, and
> they're in a common cause, and it's changed their life.
> They're on social media. Every day, they have action
> they have to do.
>
> Brooks: This was Hannah Arendt's point that loneliness
> is a seedbed for authoritarianism. But you're not
> about conversing with the other side, you're just
> fighting with the other side.
>
> Bannon: What do you mean, not conversing with?
> There's nothing to talk about.[1]

This book is, of course, not an argument that we should think like Steve Bannon. Indeed, on basically every issue of substance I am radically opposed to what he stands for. Nor do I agree with him on points of strategy in the narrow sense. (I am, for example, opposed to racist, conspiracy-driven attempted overthrows of the government). I am, however, struck by how precisely Bannon has identified what makes people commit to political ideas and take action, how well his movement has weaponized this insight. *They have friends that they never had met before, and they're in a common cause, and it's changed their life... Every day, they have action they have to do.*

True, social media is part of his scheme – but only as a way (Bannon explained) to organize those same folks to go offline and take over local branches of the Republican party and engage in 'spiritual war.' As for the debating society of mainstream politics, forget it. I often consider this quote when people ask me: if listening to ideas does little for people, why was someone I know radicalized on the internet? I explain that it is more likely that these people's social networks were so fractured, and their day-to-day life possibilities constrained enough, that reactionary ideas could be persuasive because they aligned with something (the loneliness, the stuckness, the limited view) of that person's lived experience. And that social media seems very good at leading people in this direction, but isn't very good at bringing them back towards tolerance, solidarity with others, and so on. To change minds as progressives or radicals, we probably still have to change lives. And we will probably have to do this offline.

In one sense, I don't think Bannon's insights about doing politics, about organizing people to change the world, are terribly astute. They are the same insights long developed by those who run cults, military groups or local churches. But these are insights that many in politics miss again and again because they are so caught up in the myth that we should be *talking* about politics to bring people round to our side – rather than *doing* it, and giving people ways to join.

I don't want people like Bannon to run the US, or any country. Precisely in order to prevent this, we need to understand what they do about what motivates people to engage in politics, and what doesn't help even if it seems to.

Which is to say: those of us who want a more equal, just and sustainable world need to rethink whether and how we talk about politics. We have to understand public discourse in terms of its infrastructure, rather than trusting in it as an ideal. This is especially true because of who has already realized this and is busy using this insight to engineer discourse: the far right. As Meredith Whittaker, the president of the secure messaging app Signal, put it:

> The right ... understand social media platforms as critical infrastructure capable of shaping and distorting our shared information ecosystem, and they recognize

that controlling how this ecosystem is 'distorted' is a better use of their time – in pursuit of power and influence – than trying to create a magic formula that can 'democratize' or 'balance' the influence these platforms exert. ...They [also] take to their streams and feeds to decry as censorship any move by these actors that might curtail their content and reach, while legislators and pundits echo and amplify these claims.[2]

These right-wing actors already see the importance of taking over the communications infrastructure. They play for power, only not in a democratic way. And, notably, they mask their grab at power with claims about censorship and free speech, using the myths of a marketplace of ideas and debate to counteract any attempts to curtail them.

This brings me to a couple of caveats I want to make as I finish this book. I want to acknowledge two wrong turns we could take after accepting that reasoning is, in fact, interdependent and active: condoning manipulation and romanticizing community.

First, condoning manipulation. Whenever I give a lecture, there is always one person who comes up to me afterwards and asks, 'Aren't you basically saying that all we can do is try to manipulate each other?' It's a valid concern. Part of what I am suggesting is that progressives and left-wing people should effectively engineer the social world, giving people social groups and gateway actions that can bring them into movements so they can do good in the world. In some sense, yes, this is 'manipulation', in that much of it involves creating psychological incentives and structures for people to change their minds in ways they may not be aware of.

I don't worry about this too much. Suppose someone invites you to run the local composting programme and admits, a bit later on, that they are hoping this gets you more invested in environmental action generally. To me, this is not such a huge deception in the first place, nor does it wreck anyone's life. It's generally possible to restore the social fabric and provide people with the opportunity to engage in political action – and be honest about your motivations in a reasonable span of time.

In a way, also, it is more fair, not less so, to the person you're trying to persuade if you give them not only an idea but a trellis for them to grow in that direction, an opportunity or the ability to live that idea in the world.

But more importantly, on a more fundamental level (as I've shown) our views don't come from a sacred, autonomous, uninfluenced place to begin with. Most of us are already being manipulated or at least profoundly shaped by our environment, our economy, our social world – and largely in the interests of the rich and powerful. So we are already having our lives shaped in profound ways by people who have far more influence than us. We are being made to go to work, follow laws, conform to social norms, all the time. My hope is that what I am offering is a way for people to have the chance to serve the interests of the many and the planet to create a better life for everyone. Offering new possibilities is certainly less manipulative than limiting their action-possibilities, as so many recent historical changes have done, often owing to the political calculations of devious actors.

What I do worry about is whether this analysis could strengthen those in power. Should a person who disagrees with me politically read my research, they might well use the same insights to engineer things in a direction I do not like, especially from an authoritarian angle. Let's hope they get here second.

Now, the question of romanticizing community. The word 'community' should, as a rule, never be used blithely. I love being part of many different communities, and sometimes I long to belong to more, but it's precisely because belonging is so very desirable for many and so powerful that we should approach it with some scepticism.

I grew up in a liberal Jewish community outside Washington, DC. The kids of the community were friends, and the parents of the kid-friends were friends because their kids were friends. I was very lucky. I was loved and raised by many. I was taken to synagogue despite my parents' atheism, and attended a hundred shabbat dinners and dozens of holiday events. Judaism is much more than a religion, of course, and so much more than this was given to me as a child: a group of people who would have my back implicitly; a certain shared humour; an ethos about how books should live at the centre of the home; a shared sensibility about a thousand almost indescribable things. All of this I carry with me like a sixth sense to this day.

But I am a left-wing Jew. To some in the community, if I even question (say) the actions of the Israeli state and military, I am a traitor. More broadly, my politics and indeed my personal life probably seem quite odd to some of these folks. And I moved away, to another country. Do I belong? Those in my community, who do not blink at the ads for military weapons on the radio, sometimes ask me, 'Don't you plan to ever move back?'

All of which is a way of saying what anyone who fits uneasily in a community has to say: I have seen both sides of the power of community. I am always a little afraid of being disowned, shamed, turned away. I am always afraid because I love the people and the sense of place so deeply. I think, *I hope*, that the people who love me most might still let me belong. But one never quite knows.

All of us who seek to build community should admit it: communities wield a double-edged sword, in reasoning and in so much else, as they grant us belonging. Communities teach you what you need to know; they help you up when you fall. Communities meet our most fundamental needs and tell us who we are, from the weekly gossip to our funeral. They also police you, powerfully shame you and care about who you pair up with and how you raise your children.

And shame really is powerful because it is the opposite of connection. I recall once listening to a panel on privacy and technology and hearing one of the panellists make this point beautifully. Sure, he said, privacy experts like him worried about the effects of tech companies collecting data. But actual individual people do not care about privacy, he said. They would 'give their left kidney' for connection, for a chance to share everything with the right people. They would give nearly anything, including their selfies, nudes and real-time locations, to find friends or approval. And this is why, despite the official liberal line about the importance of individual autonomy and privacy, many modern subjects happily bare all, when it suits them, and bend over backwards to belong.

But this immense power, driven by our profound relational motivation, can be used for ill or good.

I am in no way particularly singling out the community I grew up in (remember, I love them). All communities are like this, even our 'chosen' communities. As I grew up and moved away, I joined other communities, some temporary (such as universities and companies, cheery yet artificial as corporate flowerbeds), some nebulous and highly critical (such as 'lefty folks': the activists and intellectuals on the left in London). All these communities have worked their magic via strong and weak ties. All brought support and companionship, but of course also gatekept and gossiped. All brought people in line, not only when they'd done serious moral wrong but also for lesser sins such as having an 'unacceptable' view on a particular political issue or simply behaving weirdly.

So it's not that communities are purely or even largely benevolent forces when it comes to reason. Having strong social ties seems (mostly) to keep people from certain kinds of extreme beliefs, whether religious, political or conspiratorial; this could, however, be good or bad, as all conformity can swing either way.[3] I'm well aware of all the groupthink, the backbiting and infighting, and the silencing that happens because of community. Unfortunately, it's just that, especially given the effects of social atrophy, I have come to the conclusion that *not having a community is worse*.

If human beings do best in community, then we should try to arrive at a vision of political reasoning that includes this. We shouldn't only conduct our interdependent thinking in our insider groups or communities, but communities are absolutely going to be a major part of how we reason. Our need for community is not escapable, and therefore we must account for it and design for it if we want a better politics. And this point is not only empirical but also theoretical. We need communities to reason not only because of our social nature but because, without a community, a sense of collective good is extremely abstract. Without actually having lived in a particular community, it's difficult to know how we could begin to know a collective 'we', or a sense that there is a shared project of the good life. Belonging with others in this way is a key part of how we add other people to our mental model, and count their fate as part of our own. And that, in a way, is what political life is about.

What to do, then? The best we can do, I suspect, is to create a world with enough social infrastructure for all of us to belong to multiple communities at the same time, and many over the course of our lives, and for no one community to have too much power over our beliefs. Perhaps the best goal would be to create social infrastructure that allows everyone to access and belong to multiple communities at once. The best we can do is make sure we can leave, and that no one community can wreck our lives. This, ideally, can provide a check on the intuitions and values of any single community we are part of, contribute to our personal well-being and provide a minimum viable level of tolerance and respect so that we can learn, via relationships and action, about the world and thus think more wisely about politics.

Now back to the main point of this book: we need to overcome the myth of politics as a 'pure' form of discourse and instead look at things the way they really are, not the way we wish they were. And once we've done that, we need to build various kinds of infrastructure.

But, as you may have already discovered, turning away from this idealized vision of discourse as commerce or debate is far more difficult than it looks. That's because ideas continue to live in our lives and shape our behaviour even when we disavow them. If that seems odd, allow me to furnish an example from another area of life. Readers will have noticed that I am a woman. I was raised in a feminist family, one that emphasized that women shouldn't be valued for their looks. I was praised for reading books and being kind, not for looking cute. As an adult, my considered view is that women don't owe anyone pretty.[4]

All that has mattered remarkably little in practice. Although I was not allowed to own a Barbie doll, some of my earliest memories are of wanting to look like one, disliking my dark, curly hair and dark eyes, longing for more girly clothing. God knows I keep a watchful eye over the scales, and I always have. In the age of the smartphone, where I regularly create videos of my face as part of my professional work, I find I wear far more make-up than my mother ever did.

And, frankly, it would be weirder if I didn't. I self-police in the area of beauty even as I decry it because it benefits me in the areas of my life that matter most: work, love and the esteem of others. Even if I could magically set aside the question of love and sex when it comes to beauty (as if!), the psychology studies I read suggest I'm more likely to be taken seriously at work and have more friends if I succeed at attaining a certain level of conventional attractiveness.[5] So while I *intellectually* reject the idea that women should be beautiful, I begrudgingly find myself pursuing beauty sometimes anyway, even though doing so is consuming, anxiety-producing and annoying, even though it is oppressive, even though it is a trap. Often people who experience dissonance change their ideas to match their actions; I've refused to ideologically rationalize to myself that my beauty-pursuing actions are morally good, but this does mean I have to live with a certain amount of cognitive dissonance. As is often the case, I live strung between the contradictions.

And – to return to my main point, which is about the myths that we can't shake – that is how ideology works. It is not just a set of ideas to be examined and accepted intellectually; it structures our lives through many mechanisms whether we want it to or not, and tells us what possibilities we can inhabit in the social world. We cannot opt out of ideology through thought alone, because ideology structures our lives through many mechanisms other than thoughts. That is why it is entirely possible to believe one thing intellectually, even emphatically, while at the same time living one's life in contradiction to those ideas. (And yes, doing so causes discomforting cognitive dissonance.) One can have accepted all the right ideas but still not be able to live by them, and especially not without consequences. That's part of the pain of political consciousness, for all of us, especially those of us who define ourselves by our politics.

The same problem with shaking off myths is also true when it comes to our cultural obsession with discourse, with our reflexive tendency to turn to 'debate' or a 'marketplace of ideas'. It is likely that, even if you come away agreeing with much of this book, you may find it difficult to change the way you relate to arguments and debate and political conversations in real life; in fact, you will probably find yourself returning again and again to our culture's sentimental hopes about the power of exposing each other to ideas.

It's perhaps worth taking a step back and asking once again why these ideals and myths of discourse, whether warlike debate or the marketplace of ideas, are quite so entrenched. It's hard to overestimate how attached to them we are, as can be seen in all the fearful clamour about echo chambers, polarization and cancel culture in recent years. Of course, part of this is simply that this tendency is baked into our daily actions required of us (e.g. through our schooling) and our relationships with others (and the way they expect us to engage with them). But I also suspect that what all this upset represents is not just a passionate attachment to politics as discourse or a reasonable fear about the rise of authoritarianism but also a broader doubling down, a fervent attempt to make the world 'reasonable again'. Because, if we're honest, for many in the global north, the last few decades have been marked by the sense that the political order no longer makes sense. There are right-wing insurgencies. There are threats of boxing matches between billionaires. Conspiracy theories are mainstream. Reality TV stars become president and dismantle democracy.

At the same time, we're facing catastrophic climate change, deadly pandemics, widening inequality and so many other grave threats. This is all scary.

To insist on discourse as the framework for politics is a symptom of our frustration with how irrational the world is. It is a plea for the world to be intelligible. Who can blame so many of us for wanting that? If only it worked.

If you, like me, are a lover of ideas, it might be more than a little devastating to accept that words and ideals do not have power on their own but, rather, take power as they become rooted in our material, social world. All I can say is that, if it is – I sympathize. And also, we can still love ideas. We just need to love them by living them in the world. Anything less than that is ineffective.

Knowing this is bitter, but it is also helpful and demystifying.

In fact, the joy of giving up these myths is that although I am upset by the swing towards nationalist and reactionary politics, I am no longer surprised that the public sphere is, in an increasingly obvious way, fracturing. There is nothing that surprising about people spreading fake news, getting sucked into conspiracy theories, arguing past each other and much more. The economic system in which we live has systematically gobbled up the delicate ecosystem of shared space, relationships and possibilities for action that allows people to think deeply and differently about politics. To put it another way, we've destroyed the social and economic grounds on which it might be possible to have a functioning democracy. The solution to this is collective care for each other, the mending of the social fabric and, in many cases, public or collective ownership of the infrastructure of our shared lives, especially of services and goods that support crucial forms of relationships. Without this, arguably, one does not really have a society at all: after all, what is still public about the public sphere if everything we're using is privately owned?

This action-and-relationships, infrastructure-led approach unquestionably has some downsides. Strategically, like almost everything else worth doing, it's difficult to put into practice. It's endless hard work to organize human beings. And it is difficult to get governments to provide infrastructure, and some forms of infrastructure are functionally impossible to create without governments. Nevertheless, organizing people is probably what politics is, far more than talking about it. And infrastructure of all kinds is a clear, concrete and achievable demand that moves the responsibility for democratic life away from individual choices, redirecting our focus away from the moralizing that often makes it harder, not easier, to understand what is happening in politics.[*] We can also consider non-governmental ways of creating collectively owned infrastructure.

It is tempting to want to fix how we *speak*, since speaking is the place where we culturally place our hopes, and often where we encounter the most frustration. But this will not help us mend the broader societal problems we are facing. Making the 'warfare' within debate more fair or regulating the 'marketplace' of ideas so it can function better may sound appealing, easier than truly rebuilding the infrastructure of the public sphere. But these solutions overlook any serious considerations of the infrastructural problems that are

---

[*] I realize there is an irony to the way I am using studies about individual psychology to make this point about the need for structural change, but the studies I use in my research do tend to suggest that structures shape our thinking in profound ways, even if they demonstrate this through the individual.

behind the destabilization of discourse.* They start with the assumption that politics is talking and that the goal is to talk or reason in the abstract more effectively. This does not serve us well, given that it is relationships and actions that most strongly shape our political worldview. Many serious political problems simply cannot be solved by a speech-first approach. Current obsessions over the question of 'free speech' ignore the real challenges that prevent people thinking well about politics. Thinking freely isn't just about having access to ideas: we need to be able to live our ideas in the world. It's therefore time to stop trying to 'teach critical thinking' by itself and to start literally building a world where people's lives and relationships consistently enable them to think.

Despite the playful title I have given it, none of this book is an argument for simply restricting speech. Instead, it's a plea to support political discourse responsibly with adequate infrastructure and account for the social costs that discourse often entails. We've destroyed the social and economic grounds on which it might be possible to have a functioning public sphere. Debate and a 'marketplace of ideas' contribute to some of the fracturing of our social world, but this doesn't mean we should ban them. What we need to do is rebuild the social fabric so it can withstand the wear and tear that all this talking, and the rest of political life, require.

---

*I have gone back and forth in writing this book about whether to specifically list and name the types of people who do this; there is certainly a long list of mainly older, mainly white, mainly male, often psychology professors who make this sort of claim repeatedly in their books for the public. But, in truth, I did not write this book to make enemies or spark 'debate', not least because my point is that, when it comes to strongly held views related to politics, debate is very ineffective. I therefore instead trust the reader to locate people who make this claim as necessary.

We also need to understand the work involved in thinking about politics and take it more seriously. For, in contrast to the mythic models of political thought described earlier in this book, in reality, thinking about politics is hard work. It requires a certain kind of painful self-consciousness, disorientation and reorientation that other forms of reasoning may not. It is a form of surgery on the self. It is, in fact, a kind of labour, where we make not only new ideas, but a new version of ourselves.

I am aware how much work and discomfort thinking really involves because I work in the tech industry. It is common knowledge there that people find even the most basic cognitive tasks gruelling when they have to do too many in a row. Designers are constantly seeking to reduce the user's 'cognitive load' as they interact with a product, so that everything takes fewer steps, fewer moments of deliberation. That is why we have moved from flashy 1990s-style websites to the relative minimalism of web interfaces today. It is also, I suspect, the driving force behind the algorithm and AI boom – most products that use either are, in effect, curating or generating content, so that we no longer have to hop between news sites, create our own playlists, draft a cover letter or decide what to have for dinner.

When I first started working in tech, I was annoyed by this assumption that people find thinking stressful and difficult. Surely thinking could be fun? Indeed it can, but after just a few weeks of looking at analytics data, I saw how quickly people turn their minds away from their stated task to other matters. Especially if they're already overloaded by, well, everything else in life. If you've ever opened an email and immediately concluded it was TLDR ('too long, didn't read!'), if you've ever found yourself too tired to think straight, then you know about the limits to your own cognitive load.[6] Studies also suggest that we tire when asked to make multiple decisions, a phenomenon known as 'decision fatigue'. We all struggle to process more information than we can absorb at any given time. Now consider the amount of information and opinions on your average newsfeed, and the problem when it comes to politics is obvious: there's just so much of it. If deciding what to have for dinner after a long day at work is hard, then deciding what to think about political issues is much harder. We struggle because, as it's often put, there are too many tabs open in the brain.[7]

And, of course, it's not just the load of thinking that can make it painful but precisely the kinds of contradictions and questions about ourselves that tend to come up when we think about politics. For our brains particularly struggle with ambiguity, contradiction and uncertainty. As I've described in previous chapters, studies that look at how the human mind responds to ambivalence find that people often prefer to know negative outcomes will happen for sure than live in uncertainty. Ambiguity is unbearable. Some studies suggest those who experience more uncertainty tend to turn to conspiracy theories, and this may be one of the reasons.[8] No wonder so many of us turn to polemical social media posts and polarized news sources. Indeed, our news industry has already cottoned on to the problems we have with ambiguity (especially in an 'increasingly uncertain world', as the phrase goes) and begun catering to it by providing over-simplified stories that offer false certainty, distraction and entertainment. And then, of course, there's the pain of conflict with others, questions about one's own identity and the matter of cognitive dissonance.

What all of this has led to is a peak level of political disengagement for many. The Hansard Society, a British think tank founded nearly 80 years ago to promote democracy, measures political engagement via 13 core political activities, which include things such as voting, attending political meetings, contacting the media and boycotting products. In 2019, 53 per cent of the public reported not having taken part in any form of political activity in the last year. The number of people saying they would be prepared to do 'none' of the core political activities on the survey was up ten points in a year. During COVID the survey was discontinued, and it has not been resumed. But other measures of civic engagement have yet to show significant improvement.[9] And in the US, rather similarly, 65% of Americans say they 'always or often feel exhausted when thinking about politics.' As an American, I feel about the same.

Interestingly, this disengagement often comes with anger. In the same study of Americans, nearly as many felt always or often angry. The same study found the majority of people found conversations about politics with people they disagreed with stressful and difficult, rather than interesting or informative.[10]

Those on both the right and left accuse one another of being fragile, easily upset and triggered by a variety of ideas. They are right. As I have shown repeatedly in this book with a variety of studies and disciplines, people find the process of reasoning, from revising one's beliefs to disagreeing with others, a real struggle – especially when it comes to facing contradictions in their worldview.

This is an important and under-addressed phenomenon. Serious think tanks and government bodies are currently grappling with how to make sure that reporting is 'fair', that information is fact-checked and that people are taught media literacy. This is all important but, so far, there has been relatively little work on the other end of the issue – the fact that even with the best information in the world, people are often reluctant to think about politics, because it's hard and painful work. And if you personally find it enjoyable, that means you are an outlier, the wrong sort of person, in fact, to estimate or easily understand what it means for most people to do the work of thinking about these issues.

Many common-sense theories about politics only work if we believe that thinking is easy, but it's not. And this matters. That does not mean we should not value people thinking through political ideas, it means that we cannot expect that it will be easy for people to stick with the process of thinking through a conflict-ridden topic. It means if we want to build a world where people can rethink things, we need to build structures that support that.

We should try to create media that helps people with the difficulty of reasoning, so that they are able to think through the grey areas rather than rushing to find a way out of the discomfort. Our highly conflict-driven formats for discussion (from radio shows to Twitter algorithms) disengage those who don't like conflict and trap those who can just about stand it in cycles of thinking about it more or less as war. Yet it is possible to imagine other types of content that appeal to the human mind while allowing for a greater degree of imagination and ambiguity.

It is possible to imagine other types of media that also appeal to the human mind but allow for at least some greater degree of imagination and ambiguity. Storytelling is a classic one, as are visual and theoretical maps. We should be helping people to live with ambiguity, not helping them to repress and erase it. More than teaching people to 'check their sources' or 'listen to both sides', it might be powerful to teach people to recognize the discomfort they feel when questioning their own beliefs, and to support them learning to tolerate this discomfort as in the 'motivational interviewing' conversations described in earlier chapters.

But perhaps, most of all, if we wish to have a functioning democracy, we need to reserve more time and space for this thinking, doing, relationship-building process that is politics. At present, our economic system functions around efficiency and profit, which means that our attention is monetized and we work long hours. This takes a huge toll on the foundations of reasoning, whether that's our time, attention, relationships or energy. Capitalism is rife with these hidden costs, uncalculated but real: just as working long hours negatively impacts our relationships and health, so it too erodes our democracy. Economic austerity limits our actions and leads to an austerity of thought, in the worst way.

We won't be able to change the way we meet, build relationships and reason about politics without a massive restructuring of our society. Without this, any other interventions (educational programmes, 'critical thinking' training, media reforms) are unlikely to be effective. Recall, from a previous chapter, that inequality accounted for half of the fall in social trust, that housing policies are leading to increasing segregation of communities, that people spend more and more time alone and have fewer friends, in part because it is expensive and time-consuming to go to places where they would make new ones. These are material problems, about physical space and money and infrastructure, and they require material solutions: the reduction of inequality, the restructuring of housing, the reclaiming and creating of public space.

In a way, I am suggesting that change must happen in the reverse order of what many liberals and progressives might imagine: that economic changes come first, and democratic life follows from that. We can't talk our way around to equality so much as we can build equality and then do democracy better. Or, to be entirely blunt, we might put it this way: this century, it's capitalism (especially unbridled capitalism) vs. democracy. If we continue to let capitalism privatize our collective life, if we continue to let it separate us from each other and limit the possibilities of our individual lives, keeping us away from action and experimentation, then we cannot expect that our governments will ever serve the interests of anyone but the very wealthy and powerful. For all the talk by fans of free markets about how democracy and capitalism go together, when inequality becomes entrenched, as it has done over the last few decades, it destroys the specific kinds of life experiences that allow people to meaningfully evaluate political ideas together.

Books are mostly politically important insofar as they provide affordances for the reader. If you, like me, want a more just and sustainable form of life on planet Earth, I hope this book has provided some affordances for you – that is, given you a sense of new and hopeful action-possibilities.

It is always easy, after having read something, to simply mull it over or text a friend a particularly striking passage. I hope you'll do more: put down this book and do something in your community, or with a social movement. As I have demonstrated, much of the most important work is the steady, everyday stuff of building up the social world so people can think together. It's hard work, yes, and less glamorous than some other gestures, but it desperately needs doing. Some activists are willing to die to prevent authoritarian governments or catastrophic climate change. But in truth, for most of us, this is the wrong way of thinking about what is required. The right one is: what are you willing to live for? Might you be willing to build things slowly, day by day?

I also hope that in reading this it has become possible to have a different conception of what a good thinker is. Those who can think well about politics might not look like academics or debate champions. (There are enough of those anyway, populating the 'public sphere'.) Instead good political thinkers might be the kind of people who are good at building communities and social relationships, who can steadily take action in various ways to try out new ideas. Perhaps we can all strive to be this type of person, to build these habits and skills. Perhaps we can also lift up the people we know who already do this, so that they can have more influence in this world.

I have suggested that we need to abandon some myths that have come with liberalism. But I am not suggesting we need to abandon every liberal idea or ideal. In political theory, there is a German term, *Aufhebung*, that was used most famously by the early nineteenth-century German philosopher Georg Wilhelm Friedrich Hegel, a famous theorist of modern societies and governments. *Aufhebung* is a curious word that means both 'abolition' and 'transcendence'.[*] Hegel suggested that, as major historical political shifts occur, one can observe this contradictory (or rather, dialectical) phenomenon. Older systems are overcome, but some core part of them is also meaningfully preserved, even made more true than before. When states moved from monarchies to liberal democracies, monarchies were overcome, but something, perhaps, of their

---

[*] It is also the verb used to describe the making of jam, where one, I suppose, abolishes the fruit to make something else, something that is at the same time even more the essence of that fruit. See a discussion of this (the meaning of *Aufhebung*, but especially its relationship to jam) in Hugh Silverman, ed. (1997), *Philosophy and Non-Philosophy since Merleau-Ponty*. Northwestern University Press, 37.

sense of nationhood and collective identity lived on, and lived on in a more just way within the new systems. The hope is that we can also do this with liberalism: that we can, by understanding the reality of reason and rebuilding it, transcend what doesn't work about our current system (especially its emphasis on the private ownership of capital) while retaining, or even more wisely and truly expressing, its most meaningful elements: a belief in collective self-governance and freedom.

We can love some liberal ideals (say, the conviction that good ideas are important, or that we can improve the world over time) and leave the rest (the individualism, the neglect of material concerns). We need to keep unlearning the unhelpful ideals over and over again because they have left such a deep legacy in our culture (and on many of us psychologically too), so that we do not legitimize the power structures that often use liberal myths about what it means to think about politics as a cover for processes of exploitation and oppression.

In an earlier chapter I described how those who join activist groups are profoundly changed as a result. One of the more striking changes is that those who are engaged in activism are happier, and they see their lives as more meaningful than do those people who otherwise hold similar views but do not engage in activism.[11] This is remarkable given how happiness data looks on the whole when it comes to politics: on average, left-wing people are less happy than right-wing people in nearly every country on earth where this is measured, and this seems true even when one holds for other variables that affect happiness, such as income level, marriage, religiosity and so on.[12] One might even argue that this makes sense, because after all, left-wing people are likely to be more unhappy with the status quo. If one looks at all the data on left-wing people, one finds lots of possible reasons why they might be more unhappy:

they see more rifts in their friendships; they are more likely to self-criticize and worry; they follow the news more closely, which lately makes everyone I know tremendously unhappy.[13] And yet, while left-wing people are more unhappy than right-wing people, activists are happier than non-activists; activists seem to be able to beat these depressing stats.

Sometimes, when I present this finding during talks, people in the audience protest. 'Happier!?' they ask. 'What about activist burnout? What about the internal splits always happening in left-wing groups? What about the difficulty of seeing everything through the lens of oppression?'

But yes, statistically activists are happier than non-activists who share their beliefs. Sure, there's measurable burnout in a not insignificant minority of this group, but this still seems to be true.[14] There's even some evidence that this is causal: that it's the activism itself that is making them happier.[15]

And this does not surprise me, because activism involves so many of the things that otherwise seem to give people meaning and joy in life: personal agency, the ability to take action on things they care about, community, a sense of meaning. This matters a lot. There is also a lot of psychological evidence that people who feel they have some agency or autonomy in their lives are a lot better off.[16] So it's likely that it's a lack of agency that matters most, that makes so many left-wing people sad, and not just their views in themselves. Thinking the world is on fire makes you a lot less psychologically well, but thinking that the world is on fire and that you can do something about it with other people makes things bearable, even inspiring and meaningful again. It allows you to be less interested in or caught up in armchair debates, to transcend some theoretical differences by taking action instead. And it returns you to a community, however difficult that community may sometimes be.

This brings us to a larger point: one of the most cherished parts of liberalism, I suspect, is a resistance to the idea that being political can make one happy, or more specifically, it is a desire for a boundary on the political, between the political and the rest of our life. The term 'the public sphere' implies, of course, that there is a private sphere, and liberal political theorists have emphasized this, pointed joyfully to the idea that in liberal societies the government and church are limited; you can (in theory) go home, close your door and enter a private world, one untouched by the state or the stress of political life.

Various recent commentators, indeed even esteemed political scientists, have suggested that perhaps part of the reason we are so polarized is that everything has 'become political', and that if we could make things less so, things could go back to the way they supposedly once were – more civil and rational, less contentious.[17] But this is a profound misrecognition of the reality we face, for two reasons. First, often these thinkers are really describing the detrimental effects of a certain kind of culturally idealized discourse: 'debate' and 'the marketplace of ideas'. They are describing not the effects of things 'being political' but rather the effects of *just* talking about politics, the outcome when people who lack much in the way of social relationships and diverse experiences collide. What polarizes us is not politics itself, nor even political discussions, but the way we've ended up doing these in a socially-atrophied, infrastructurally-poor world.

And second, it is an alluring idea, that we can exit the political, but it's a fantasy. Politics is not escapable, not even through denial. (And it never really was, except as an illusion for smaller, privileged groups.) Climate change and migration and war are at our doorstep and will dominate the next few decades. The economic system that has made nearly everyone poorer and more precarious is an unavoidable political problem. Being less political isn't really possible, and it turns out that, for those of us who are progressive or left-wing, trying to be less political will only make us unhappier anyway.

The wise or mature position, then, is not to be less political but to be *more* political. Our day-to-day lives could involve a deep care for and organizing around political issues, in particular the building and rebuilding of relationships and places of belonging, the rebuilding of infrastructure and the creation of action-possibilities for people to try out new and varied ways of living. This is the business of politics, in truth, and all the discourse in the world (all the talking about politics) sits largely downstream of that. And the good news is that this building of relationships, networks and action-possibilities is both effective and something that is likely to make us happier.

Because of this, I still feel hopeful about human beings and even sometimes about politics. Hopeful, even after abandoning the myth that simply exposing people to the right ideas will set politics on the right course. Hopeful, even after abandoning the also-common, implicit myth that progress is inevitable or likely to come from anything other than hard work. For if I had to gesture broadly and summarize what I have learned as I look at this giant body of mixed and complicated sociological and psychological evidence, it is that humans want to make meaning out of their lives, they are motivated to think and believe in ways that allow them to think of themselves as good people, they want to believe they could have agency and use it for good in the world around them.

Of course, that analysis includes everyone – those I disagree with, those on the right, those trending towards fascism, the actual fascists, those defending the indefensible. Nevertheless, this meaning-based understanding of human beings gives us reason to believe that we could politically reconfigure our world for the better. We do not have to live under a profit-maximizing system. We do not have to compete ferociously with everyone around us. We do not even have to spend all our time arguing with each other. We could choose another way – and be happier for it.

There are (at least) two ways to love ideas: to talk about them and to live them in the world. My fellow lovers of ideas: the beauty of re-understanding politics in the way I suggest here is that it is still possible to believe in ideas. Ideas do matter. But they matter through our actions and relationships. And that is a hopeful thing. Let us try to go out and live out our ideas, in relationship with other people. And let's try to build a world where it's easier for everyone to do this, because that's what it means to truly think about politics.

If we do it well, thinking about, talking about and ultimately doing politics might become less painful, exhausting and scary. It could even become, on a particularly good day, meaningful, beautiful and fun.

FURTHER READING

HIGHLY 'READABLE' HISTORICAL AND CONCEPTUAL WORKS

Alvin Chang (2023), 'The Invisible Epidemic: Understanding Loneliness in America', *The Pudding*, available at: pudding.cool/2023/09/invisible-epidemic/ (accessed 27 October 2024).

Joel Cooper (2007), *Cognitive Dissonance: 50 Years of a Classic Theory*. Sage.

David Graeber (2013), *The Democracy Project: A History, a Crisis, a Movement*, Spiegel & Grau.

Eric Klinenberg (2018), *Palaces for the People: How Social Infrastructure Can Help Fight Inequality, Polarization, and the Decline of Civic Life*, Crown.

Sheila Liming (2023), *Hanging Out: The Radical Power of Killing Time*, Melville House.

Domenico Losurdo (2014), *Liberalism: A Counter-history*, Verso Books.

David McRaney (2022), *How Minds Change: The Surprising Science of Belief, Opinion, and Persuasion*, Penguin.

Ray Oldenburg (1999), *The Great Good Place: Cafes, Coffee Shops, Bookstores, Bars, Hair Salons, and other Hangouts at the Heart of a Community*, Da Capo Press.

Jonah Peretti (2007), 'Notes on Contagious Media', *Structures of Participation in Digital Culture*, New York: Social Science Research Council.

Robert Putnam and Shaylyn Romney Garrett (2020), *The Upswing: How America Came Together a Century Ago and How We Can Do It Again*, Simon & Schuster.

Deborah Tannen (1999), *The Argument Culture: Stopping America's War of Words*, Ballantine Books.

Derek Thompson (2016), 'How America Lost Its Mojo', *The Atlantic*, 3 May, available at: www.theatlantic.com/business/archive/2016/05/how-america-lost-its-mojo/484655/ (accessed 1 November 2024).

Zeynep Tufekci (2017), *Twitter and Tear Gas: The Power and Fragility of Networked Protest*, Yale University Press.

Meredith Whittaker (2022), 'Social Media Authoritarianism and the World As It Is', *LPE Project*, available at: lpeproject.org/blog/social-media-authoritarianism-and-the-world-as-it-is/ (accessed 1 November 2024).

LESS 'READABLE' HISTORICAL AND CONCEPTUAL WORKS

Gordon Allport, K. Clark and T. Pettigrew ([1954] 1979), *The Nature of Prejudice*, Basic Books.

Jürgen Habermas (1991), *The Structural Transformation of the Public Sphere: An Inquiry into a Category of Bourgeois Society*, MIT Press.

Jürgen Habermas (1984), *The Theory of Communicative Action*, vol. 2, Beacon Press.

Stanley Ingber (1984), 'The Marketplace of Ideas: A Legitimizing Myth', *Duke Law Journal*, 1984(1): 1–91.

Robert Putnam (1995), 'Bowling Alone: America's Declining Social Capital', *Journal of Democracy* 6 (1), repr. in L. Crothers and C. Lockhart, eds. (2000), *Culture and Politics: A Reader*, 223–34.

SOCIAL-SCIENTIFIC PAPERS

Joyce Balls-Berry, L. C. Dacy and J. Balls (2016), '"Heard It through the Grapevine": The Black Barbershop as a Source of Health Information', *Western Journal of Nursing Research*, 38(10): 1409–17, available at: www.ncbi.nlm.nih.gov/pmc/articles/PMC4749262/ (accessed 1 November 2024).

David Broockman and Joshua Kalla (2016), 'Durably Reducing Transphobia: A Field Experiment on Door-to-Door Canvassing', *Science* 352(6282): 223.

Daniel A. Cox and Sam Pressler (2024), 'Disconnected: The Growing Class Divide in American Civic Life. Findings from 2024 American Social Capital Survey', American Survey

Center, 22 August, available at: www.americansurveycenter.org/research/disconnected-places-and-spaces/ (accessed 21 December 2024).

Hansard Society, 'Audit of Political Engagement 16: The 2019 Report', www.hansardsociety.org.uk/projects/audit-of-political-engagement (accessed 22 October 2024).

Miles Hewstone (2009), 'Living Apart, Living Together? The Role of Intergroup Contact in Social Integration', *Proceedings of the British Academy*. 162(2008): 243–300.

Christian Jarrett (2009), 'Political Activism Is Good for You', *British Psychological Society Research Digest*, 30 September, available at: www.bps.org.uk/research-digest/political-activism-good-you (accessed 25 October 2024).

Mohsen Joshanloo (2024), 'Loneliness Leads to Changes in Personality over Time', *PsyPost*, 27 March, available at: www.psypost.org/loneliness-leads-to-changes-in-personality-over-time/ (accessed 27 October 2024).

John T. Jost et al. (2003), 'Social Inequality and the Reduction of Ideological Dissonance on Behalf of the System: Evidence of Enhanced System Justification among the Disadvantaged', *European Journal of Social Psychology* 33(1): 1.

Jonas T. Kaplan, Sarah I. Gimbel and Sam Harris (2016), 'Neural Correlates of Maintaining One's Political Beliefs in the Face of Counterevidence', *Scientific Reports* 6: 39589.

Kristin Laurin (2018), 'Inaugurating Rationalization: Three Field Studies Find Increased Rationalization when Anticipated Realities Become Current', *Psychological Science*, 29(4): 483–95.

Douglas A. Marshall (2002), 'Behavior, Belonging, and Belief: A Theory of Ritual Practice', *Sociological Theory* 20(3): 360–80.

J. Mewes, M. Fairbrother, G. N. Giordano, C. Wu and R. Wilkes (2021), 'Experiences Matter: A Longitudinal Study of Individual-level Sources of Declining Social Trust in the United States', *Social Science Research*, 95: 102537.

J. De Moor and S. Verhaegen (2020), 'Gateway or Getaway? Testing the Link between Lifestyle Politics and Other Modes of Political Participation', *European Political Science Review*, 12(1): 91–111.

Esteban Ortiz-Ospina (2019), 'Is There a Loneliness Epidemic?', Our World in Data, available at: ourworldindata.org/loneliness-epidemic.

ACKNOWLEDGEMENTS

This book is dedicated to my parents Debbie Stein and Mike Lubrano, who have always loved and supported me unconditionally, enthusiastically and with deep curiosity. They also graciously forgave me for moving an ocean away (and using their and my resources to write social theory for the public.)

I think with my friends, as we all should. I am extremely grateful to too many friends to name, but here are some who especially helped with this book: Ben, Charlotte, Dan, Jack, Jackie, Joey, Laurel, Melissa, Matt, Nas, Shulamith, Thalie, and my siblings Ben and Khadijah. Max Haiven has been an ideal professional and intellectual collaborator and a most excellent friend. Chapter Five in particular could not have hit its mark without his co-thinking.

My wonderful partners supported me unflaggingly in this process, especially Dan, who was there from the very start, and who has sacrificed our time together without hesitation, talking me through every up and down and hurdle. Thank you E, Kirsten and other partners for putting up with the version of me that is always on a writing deadline.

Thank you to my agent, Charlotte Merritt, who reached out to me across the internet many years ago, back when I had not truly thought of writing a book, who believed in it all when I couldn't, and who gracefully and kindly managed some very un-British tears from me on a regular basis. Thank you to my editors: Tomasz Hoskins, who saved this book from oblivion and understood why critical theory is needed more than ever, and Octavia Stocker, who edited with great enthusiasm, which matters enormously for a first book.

Many friends kindly listened to me read chapters aloud on Zoom. Thank you to Brianna, Dalumuzi, Danny, Daniel, Guillermo, Ilana, Juli, Kat, Laura, and Marina. And thank you to Elizabeth, Anthea, and others who generously read the book around the same time.

David McRaney helped me connect with social scientists and psychology researchers to check and deepen my understanding of research in the field. I am very grateful to him and to the researchers, including John T. Jost, Josh Kalla, Andy Lutrell, Brendan Nyhan, Richard Petty, Debbie Prentice, Laurie Santos and Tom Stafford.

This book's highly interdisciplinary approach is the slow-ripening fruit of the Harvard Social Studies Department, and I am so grateful for the life and support of Anya Bernstein, who is deeply missed. Thank you also to Chris Brooke, Bo-Mi Choi, and Bonnie Talbert. This book came after, and in some ways directly from, a DPhil at the University of Oxford. I am very grateful for the support of my supervisor, Lois McNay. I am also very grateful to David Leopold, Sophie Smith, and Amia Srinivasan for the skills and training I needed to write it. The book was written at times on writing retreats with our unnamed collective of radical writers, and I am especially grateful for their support; thank you Adele, Aviah, Brett, Emily, Leah, Lola, Marcus, Sita, Sophie and Zara.

In everything I write about politics I am thinking of Otto Stein, a genocide survivor, refugee and scholar. I also hope Mario Lubrano would be proud that I follow in the tradition of radical writing. I hope we can love ideas well enough to make the kind of world they worked towards.

NOTES

INTRODUCTION: THE REQUIREMENT

1. Juan López de Palacios Rubios (1513), *National Humanities Center Resource Toolbox: American Beginnings: The European Prescence in North America, 1492–1690*, available at: nationalhumanitiescenter.org/pds/amerbegin/contact/text7/requirement.pdf (accessed 1 October 2024).
2. Ibid.; see historical note about the lack of translation.
3. William V. Crockett and James G. Sigountos, eds. (1993), *Through No Fault of Their Own? The Fate of Those Who Have Never Heard*, Baker Book House.
4. Stacey Clifford Simplican (2009), 'Disabling Democracy: How Disability Reconfigures Deliberative Democratic Norms', APSA Toronto Meeting Paper (published online 13 August), available at: papers.ssrn.com/sol3/papers.cfm?abstract_id=1451092 (accessed 1 October 2024). Jürgen Habermas (2006), *Between Naturalism and Religion: Philosophical Essays*, Polity Press.
5. *Times Higher Education* (2009), 'Most Cited Authors of Books in the Humanities, 2007', 26 March, available at: www.timeshighereducation.com/news/most-cited-authors-of-books-in-the-humanities-2007/405956.article?storyCode=405956&sectioncode=26 (accessed 9 October 2024).
6. Jürgen Habermas (1991), *The Structural Transformation of the Public Sphere: An Inquiry into a Category of Bourgeois Society*, MIT Press, 52; Hannah Arendt (1958), *The Human Condition*, University of Chicago Press, 52.
7. Jürgen Habermas (1984), *The Theory of Communicative Action*, vol. 2, Beacon Press, 355.

CHAPTER ONE: DON'T ENTER THE 'MARKET' FOR IDEAS

1. Ellen McCarthy (2005), 'Contractors Take Message to Their People', *Washington Post*, 28 November, available at: www.washingtonpost.com/archive/business/2005/11/28/contractors-take-message-to-their-people/4956616e-4f92-456c-adee-278b2cc3f90c/ (accessed 9 October 2024).
2. David Schultz (2009), *Marketplace of Ideas*, The Free Speech Center, available at: firstamendment.mtsu.edu/article/marketplace-of-ideas/ (accessed 8 October 2024).
3. United States v. Rumely (1953), US Supreme Court, 345 U.S. 41. *Justia*, available at: supreme.justia.com/cases/federal/us/345/41/ (accessed 9 October 2024).
4. Brandenburg v. Ohio (1969) US Supreme Court, 395 U.S. 444. *Justia*. available at: supreme.justia.com/cases/federal/us/395/444/ (accessed 9 October 2024); Citizens United v. FEC (2010), US Supreme Court, 558 U.S. 310. Justia, available at: supreme.justia.com/cases/federal/us/558/310/ (accessed Feb 26 2024.
5. See my discussion in Chapter 6 below.
6. See, for example: John Stuart Mill ([1859] 1998), *On Liberty and Other Essays*, Oxford University Press; and Thomas Jefferson (1801), 'First Inaugural Address', The Avalon Project,

Yale Law School, available at: avalon.law.yale.edu/19th_century/jefinau1.asp (accessed 11 October 2024).

7 David Schultz (2009), *Marketplace of Ideas*. The Free Speech Center, available at: firstamendment.mtsu.edu/article/marketplace-of-ideas/ (accessed 8 October 2024).

8 Olúfẹ́mi O. Táíwò (2022), *Elite Capture: How the Powerful Took Over Identity Politics (and Everything Else)*. Haymarket Books, 24.

9 Stanley Ingber (1984), 'The Marketplace of Ideas: A Legitimizing Myth', *Duke Law Journal*, 1984(1): 1–91.

10 Ibid., 85.

11 Jamillah Bowman Williams and Elizabeth Tippett (2022), 'Five Years On, Here's What #MeToo Has Changed.' *Politico*, 14 October 2022, available at: www.politico.com/newsletters/women-rule/2022/10/14/five-years-on-heres-what-metoo-has-changed-00061853 (accessed 8 October 2024).

12 Pew Research Center (2018), *14% of Americans Have Changed Their Mind about an Issue Because of Something They Saw on Social Media*, 15 August, available at: www.pewresearch.org/short-reads/2018/08/15/14-of-americans-have-changed-their-mind-about-an-issue-because-of-something-they-saw-on-social-media/ (accessed 11 October 2024).

13 For an extensive description of this phenomenon (confirmation bias) and the next (rationalization) for the non-psychologist, I suggest Joel Cooper (2007), *Cognitive Dissonance: 50 Years of a Classic Theory*. Sage.

14 For evidence of this, see Silvia Knobloch-Westerwick and Jingbo Meng (2009), 'Looking the Other Way: Selective Exposure to Attitude-Consistent and Counterattitudinal Political Information', *Communication Research*, 36(3): 426–48.

15 Aaron Blake (2024), 'GOP Voters Have Flip-Flopped Fast on Questions about Trump and Crime', *Washington Post*, 5 June, available at: www.washingtonpost.com/politics/2024/06/05/gop-voters-have-flip-flopped-fast-questions-about-trump-crime/ (accessed 12 October 2024).

16 YouGov (2024), 'Opinion Change Post-Trump Hush-Money Guilty Verdict', Today.yougov.com, 4 June, available at: today.yougov.com/politics/articles/49617-opinion-change-post-trump-hush-money-guilty-verdict (accessed 12 October 2024).

17 Ozan Varol (2019), 'Facts Don't Change People's Minds. Here's What Does', Next Big Idea Club, available at: nextbigideaclub.com/magazine/facts-dont-change-peoples-minds-heres/16242/amp/ (accessed 12 October 2024).

18 I would spend more time on each of these points here, but to do so would be almost redundant, given the field I work in. There is a vast and growing sea of literature in popular psychology that makes these points in greater detail than I ever could in this book, and some of it has even held up nicely in the face of the recent replication crises in these fields. I particularly recommend the now old and 'classic' book *Thinking, Fast and Slow*, by Daniel Kahneman, as well my friend David McRaney's book *How Minds Change*, which is more modern and nuances older points, as well as showing how some of these errors in reasoning can be overcome in a political context. In any case, although I do not linger on these points about human psychology here, I will return to them and examples of them over and over throughout the book. Daniel Kahneman (2011), *Thinking, Fast and Slow*, Farrar, Straus and Giroux. David McRaney (2022), *How Minds Change: The Surprising Science of Belief, Opinion, and Persuasion*, Penguin, 44.

19 Dan Kahan, H. Jenkins-Smith and D. Braman (2011), 'Cultural Cognition of Scientific Consensus', *Journal of Risk Research*, 14(2): 147–74. There are, in fact, a number of other paradoxes about how we feel about climate change versus how we behave; for example, oddly (or arguably oddly) those who know more about how the environment works are less anxious about climate change, and those who are angry are no more likely to engage in individual mitigation efforts. We are, in other words, perfectly capable of feeling one way in theory and having our actions be entirely different in practice. See also: Thea Gregersen, G. Andersen and E. Tvinnereim (2023), 'The Strength and Content of Climate Anger',

Global Environmental Change, 82: 102738; and Hannes Zacher and C. W. Rudolph (2023), 'Environmental Knowledge is Inversely Associated with Climate Change Anxiety', *Climatic Change*, 176(4): 32.

20 Similarly, evolutionary biologist Hugo Mercier and his colleague Dan Sperber argue that reason is in fact an adaptation that hypersocial humans evolved as a way of convincing others to follow one strategy or another, so that collaboration could take place (they term this an 'interactionist', rather than 'intellectualist', concept of reason). When we reason this way, it is more about figuring out what will appeal to others, or reaching good compromises, than pursuing an objective truth. As a result, some of the kinds of behaviour that the 'marketplace of ideas' model suggests, such as immediately revising beliefs on one's own, are less likely to occur. Hugo Mercier and Dan Sperber (2017), *The Enigma of Reason*, Harvard University Press.

21 Joanne Lipman (2019), 'Tech Overlords Google and Facebook Have Used Monopoly to Rob Journalism of Its Revenue', *USA TODAY*, available at: eu.usatoday.com/story/opinion/2019/06/11/google-facebook-antitrust-monopoly-advertising-journalism-revenue-streams-column/1414562001/ (accessed 12 October 2024).

22 Ezra Klein (2024), 'Pitchforks and GQ: The Internet's Media Crisis', *New York Times*, 21 January, available at: www.nytimes.com/2024/01/21/opinion/pitchfork-gq-internet-media.html (accessed 12 October 2024).

23 Jia Tolentino (2020), *Trick Mirror: Reflections on Self-Delusion*, Random House Trade Paperbacks, 30.

24 DataReportal (2024), 'Digital around the World', DataReportal, 12 July, available at: datareportal.com/global-digital-overview (accessed 12 October 2024).

25 Jonah Peretti (2007), 'Notes on Contagious Media', *Structures of Participation in Digital Culture*, New York: Social Science Research Council, 159.

26 John Rawls (1999), *A Theory of Justice*, rev. edn, Belknap Press of Harvard University Press.

27 Nancy Hartsock (1998), 'The Feminist Standpoint Revisited', *The Socialist Feminist Project: A Contemporary Reader in Theory and Politics*, Monthly Review Press, 350–60.

28 David Graeber (2013), *The Democracy Project: A History, a Crisis, a Movement*, Spiegel & Grau.

29 Ibid.

30 David McRaney, *How Minds Change*, 3 (emphasis mine).

31 See discussion, for example, in Ralph Raico (1994), 'Intellectuals and the Marketplace', *Mises Institute*, available at: mises.org/library/book/intellectuals-and-marketplace (accessed 13 October 2024).

32 Stephen Bush (2023), 'There is No Such Thing as a "Marketplace of Ideas"', *Financial Times*, 2 January, available at: www.ft.com/content/40582980-8561-493b-ae91-7ceec7e2bfa5 (accessed 13 October 2024).

33 Giulia Carbonaro (2024), 'America's Middle Class is Shrinking', *Newsweek*, 20 June, www.newsweek.com/america-middle-class-shrinking-1913772 (accessed 13 October 2024).

34 In any case, I harbour no special distrust of science itself. Certainly there is plenty that is wrong with how current science operates: for example, the way that scientists progress in their careers based only on positive findings of results creates pressure for them to find, tweak or fake findings.

35 Shai Agmon (2022), 'Two Concepts of Competition', *Ethics*, 133(1): 5–37.

CHAPTER TWO: DON'T DEBATE IT

1 Brianna Scott (2024), 'So Long, Presidential Debates? Why We May Not See Trump, Biden or Haley on Stage Together', *NPR*, 25 January, available at: www.npr.org/2024/01/25/1226440031/donald-trump-joe-biden-nikki-haley-debates-primary-election (accessed 13 October 2024).

NOTES

2. Colby Galliher (2022), 'The Worrying Decline of the Senate Candidate Debate', *Brookings*, 10 October, available at: www.brookings.edu/articles/the-worrying-decline-of-the-senate-candidate-debate/ (accessed 13 October 2024).

3. Peter Walker (2022), 'Rishi Sunak and Liz Truss Set to Miss Third Tory Leadership Debate', *Guardian*, 18 July, available at: www.theguardian.com/politics/2022/jul/18/rishi-sunak-liz-truss-set-to-miss-third-tory-leadership-debate-sky (accessed 13 October 2024).

4. History.com (n.d.), *Kennedy–Nixon Debates*, available at: www.history.com/topics/us-presidents/kennedy-nixon-debates (accessed 13 October 2024).

5. Andrew Glass (2017), *Kennedy and Nixon Hold First Televised Debate, Sept. 26, 1960*, Politico, 26 September, available at: www.politico.com/story/2017/09/26/kennedy-and-nixon-hold-first-televised-debate-sept-26-1960-243075 (accessed 13 October 2024).

6. David Smith (2022), 'The End of the Debate: Republicans and the Midterms', *Guardian*, 18 September, available at: www.theguardian.com/us-news/2022/sep/18/the-end-of-the-debate-republicans-midterms (accessed 13 October 2024).

7. See, for example, CBC (2015), 'From the CBC Vault: Viewers Panned the First Televised Election Debate', *CBC News*, available at: www.cbc.ca/news/politics/canada-election-2015-vault-leaders-debate-1.3232272 (accessed 13 October 2024).

8. Caroline Le Pennec and Vincent Pons (2019), *How Do Campaigns Shape Vote Choice? Multi-Country Evidence from 62 Elections and 56 TV Debates* (no. w26572), National Bureau of Economic Research.

9. Rachel Nuwer (2020), 'Presidential Debates Have Shockingly Little Effect on Election Outcomes', *Scientific American*, 20 October, available at: www.scientificamerican.com/article/presidential-debates-have-shockingly-little-effect-on-election-outcomes/ (accessed 13 October 2024).

10. Dylan Matthews (2012), 'What Political Scientists Know about Debates', *Washington Post*, 3 October, available at: www.washingtonpost.com/news/wonk/wp/2012/10/03/what-political-scientists-know-about-debates (accessed 13 October 2024).

11. Cody Mello-Klein (2024), 'Biden's Debate Performance Could Shape Voter Preferences, Northeastern Expert Says', *Northeastern University News*, 9 July, available at: news.northeastern.edu/2024/07/09/biden-debate-performance-voter-preferences/ (accessed 13 October 2024).

12. I refer the reader, as in the last chapter, to Joel Cooper's book on cognitive dissonance.

13. M. Avalle, N. Di Marco, G. Etta, E. Sangiorgio, S. Alipour, A. Bonetti, L. Alvisi, A. Scala, A. Baronchelli, M. Cinelli and W. Quattrociocchi (2024), 'Persistent Interaction Patterns across Social Media Platforms and Over Time', *Nature*, 628(8008): 582–9.

14. Donna Zuckerberg (2019), 'What's Wrong with Online "Debate Me" Culture', *Washington Post*, 29 August, available at: www.washingtonpost.com/outlook/whats-wrong-with-online-debate-me-culture/2019/08/29/c0ec8aa2-c9ca-11e9-8067-196d9f17af68_story.html (accessed 13 October 2024).

15. David Knight Legg (2022), 'Debates Are Dangerous: Time to Legislate Them', *Politico*, 10 June, available at: www.politico.com/news/magazine/2022/10/06/debates-are-dangerous-time-to-legislate-them-00060722 (accessed 13 October 2024).

16. Walker, 'Rishi Sunak and Liz Truss Set to Miss Third Tory Leadership Debate'.

17. Toby Helm (2022), 'The More Tory Voters See of Liz Truss, the Less They Like Her, Polls Show', *Guardian*, 3 September, available at: www.theguardian.com/politics/2022/sep/03/the-more-tory-voters-see-of-liz-truss-the-less-they-like-her-polls-show (accessed 13 October 2024).

18. Roper Center for Public Opinion Research (2024), 'Presidential Approval Highs & Lows', *Cornell University*, available at: ropercenter.cornell.edu/presidential-approval/highslows (accessed 18 October 2024).

19. IPPR (2024), 'Revealed: Trust in Politicians at Lowest Level on Record', available at: www.ippr.org/media-office/revealed-trust-in-politicians-at-lowest-level-on-record (accessed 18 October 2024).

20 Karin Brulliard (2024), 'Empty Chairs at Candidate Debates a Sign of These Very Partisan Times', *Washington Post*, 12 August, available at: www.washingtonpost.com/nation/2024/08/12/candidates-decline-debates-league-women-voters/ (accessed 18 October 2024).

21 Deborah Tannen (1999), *The Argument Culture: Stopping America's War of Words*, Ballantine Books.

22 T. A. Ito, J. T. Larsen, N. K. Smith and J. T. Cacioppo (1998), 'Negative Information Weighs More Heavily on the Brain: The Negativity Bias in Evaluative Categorizations', *Journal of Personality and Social Psychology*, 75(4): 887–900.

23 P. Fournier, S. Soroka and L. Nir (2020), 'Negativity Biases and Political Ideology: A Comparative Test across 17 Countries', *American Political Science Review*, 114(3): 775–91.

24 Jürgen Habermas (1975), *Legitimation Crisis*, Beacon Press, 108.

25 Simon Jenkins (2024), 'Keir Starmer's Prime Minister's Questions: A Lesson in Politics', *Guardian*, 25 July, available at: www.theguardian.com/commentisfree/article/2024/jul/25/keir-starmer-prime-ministers-questions-politics-parliament (accessed 18 October 2024).

26 Hugh Schofield (2019), 'Gilets Jaunes: Will Macron's Grand Debate Tackle French Crisis?', *BBC News*, 12 March, available at: www.bbc.co.uk/news/world-europe-46878317 (accessed 18 October 2024).

27 Renaud Thillaye (2019), 'Is Macron's Grand Débat a Democratic Dawn for France?' *Carnegie Europe*, 26 April, available at: carnegieendowment.org/research/2019/04/is-macrons-grand-debat-a-democratic-dawn-for-france?lang=en&center=europe (accessed 18 October 2024).

28 Elena Souris (2019), 'What Can We Learn from the Grand Débat's Grand Ambition?' *New America*, 14 November, available at: www.newamerica.org/weekly/what-can-we-learn-from-the-grand-d%C3%A9bats-grand-ambition/ (accessed 18 October 2024).

29 Bonnie A. Powell (2003), 'Framing the Issues: UC Berkeley Professor George Lakoff Tells How Conservatives Use Language to Dominate Politics', *UC Berkeley News*, 27 October, available at: newsarchive.berkeley.edu/news/media/releases/2003/10/27_lakoff.shtml (accessed 18 October 2024).

30 Shon Faye (2021), *The Transgender Issue: An Argument for Justice*, Allen Lane.

31 Personal interview, 2024.

32 Thomas Baerthlein (2016), 'Brexit Lessons: We Need European Media for a European Public Sphere', *OpenDemocracy*, 4 July, available at: www.opendemocracy.net/en/can-europe-make-it/brexit-lessons-we-need-european-media-for-european-public-spher/ (accessed 19 October 2024).

33 Raymond Geuss (2019), 'A Republic of Discussion: Habermas at Ninety', *The Point Magazine*, 18 June, available at: thepointmag.com/politics/a-republic-of-discussion-habermas-at-ninety/ (accessed 19 October 2024).

34 Emily Maitlis (2022), 'When an Agent of the Tory Party Decides the BBC's "Bias", It's a Huge Problem', *Guardian*, 25 August, available at: www.theguardian.com/commentisfree/2022/aug/25/bbc-agent-tory-party-bias-news-media-emily-maitlis-mactaggart-lecture (accessed 19 October 2024).

35 'I Can Change Your Mind on Climate', *The Science Show*, radio programme transcript, ABC Radio National, 21 April 2012, www.abc.net.au/listen/programs/scienceshow/i-can-change-your-mind-on-climate/3963066 (accessed 20 October 2024).

36 Ibid.

37 Aaron Huertas (2021), 'We Need to Talk about Reactionary Centrists', available at: www.aaronhuertas.com/we-need-to-talk-about-reactionary-centrists/ (accessed 20 October 2024).

38 See, for example, Chantal Mouffe (2013), *Agonistics: Thinking the World Politically*, Verso Books.

39 This tool was developed by George Lakey at Training for Change. See Nadine Bloch (n.d.), 'Spectrum of Allies', *The Commons Social Change Library*, available at: commonslibrary.org/spectrum-of-allies/ (accessed 20 October 2024).

40 Georg C. Lichtenberg (2000), *The Waste Books*, New York Review of Books Classics.

NOTES

CHAPTER THREE: ACT FIRST, THINK LATER

1. Belinda Archibong (2022), 'Do Protests Matter at All for Shifting Government Policy around Economic Redistribution?' *ProMarket*, 16 May, www.promarket.org/2022/05/16/do-protests-matter-at-all-for-shifting-government-policy-around-economic-redistribution/ (accessed 21 October 2024).
2. Martin Gilens (2012), *Affluence and Influence: Economic Inequality and Political Power in America*, Princeton University Press.
3. *PBS NewsHour* (2003), 'Bush: War Remains "Last Resort" Despite Protests', 18 February, available at: www.pbs.org/newshour/politics/middle_east-jan-june03-iraq_02-18 (accessed 21 October 2024).
4. Amory Gethin and Vincent Pons (2024), 'Social Movements and Public Opinion in the United States' (No. w32342), National Bureau of Economic Research, April, available at: www.nber.org/papers/w32342, (accessed Jan 5 2025).
5. D. Bugden (2020), 'Does Climate Protest Work? Partisanship, Protest, and Sentiment Pools', *Socius: Sociological Research for a Dynamic World*, 6, available at: journals.sagepub.com/doi/full/10.1177/2378023120925949 (accessed 21 October 2024).
   Similarly, right-wing Tea Party protests have an effect on support for and turnout for Tea-Party-style Republicans, but they had no effect in either direction on the behaviour of Democrats (who become neither alarmed and eager to vote against these types of candidates nor disheartened so as to vote less). A. Madestam, D. Shoag, S. Veuger and D. Yanagizawa-Drott (2013), 'Do Political Protests Matter? Evidence from The Tea Party Movement', *Quarterly Journal of Economics*, 128(4): 1633–85.
6. Pew Research Center (2023), 'Support for the Black Lives Matter Movement Has Dropped Considerably from Its Peak in 2020', 14 June, www.pewresearch.org/social-trends/2023/06/14/support-for-the-black-lives-matter-movement-has-dropped-considerably-from-its-peak-in-2020/ (accessed 21 October 2024).
7. S. Vestergren, J. Drury and E. H. Chiriac (2016), 'The Biographical Consequences of Protest and Activism: A Systematic Review and a New Typology', *Social Movement Studies*, 16(2): 203–21, doi: 10.1080/14742837.2016.1252665.
8. The same research suggests a large minority ultimately experience the opposite effect and 'burn out' psychologically on activism.
9. Larry Buchanan, Quoctrung Bui and Jugal K. Patel (2020), 'Crowd Size at George Floyd Protests', *New York Times*, 3 July, available at: www.nytimes.com/interactive/2020/07/03/us/george-floyd-protests-crowd-size.html (accessed 21 October 2024).
10. Zeynep Tufekci (2020), 'Do Protests Even Work?', *The Atlantic*, 24 June, available at: www.theatlantic.com/technology/archive/2020/06/why-protests-work/613420/ (accessed 12 November 2024).
11. Kristin Laurin (2018), 'Inaugurating Rationalization: Three Field Studies Find Increased Rationalization when Anticipated Realities Become Current', *Psychological Science*, 29(4): 483–95.
12. Kristin Laurin, A. C. Kay and G. J. Fitzsimons (2012), 'Reactance versus Rationalization: Divergent Responses to Policies that Constrain Freedom', *Psychological Science*, 23(2): 205–9. Kristin Laurin, A. C. Kay, D. Proudfoot and G. J. Fitzsimons (2013), 'Response to Restrictive Policies: Reconciling System Justification and Psychological Reactance', *Organizational Behavior and Human Decision Processes*, 122(2): 152–62.
13. John T. Jost et al. (2003), 'Social Inequality and the Reduction of Ideological Dissonance on Behalf of the System: Evidence of Enhanced System Justification among the Disadvantaged', *European Journal of Social Psychology* 33(1): 1.
14. Ibid., p. 1.
15. See John T. Jost, B. A. Nosek and S. D. Gosling (2008), 'Ideology: Its Resurgence in Social, Personality, and Political Psychology', *Perspectives on Psychological Science*, 3(2): 126–36.

16. See, for example, A. Godefroidt (2023), 'How Terrorism Does (and Does Not) Affect Citizens' Political Attitudes: A Meta-Analysis', *American Journal of Political Science*, 67(1): 22–38.
17. There were numerous interesting differences when it came to the mental health and overall well-being of these respective pools of women (I recommend the read). Diana Greene Foster (2021), *The Turnaway Study: Ten Years, A Thousand Women, and The Consequences of Having—or Being Denied—an Abortion*, Simon & Schuster.
18. Foster, *The Turnaway Study*, p. 171.
19. Matthew T. Ballew, Jennifer Marlon, Matthew Goldberg, Edward Maibach, Seth Rosenthal, Emily Aiken and Anthony Leiserowitz (2022), 'Experience with Global Warming Is Changing People's Minds about It', *Climatic Change*, 7 September, available at: climatecommunication.yale.edu/publications/experience-with-global-warming-is-changing-peoples-minds-about-it/ (accessed 21 October 2024). See also M. Bergquist, A. Nilsson and P. W. Schultz (2019), 'Experiencing a Severe Weather Event Increases Concern about Climate Change', *Frontiers in Psychology*, 10.
20. Laurin et al., 'Response to Restrictive Policies'.
21. Ibid.
22. Personal conversations over the course of 2023.
23. Stephanie Hinnershitz (2020), 'Maxwell opened my eyes to Rosa Parks: WWII defense worker', *The National WWII Museum*, available at: www.nationalww2museum.org/war/articles/maxwell-opened-my-eyes-rosa-parks-wwii-defense-worker (Accessed: 8 January 2025).
24. Much gratitude to Shalmy and others in the cooperative for allowing these visits over 2023 and 2024.
25. Thomas Metzinger (2010), *The Ego Tunnel: The Science of the Mind and the Myth of the Self*, reprint edn, Basic Books, 115.
26. Ibid., 118.
27. For more on this model, see Andy Clark (2015), *Surfing Uncertainty: Prediction, Action, and The Embodied Mind*, Oxford University Press.
28. Richard Petty and P. Briñol (2011), 'The Elaboration Likelihood Model', *Handbook of Theories of Social Psychology*, 1: 224–45.
29. Mark Fisher (2022), *Capitalist Realism: Is There No Alternative?*, John Hunt Publishing, 2.
30. Consider, for example, people's willingness in tests to pay a tax if they are allowed to offer suggestions for how that tax should be spent. See C. P. Lamberton, J. E. De Neve and M. I. Norton (2014), 'Eliciting Taxpayer Preferences Increases Tax Compliance', *Journal of Consumer Psychology*, 1057-7408/2018/1532-7663/28(2)/310-328 doi: 10.1002/jcpy.1022.
31. Joel Cooper (2007), *Cognitive Dissonance: 50 Years of a Classic Theory*, Sage, 22.
32. Douglas A. Marshall (2002), 'Behavior, Belonging, and Belief: A Theory of Ritual Practice', *Sociological Theory* 20(3): 360–80.
33. See J. De Moor and S. Verhaegen (2020), 'Gateway or Getaway? Testing the Link between Lifestyle Politics and Other Modes of Political Participation', *European Political Science Review*, 12(1): 91–111.
34. Pierre Bourdieu (1977), *Outline of a Theory of Practice*, Cambridge University Press, 86.
35. *American Libraries Magazine* (2012), 'The Librarians of Occupy Wall Street', 21 January, available at: americanlibrariesmagazine.org/blogs/the-scoop/the-librarians-of-occupy-wall-street/ (accessed 21 October 2024).
36. Zeynep Tufekci (2022), 'I Was Wrong about Why Protests Work', *New York Times*, 21 July, available at: www.nytimes.com/2022/07/21/opinion/zeynep-tufekci-protests.html (accessed 23 October 2024).
37. Nick Srnicek and Alex Williams (2015), *Inventing the Future: Postcapitalism and a World without Work*, Verso Books.
38. Alasdair Roberts (2017), *The End of Protest: How Free-Market Capitalism Learned to Control Dissent*, Cornell University Press, 60.
39. J. Long (2022), 'Organized Labor and the Vietnam Antiwar Movement: Early Union Mobilization', *Crimson Historical Review*, 5: 13–32.

NOTES

40 See an interview with Thomas Sugrue on *All Things Considered* (2013), 'Labor Movement Was Critical Ally to Civil Rights Movement', *NPR*, 27 August, available at: www.npr.org/2013/08/27/216191855/labor-movement-was-critical-ally-to-civil-rights-movement (accessed 23 October 2024). Also H. Collins, G. Lester and V. Mantouvalou, eds. (2018), *Philosophical Foundations of Labour Law*, Oxford University Press.

41 A. Dean, J. McCallum and J. Grumbach (2024), 'Decline of Labor Unions Weakens American Democracy', Economic Policy Institute, 23 October, available at: www.epi.org/blog/decline-of-labor-unions-weakens-american-democracy/ (accessed 23 October 2024). G. Lyon and B. F. Schaffner (2021), Labor Unions and Non-Member Political Protest Mobilization in the United States', *Political Research Quarterly*, 74(4): 998–1008. doi.org/10.1177/1065912920950826.

42 Zeynep Tufekci (2017), *Twitter and Tear Gas: The Power and Fragility of Networked Protest*, Yale University Press.

CHAPTER FOUR: THINK WITH YOUR FRIENDS

1 National Archives (2024), 'Executive Order 9981: Desegregation of the Armed Forces (1948)', *National Archives*, 26 July, available at: www.archives.gov/milestone-documents/executive-order-9981 (accessed 23 October 2024).

2 Gordon Allport, K. Clark and T. Pettigrew ([1954] 1979), *The Nature of Prejudice*, Basic Books, 2.

3 M. S. Gou, T. L. Webb and T. Prescott (2021), 'The Effect of Direct and Extended Contact on Attitudes towards Social Robots', *Heliyon*, 7(3).

4 Miles Hewstone (2009), 'Living Apart, Living Together? The Role of Intergroup Contact in Social Integration', *Proceedings of the British Academy*. 162(2008): 243–300.

5 Christopher Scalia (2020), 'My Father's Relationship with Justice Ginsburg: Best of Friends', *American Enterprise Institute*, 21 September, available at: www.aei.org/articles/my-fathers-relationship-with-justice-ginsburg-best-of-friends/ (accessed 25 October 2024).

6 John Whitesides (2017), 'From Disputes to a Breakup: Wounds Still Raw After U.S. Election', *Reuters*, 7 February, available at: www.reuters.com/article/us-usa-trump-relationships-insight/from-disputes-to-a-breakup-wounds-still-raw-after-u-s-election-idUSKBN15M13L/ (accessed 25 October 2024).

7 Gwen Aviles (2018), 'Just One Gay Acquaintance Can Change Hearts and Minds on LGBTQ Rights', *NBC News*, 17 September, available at: www.nbcnews.com/feature/nbc-out/just-one-gay-acquaintance-can-change-hearts-minds-lgbtq-rights-n948911 (accessed 25 October 2024).

8 Gallup (2024), 'Gay and Lesbian Rights', available at: news.gallup.com/poll/1651/gay-lesbian-rights.aspx (accessed 25 October 2024). Gallup didn't even poll on gay marriage before 1996, and when they polled on whether gay *relations* should be legal in 1986 only a third thought they should be legal.

9 Samantha Schmidt (2019), 'Americans' Views Flipped on Gay Rights: How Did Minds Change So Quickly?', *Washington Post*, 7 June, available at: www.washingtonpost.com/local/social-issues/americans-views-flipped-on-gay-rights-how-did-minds-change-so-quickly/2019/06/07/ae256016-8720-11e9-98c1-e945ae5db8fb_story.html (accessed 25 October 2024).

10 Everything in this paragraph is from Miles Hewstone's aforementioned and previously cited summary of the mechanics of social contact theory, 'Living Apart, Living Together?'.

11 A similar French study from 2020, where once again students were randomly assigned to study together for a year, found related but slightly different results. This study did not look directly at the effects of having politically *engaged* friends (it thus did not measure whether this increased one's engagement) but did find that one's friends tended to exert some gravitational effect on one's political views, especially if friends were already close in views to oneself. There are a number of ways of explaining this difference, but one seems particularly possible: this study was conducted at Sciences Po, and this school is one of the most political and elite schools in France, so it is likely that the students were already mostly

all talking about politics, all the time. Thus they were, in a way, most similar to the students in the Brazilian study who had already become highly engaged, and who also consequently understood their own views better and moved slightly towards one another on the political axis. Yann Algan, Nicolò Dalvit, Quoc-Anh Do, Alexis Le Chapelain and Yves Zenou (2019), 'Friendship Networks and Political Opinions: A Natural Experiment among Future French Politicians', HAL Open Science, available at: sciencespo.hal.science/hal-03393089/file/2019-algan-et-al-friendship-networks-and-political-opinions-a-natural-experiment-among-future-french-politicians.pdf (accessed 24 October 2024).

12 See Stanford University (2023), 'The Strength of Weak Ties', *Stanford News*, 24 July, available at: news.stanford.edu/stories/2023/07/strength-weak-ties (accessed 25 October 2024).

13 See T. König (1999), 'Patterns of Movement Recruitment: Why Dense Networks Help Recruitment to New Social Movements but Obstruct Recruitment to the New Age Movement', 6. Presented at the American Sociological Association Annual Meeting 1999, available at www.restore.ac.uk/lboro/staff/thomas/papers/recruitment_patterns.pdf (accessed 3 November 2024). Also D. Freeman and R. P. Bentall (2017), 'The Concomitants of Conspiracy Concerns', *Social Psychiatry and Psychiatric Epidemiology*, 52(5): 595–604, available at: pmc.ncbi.nlm.nih.gov/articles/PMC5423964/ (accessed 23 October 2024). And J. M. Curtis and M. J. Curtis (1993), 'Vulnerability to Cults: What We Know and How We Know It', *Cultic Studies Journal*, 11(2): 217–29, available at: pubmed.ncbi.nlm.nih.gov/8234595/ (accessed 23 October 2024).

14 N. M. Somma (2009), 'How Strong Are Strong Ties? The Conditional Effectiveness of Strong Ties in Protest Recruitment Attempts', *Sociological Perspectives*, 52(3): 289–308.

15 M. J. Coren (2023), 'The Surprisingly Simple Way to Convince People to Go Green', *Washington Post*, 5 December, available at: www.washingtonpost.com/climate-environment/2023/12/05/improve-sustainability-help-climate-change/ (accessed 29 October 2024).

16 Jeroen Van Laer (2017), 'The Mobilization Dropout Race: Interpersonal Networks and Motivations Predicting Differential Recruitment in a National Climate Change Demonstration', *Social Movement Studies*, 12(4): 420–34. J. van Stekelenburg and B. Klandermans (2023), *A Social Psychology of Protest: Individuals in Action*, Cambridge University Press, 86, 95.

17 Ibid., p. 121.

18 See discussion in C. Corrigall-Brown (2011), *Patterns of Protest: Trajectories of Participation in Social Movements*, Stanford University Press.

19 See, for example, Rickard Sandell (1999), 'Organizational Life aboard the Moving Bandwagons: A Network Analysis of Dropouts from a Swedish Temperance Organization, 1896–1937', *Acta Sociologica* 42: 3–15.

20 Many thanks to Ayla Newhouse for speaking with me about this project in January 2024, and for consultation from her former colleague Sarah Sullivan.

21 For a learning-design-oriented description of the importance of affective context, see Nick Shackleton-Jones (2019), *How People Learn: Designing Education and Training that Works to Improve Performance*, Kogan Page.

22 See a discussion in Hewstone, 'Living Apart, Living Together?', 250. Also Stephen C. Wright, Arthur Aron, Tracy McLaughlin-Volpe and Stacy A. Ropp (1997), 'The Extended Contact Effect: Knowledge of Cross-Group Friendships and Prejudice', *Journal of Personality and Social Psychology*, 73(1): 73–90.

23 Martijn van. Zomeren (2016), 'Selvations Theory II: Coping with Value-Infused Events', in *From Self to Social Relationships: An Essentially Relational Perspective on Social Motivation*, Cambridge University Press (Studies in Emotion and Social Interaction), 115.

24 Ibid., p. 5.

25 For evidence of this see J. L. Kalla, and D. E. Broockman (2018), 'The Minimal Persuasive Effects of Campaign Contact in General Elections: Evidence from 49 Field Experiments', *American Political Science Review*, 112(1): 148–66.

26 David McRaney (2022), *How Minds Change: The Surprising Science of Belief, Opinion, and Persuasion*, Penguin, 44.

27 David Broockman and Joshua Kalla (2016), 'Durably Reducing Transphobia: A Field Experiment on Door-to-Door Canvassing', *Science* 352(6282): 223.

28 Yale Center for Environmental Communication (2023), 'Deep Canvassing on Climate: The Power of Listening to Persuade', 1 December, available at: climatecommunication.yale.edu/news-events/deep-canvassing-on-climate-the-power-of-listening-to-persuade/ (accessed 26 October 2024).

29 Many thanks to Joshua Kalla for agreeing to this interview, which took place in 2023.

30 Thanks to Stephanie Bastek and Stomp Out Slumlords for their assistance. Interviews happened across 2023 and 2024.

31 You can read his horror about this in Gustave le Bon (1896), *Crowd: A Study of the Popular Mind*, Macmillan & Co.

32 Geoff Eley (2008), *Citizenship and National Identity in Twentieth-Century Germany*, Stanford University Press, 284. Jaap van Ginneken (1992), *Crowds, Psychology, and Politics, 1871–1899*, Cambridge University Press, 186.

33 Stuart Ewen (1996), *PR!: A Social History of Spin*, Basic Books, 63.

34 Fredric Jameson (2020), *Valences of the Dialectic*, Verso Books, 211.

35 Elijah Millgram (2015), *The Great Endarkenment*, Oxford University Press, 36.

36 R. B. Siegel (2004), 'Introduction: A Short History of Sexual Harassment', in *Directions in Sexual Harassment Law*, Yale University Press. Those who theorized about consciousness-raising are perhaps important exceptions to the general way that political theorists have ignored the benefits of reasoning together, especially and including the way that those in the group learn by doing things together in ways they could not do alone.

37 Kathleen M. Carley (2009), 'A Friend like Me', *Scientific American*, 26 September, available at: www.scientificamerican.com/article/a-friend-like-me/ (accessed 26 October 2024).

38 C. Hepçağlayan (2024), 'Political Friendship as Joint Commitment: Aristotle on *Homonoia*', *Inquiry*, 1–34, doi: 10.1080/0020174X.2024.2392612.

39 See discussion in Chapter Ten of P. P. Craig (1991), *Public Law and Democracy in the United Kingdom and the United States of America*, Oxford University Press. Also J. Medina (2013), *The Epistemology of Resistance: Gender and Racial Oppression, Epistemic Injustice, and the Social Imagination*, Oxford University Press.

CHAPTER FIVE: TAKE BACK TWITTER (AND OTHER INFRASTRUCTURE)

1 Throughout this text I use both the old name of this company and the new one, as seems appropriate to the context.

2 Matt O'Brien (2022), 'Musk Doesn't Want Twitter "Free-for-all Hellscape," He Tells Advertisers', *PBS NewsHour*, 27 October, available at: www.pbs.org/newshour/politics/musk-doesnt-want-twitter-free-for-all-hellscape-he-tells-advertisers (accessed 27 October 2024).

3 Michelle Toh and Juliana Liu (2023), 'Elon Musk's BBC Interview: What He Said about Twitter and Free Speech', *CNN*, 12 April, available at: edition.cnn.com/2023/04/12/tech/elon-musk-bbc-interview-twitter-intl-hnk/index.html (accessed 27 October 2024). Alexia Fernández Campbell (2019), 'Elon Musk's Labor Violation Case: What You Need to Know', *Vox*, 30 September, available at: www.vox.com/identities/2019/9/30/20891314/elon-musk-tesla-labor-violation-nlrb (accessed 27 October 2024).

4 Walter Isaacson (2023), 'Elon Musk Moved Twitter Servers Himself in the Night, New Biography Details His "Maniacal" Sense of Urgency', *CNBC*, 11 September, available at: www.cnbc.com/2023/09/11/elon-musk-moved-twitter-servers-himself-in-the-night-new-biography-details-his-maniacal-sense-of-urgency.html (accessed 27 October 2024). Kevin Poireault (2023), 'Elon Musk in the Crosshairs of FTC over Twitter Privacy Issues',

Infosecurity Magazine, 14 September, available at: www.infosecurity-magazine.com/news/elon-musk-ftc-twitter-x-privacy/ (accessed 27 October 2024). Jon Brodkin (2023), 'After Musk's Mass Layoffs, One Engineer's Mistake Broke the Twitter API', *Ars Technica*, 7 October, available at: arstechnica.com/tech-policy/2023/03/after-musks-mass-layoffs-one-engineers-mistake-broke-the-twitter-api/ (accessed 27 October 2024). Kali Hays (2022), 'Twitter's Payroll and Finance Department Resigns en Masse under Elon Musk', *Business Insider*, available at: www.businessinsider.com/twitter-payroll-finance-department-resigns-en-masse-under-elon-musk-2022-11 (accessed 27 October 2024).

5 Julianne McShane (2023), 'Elon Musk, New Owner of Twitter, Tweets Unfounded Conspiracy Theory about Paul Pelosi', *NBC News*, 30 October, available at: http://www.nbcnews.com/news/us-news/elon-musk-new-owner-twitter-tweets-unfounded-conspiracy-theory-paul-pe-rcna54717 (accessed 27 October 2024).

6 Shayan Sardarizadeh (2022), 'Twitter Chaos after Wave of Blue Tick Impersonations', *BBC News*, 12 November, available at: www.bbc.co.uk/news/technology-63599553 (accessed 27 October 2024).

7 Drew Harwell (2022), 'A Fake Tweet Sparked Panic at Eli Lilly and May Have Cost Twitter Millions', *Washington Post*, 14 November, available at: www.washingtonpost.com/technology/2022/11/14/twitter-fake-eli-lilly/ (accessed 27 October 2024).

8 Kate Conger, Ryan Mac and Mike Isaac (2022), 'Elon Musk Fires Twitter Employees Who Criticized Him', *New York Times*, 15 November, available at: www.nytimes.com/2022/11/15/technology/elon-musk-twitter-fired-criticism.html (accessed 27 October 2024).

9 David Klepper (2024), 'Report: Tweets with Racial Slurs Soar Since Musk Takeover', *Associated Press*, available at: apnews.com/article/elon-musk-technology-business-government-and-politics-2907d382db132cfd7446152b9309992c (accessed 3 December 2024).

10 Ryan Mac and Kate Conger (2023), 'X May Lose up to $75 Million in Revenue as More Advertisers Pull Out', *New York Times*, 24 November, available at: www.nytimes.com/2023/11/24/business/x-elon-musk-advertisers.html (accessed 27 October 2024). Matt Egan (2024), 'Elon Musk's X is Worth Nearly 80% Less than When He Bought It, Fidelity Estimates', *CNN*, 2 October, available at: edition.cnn.com/2024/10/02/business/elon-musk-twitter-x-fidelity/index.html (accessed 27 October 2024). Dan Milmo (2022), 'How "Free Speech Absolutist" Elon Musk Would Transform Twitter', *Guardian*, 14 April, available at: www.theguardian.com/technology/2022/apr/14/how-free-speech-absolutist-elon-musk-would-transform-twitter (accessed 27 October 2024).

11 Jacob Kastrenakes and Mia Sato (2023), 'Elon Musk Tells Ad Agencies to 'Go Fuck Yourself' Amid Boycott of X', *The Verge*, 30 November, available at: www.theverge.com/2023/11/29/23981928/elon-musk-ad-boycott-go-fuck-yourself-destroy-x (accessed 3 December 2024).

12 Elon Musk (2022), 'Tweet about X Platform' [Twitter/X], available at: x.com/elonmusk/status/1593767953706921985?lang=en (accessed 3 December 2024).

13 Jill Colvin (2023), 'Trump Returns to Site Formerly Known as Twitter, Posts His Mug Shot Shortly after Georgia Surrender', *Associated Press*, 25 August, available at: apnews.com/article/trump-twitter-tweets-return-49594b9f72c68a309758e19bc9cdceof (accessed 3 December 2024).

14 Sheila Dang (2022), 'Twitter Dissolves Trust and Safety Council', *Reuters*, 13 December, available at: www.reuters.com/technology/twitter-dissolves-trust-safety-council-2022-12-13/ (accessed 3 December 2024).

15 Peter Eavis and Isabella Simonetti (2022), 'Elon Musk's Twitter Role Puts Tesla Board under New Scrutiny', *New York Times*, 22 November, available at: www.nytimes.com/2022/11/22/business/elon-musk-tesla-board-twitter.html (accessed 27 October 2024). Kari Paul, Lois Beckett and Josh Taylor (2022), 'Twitter Suspends Accounts of Several Journalists Who Had Reported on Elon Musk', *Guardian*, 15 December, available at: www.theguardian.com/technology/2022/dec/15/twitter-suspends-accounts-journalists-musk (accessed

27 October 2024). Jessica Silver-Greenberg (2022), 'Twitter Bans Links to Rival Social Media Platforms, including Mastodon', *New York Times*, 18 December, available at: www.nytimes.com/2022/12/18/business/twitter-ban-social-media-competitors-mastodon.html (accessed 27 October 2024). Bryan Fung (2022), 'Elon Musk Says He Will Step Down as Twitter CEO When He Finds a Replacement', *CNN*, 19 December, available at: edition.cnn.com/2022/12/19/tech/elon-musk-twitter-ceo-poll/index.html (accessed 27 October 2024).

16 Sarah E. Needleman (2023), 'Elon Musk Casts Doubt on Poll Wanting Him Gone as Twitter Head', *Wall Street Journal*, 20 December, available at: www.wsj.com/articles/elon-musk-casts-doubt-on-poll-wanting-him-gone-as-twitter-head-11671578391 (accessed 27 October 2024).

17 Dan Milmo (2023), '"Musk Destroyed All That": Twitter's Business is Flailing after a Year of Elon', *Guardian*, 27 October, available at: www.theguardian.com/technology/2023/oct/27/elon-musk-x-twitter-takeover-revenue-users-advertising (accessed 27 October 2024). Chloe Olivia Sladden (2022), 'Elon Musk's "Weak Stance on Moderation" Is Catching Up to Him as Apple Threatens to Remove Twitter App', *Verdict*, 29 November, available at: www.verdict.co.uk/elon-musks-weak-stance-on-moderation-is-catching-up-to-him-as-apple-threatens-to-remove-twitter-app/ (accessed 27 October 2024).

18 And he not only interfered in the world via Trump and the United States; Musk also got into heated struggles with the Brazilian Supreme Court after he refused to follow their decisions about who should be banned from the platform. Notably, the Brazilian authorities eventually got Musk to back down. Al Jazeera (2024), 'Brazil Lifts Ban on Elon Musk's X platform', *Al Jazeera*, 9 October, available at: www.aljazeera.com/economy/2024/10/9/brazil-lifts-ban-on-elon-musks-x-platform (accessed 22 December 2024).

19 Kari Paul (2023), 'Elon Musk Reportedly Forced Twitter Algorithm to Boost His Tweets after Super Bowl Flop', *Guardian*, 15 February, available at: www.theguardian.com/technology/2023/feb/15/elon-musk-changes-twitter-algorithm-super-bowl-slump-report (accessed 3 December 2024).

20 Kari Paul (2023), 'Twitter (X) Updates Political Ads Policy to Combat Misinformation', *Guardian*, 29 August, available at: www.theguardian.com/technology/2023/aug/29/twitter-x-political-ads-us-policy-misinformation (accessed 3 December 2024).

21 Alex Hern (2024), 'A Week in Tweets: Elon Musk Doesn't Stop Posting But What Is He Saying?', *Guardian*, 17 August, available at: www.theguardian.com/technology/article/2024/aug/17/a-week-in-tweets-elon-musk-x (accessed 17 August 2024).

22 Tim Hanlon (2024), 'Elon Musk Called Out as Biggest Pusher of Misinformation on Own Grok AI Platform', *Mirror*, 13 December, available at: www.mirror.co.uk/news/us-news/elon-musk-called-out-biggest-34100353 (accessed 13 December 2024).

23 David Ingram (2024), 'How Elon Musk Turned X into a Pro-Trump Echo Chamber', *NBC News*, 31 October, available at: www.nbcnews.com/tech/social-media/elon-musk-turned-x-trump-echo-chamber-rcna174321 (accessed 13 December 2024).

24 Paige Oamek (2024), 'Tucker Carlson and Elon Musk Secretly Lobbied Trump for J. D. Vance as VP', *The New Republic*, 16 July, available at: newrepublic.com/post/183888/tucker-carlson-elon-musk-secretly-lobbied-trump-jd-vance (accessed 3 December 2024).

25 Ellen Ioanes (2024) 'Elon Musk Says He's Giving Away $1 Million a Day to Voters. Is That Legal?', Vox.com, November 4, available at: www.vox.com/politics/378912/musk-trump-voting-contest-million-dollars-swing-state-lottery-pennsylvania (accessed 3 December 2024). Tom Perkins (2024), 'Musk-Linked Pac Accused of Targeting Jewish and Arab Americans in Swing States', *Guardian*, 4 November, available at: www.theguardian.com/us-news/2024/nov/04/election-musk-pac-michigan-ads-israel-gaza (accessed 4 December 2024). Josh Marshall (2024), 'Elon Musk's Fake Sites and Texts Impersonating the Harris Campaign', *Talking Points Memo*, 19 October, available at: talkingpointsmemo.com/edblog/elon-musks-fake-sites-and-texts-impersonating-the-harris-campaign (accessed 4 December 2024). Peter Stone (2024), 'Alarm Grows over Trump and Musk's Blizzard of Baseless Voter-Fraud Claims', *Guardian*, 5 November, available at: www.theguardian.com/us-news/2024/nov/05/

trump-musk-election-voter-fraud-misinformation, (accessed 4 December 2024). Joseph Gedeon (2024), 'Elon Musk', *Guardian*, 6 December, available at: www.theguardian.com/technology/2024/dec/06/elon-musk-rbg-pac-abortion (accessed 13 December 2024).

26 T. Fujiwara, K. Müller and C. Schwarz (2024) 'The Effect of Social Media on Elections: Evidence from the United States', *Journal of the European Economic Association*, 22(3): 1495–1539.

27 Nada Tawfik and Kayla Epstein (2024), 'Trump Revellers Gather in Florida to Await His Arrival', *BBC News*, 5 November. Available at: www.bbc.co.uk/news/articles/c9dlg1v7jevo (accessed 4 December 2024).

28 Eric Lipton, David A. Fahrenthold, Aaron Krolik and Kirsten Grind (2024), 'U.S. Agencies Fund, and Fight with, Elon Musk. A Trump Presidency Could Give Him Power over Them', *New York Times*, 20 October, available at: www.nytimes.com/2024/10/20/us/politics/elon-musk-federal-agencies-contracts.html (accessed 4 December 2024).

29 Theo Burman (2024), 'Elon Musk Net Worth Up 69 Percent since Donald Trump Victory', *Newsweek*, 12 December, available at: www.newsweek.com/elon-musk-net-worth-donald-trump-victory-1999730 (accessed 15 December 2024).

30 Sky News (2024), 'Elon Musk on Track to Be the First Trillionaire by 2027, According to Report', *Sky News*, 9 September (accessed 15 December 2024).

31 Joe Sommerlad (2024) 'Amazon's Jeff Bezos Set to Donate $1 Million to Trump's Inaugural Fund', available at: www.independent.co.uk/news/world/americas/us-politics/amazon-jeff-bezos-trump-donation-mark-zuckerberg-meta-b2663871.html (accessed 15 December 2024).

32 Reuters (2023), 'Only Verified Accounts Can Vote in Twitter Polls from April 15, Says Musk', Reuters, 28 March, available at: www.reuters.com/technology/only-verified-accounts-can-vote-twitter-polls-april-15-says-musk-2023-03-28/ (accessed 27 October 2024).

33 L. Zaleski (2023), 'Tweet', *Twitter*, 10 March, available at: twitter.com/ZaleskiLuke/status/1772063241243349183 (accessed 27 October 2024).

34 ProgGrrl (2022), 'Tweet', *Twitter*, 2 December, available at: twitter.com/ProgGrrl/status/1598737677528047616 (accessed 27 October 2024).

35 Vincent Bevins (2023), *If We Burn: The Mass Protest Decade and the Missing Revolution*, Hachette UK.

36 Olivia Solon (2017), '"It's Digital Colonialism": How Facebook's Free Internet Service Has Failed Its Users', *Guardian*, 27 July, available at: www.theguardian.com/technology/2017/jul/27/facebook-free-basics-developing-markets (accessed 27 October 2024).

37 Euronews with AP (2024), 'What Does the Possible TikTok Ban Mean for US–China Relations?', *Euronews*, 26 April, available at: www.euronews.com/next/2024/04/26/what-does-the-possible-tiktok-ban-mean-for-us-china-relations (accessed 27 October 2024).

38 Kate Vinton (2016), 'These 15 Billionaires Own America's News Media Companies', *Forbes*, 1 June, available at: www.forbes.com/sites/katevinton/2016/06/01/these-15-billionaires-own-americas-news-media-companies/#29ae3f3e660a (accessed 27 October 2024). N. Rapp and A. Jenkins (2018), 'These 6 Companies Control Much of U.S. Media', *Fortune*, 1 August, available at: fortune.com/longform/media-company-ownership-consolidation/ (accessed 27 October 2024).

39 Susan Leigh Star (1999), 'The Ethnography of Infrastructure', *American Behavioral Scientist*, 43(3): 381.

40 See a lengthy discussion here: Shirin Ghaffary (2023), 'Elon Musk's Twitter Is Degrading in Quality as Glitches Persist and Users Complain', *Vox*, 6 March, available at: www.vox.com/technology/2023/2/16/23603155/elon-musk-twitter-worse-degrading-quality-glitches-superbowl-boost-feed (accessed 27 October 2024).

41 I think with my friends, and I'm indebted to Sita Balani for the excellent observation.

42 Aja Romano (2022), 'Saying Goodbye to Twitter: Why I'm Leaving Social Media', *Vox*, 24 July, available at: www.vox.com/culture/2022/11/22/23466381/leaving-twitter-saying-goodbye-social-media (accessed 27 October 2024).

NOTES

43 Alex Marshall (2015), 'Why the Word "Infrastructure" Replaced "Public Works"', *Governing*, 1 July, available at: www.governing.com/archive/gov-the-word-infrastructure.html (accessed 27 October 2024).

44 In this way it is much like technology. The American historian Melvin Kranzberg put it nicely when he wrote, 'Technology is neither good nor bad, nor is it neutral.'

45 It will not be lost on some of my readers that actual tech companies often end up cannibalizing and privatizing the infrastructure in the cities in which they reside, building lucrative semi-private infrastructures and destroying public ones.

46 Paris Marx (2022), 'Elon Musk Just Changed the Meaning of Twitter's Coveted Blue Check', *NBC News*, 2 November, available at: www.nbcnews.com/think/opinion/elon-musk-just-changed-be-classed-meaning-twitters-coveted-blue-check-rcna55121 (accessed 27 October 2024).

47 See Silver-Greenberg, 'Twitter Bans Links to Rival Social Media Platforms, including Mastodon.

48 Lilian Barratt (2023), 'Social Infrastructure in Two Minutes', British Academy, available at: www.thebritishacademy.ac.uk/blog/social-infrastructure-in-two-minutes/ (accessed 1 November 2024).

49 Peter Walker (2022), 'Childcare Should Be Classed as Necessary Infrastructure, Say MPs', *Guardian*, 12 December, available at: www.theguardian.com/money/2022/dec/12/childcare-should-be-classed-as-necessary-infrastructure-say-mps (accessed 27 October 2024).

50 For an interesting discussion of platform monopolies, see Nick Srnicek (2018), 'Digital Platforms and Monopolies: An Interview with Nick Srnicek', *Philonomist*, 19 October, available at: www.philonomist.com/en/entretien/nick-srnicek-platform-monopolies (accessed 27 October 2024).

51 Richard Fletcher (2021), 'Perceptions of Fair News Coverage among Different Groups', *Reuters Institute for the Study of Journalism*, 23 June, available at: reutersinstitute.politics.ox.ac.uk/digital-news-report/2021/perceptions-fair-news-coverage-among-different-groups (accessed 27 October 2024).

52 Dan Milmo (2024), 'Internet Replaces TV as UK's Most Popular News Source for First Time', *Guardian*, 10 September, available at: www.theguardian.com/media/article/2024/sep/10/internet-tv-uk-most-popular-news-source-first-time (accessed 27 October 2024).

53 Flamingo Consultancy (2023), 'How Young People Consume News and the Implications for Mainstream Media', *Reuters Institute for the Study of Journalism*, available at: reutersinstitute.politics.ox.ac.uk/our-research/how-young-people-consume-news-and-implications-mainstream-media (accessed 27 October 2024).

54 Mozilla Foundation (2023), 'Net Neutrality Timeline', Mozilla Foundation, available at: foundation.mozilla.org/en/campaigns/net-neutrality-timeline/ (accessed 27 October 2024).

55 Tom de Castella (2013), 'Have Train Fares Gone Up or Down since British Rail?', *BBC News*, 22 January, available at: www.bbc.com/news/magazine-21056703 (accessed 14 January 2025).

56 Barratt, 'Social Infrastructure in Two Minutes'.

57 Eric Klinenberg (2018), *Palaces for the People: How Social Infrastructure Can Help Fight Inequality, Polarization, and the Decline of Civic Life*, Crown, p. 14.

58 See Klinenberg's book and the sources in previous chapters.

59 See, for example, a popular discussion of academic research by Ralph Scott (2023), 'University Degrees and Political Values: How Education Shapes Political Attitudes', LSE Politics and Policy Blog, 6 June, available at: blogs.lse.ac.uk/politicsandpolicy/university-degree-political-values/ (accessed 27 October 2024).

60 See O. Christ, K. Schmid, S. Lolliot, H. Swart, D. Stolle, N. Tausch, A. Al Ramiah, U. Wagner, S. Vertovec and M. Hewstone (2014), 'Contextual Effect of Positive Intergroup Contact on Outgroup Prejudice', *Proceedings of the National Academy of Sciences*, 111(11): 3996–4000.

61 The whole of the next chapter has to do with social infrastructure, so I'll leave its importance here for now.

62 S. Graham and C. McFarlane (2014), *Infrastructural Lives*, Taylor & Francis.

63 In fact, former prime minister Rishi Sunak suggested this as a future policy in 2024, suggesting a mandatory year for all 18-year-olds. This was not exactly met with enthusiasm. But there are other ways to build public service obligations into everyday life. Associated Press (2024), 'Sunak's Plan to Make 18-Year-Olds Do National Service Grabs Attention', *NBC News*, 26 April, available at: www.nbcnews.com/news/world/sunak-national-service-18-year-olds-uk-election-rcna154155 (accessed 27 October 2024).

64 RAND Corporation (2019), 'Americans Have More Free Time than Generally Recognized: Study Suggests Lack of Leisure Time Is Not a Barrier to Physical Activity', RAND Corporation News Release, 28 October, available at: www.rand.org/news/press/2019/10/28.html (accessed 27 October 2024). Joe Pinsker (2019), 'The Surprising Relationship between Free Time and Life Satisfaction', *The Atlantic*, 26 February, available at: www.theatlantic.com/family/archive/2019/02/free-time-life-satisfaction/583171/ (accessed 27 October 2024).

65 See research on how well this works when it comes to COVID: Julia Métraux (2021), 'Talking to Doctors about the COVID Vaccine: Building Trust', *Verywell Health*, 26 March, available at: www.verywellhealth.com/talking-to-doctors-covid-vaccine-trust-5118277 (accessed 27 October 2024). And how integrated high schools decrease racism: S. Burgess and L. Platt (2021), 'Inter-Ethnic Relations of Teenagers in England's Schools: The Role of School and Neighbourhood Ethnic Composition', *Journal of Ethnic and Migration Studies*, 47(9): 2011–38.

66 In addition to sources I've cited earlier in this book, see K. Sambrook, E. Konstantinidis, S. Russell and Y. Okan (2021), 'The Role of Personal Experience and Prior Beliefs in Shaping Climate Change Perceptions: A Narrative Review', *Frontiers in Psychology*, 12: 669911.

67 Remember Stanley Ingber, the lawyer I mentioned in Chapter One, who wrote about the way the myth of a functioning 'marketplace of ideas' often merely serves to legitimize the ideas currently favoured by those in power? He too noticed how important action was for political reasoning. I was surprised to find that he not only suggested that freedom of action might be more important than certain kinds of freedom of speech but also that he believed this to be the case because of our social networks, the way actions affect our reasoning and because of cognitive dissonance, the very phenomenon I'd spent so long researching in my academic work. He wrote:

> To the Court ... people may associate to advocate certain behavior but may not associate to take action to implement the ideas advocated. Psychology has long recognized, however, that requiring behavior inconsistent with belief creates tension within an individual. That tension is often resolved by altering the belief system to make it consistent with the compelled conduct. This theory of cognitive dissonance recognizes an inalienable connection between action and belief. The Court's attempt to separate them accords with the myth of individual autonomy discussed earlier.

His point is we are not free to think if we are not free to act in alignment with new possible beliefs. Ingber also wrote:

> In addition to ecological change, new perspectives and values may be nurtured in a society that encourages, or at least permits, the development of new interests and experiences. Consequently, the status quo bias of the marketplace [of ideas] can probably be neutralized only by protecting a greater liberty of action – allowing people to choose among lifestyles offering differing roles and relationships – rather than merely supporting the freedom of speech.

I was slightly shocked, but pleasantly so, to discover that someone else had thought about these issues the same way. Perhaps because of our cultural attachment to the myth of the marketplace of ideas and our emphasis on the importance of debate, a great deal of angry energy has been spent discussing freedom of speech – but this may well distract us from other important rights, not least of which is the freedom to try out our ideas, in miniature, in the world.

68 Maik Fielitz and Holger Marcks (2019), 'Digital Fascism: Challenges for the Open Society in Times of Social Media', UC Berkeley: Center for Right-Wing Studies, available at: escholarship.org/uc/item/87w5c5gp (accessed 12 January 2025).

69 Karl Popper, E. H. Gombrich and V. Havel (2012), *The Open Society and Its Enemies*, Routledge.

70 Aaron O'Neill (2024), 'Lynching by State and Race', *Statista*, available at: www.statista.com/statistics/1175147/lynching-by-race-state-and-race/ (accessed 13 December 2024).

71 Business Standard Web Team (2022), 'Musk Announces New Changes for Twitter Blue: Here's What to Expect', *Business Standard*, 18 December, available at: www.business-standard.com/article/international/musk-announces-new-changes-for-twitter-blue-here-s-what-to-expect-1221218007431.html (accessed 27 October 2024).

72 For an interesting statistical analysis of the hierarchical nature of the network, see Zhe Liu (2014), 'Is Twitter a Public Sphere for Online Conflicts? A Cross-Ideological and Cross-Hierarchical Look', available at: arxiv.org/pdf/1410.0610. This was also true of 'academic Twitter': Chris Havergal (2024), 'Twitter Creates New Academic Hierarchies, Suggests Study', *Times Higher Education*, retrieved from www.timeshighereducation.com/news/twitter-creates-new-academic-hierarchies-suggests-study (accessed 27 October 2024). Academic research also indicates that the format of social media itself, especially Twitter, increases people's level of moral outrage and polarizes their views: W. J. Brady, K. McLoughlin, T. N. Doan and M. J. Crockett (2021), 'How Social Learning Amplifies Moral Outrage Expression in Online Social Networks', *Science Advances*, 7(33): eabe5641.

73 Rumman Chowdhury (2021), 'Sharing Learnings about Our Image Cropping Algorithm', *X Blog*, 19 May, available at: blog.x.com/engineering/en_us/topics/insights/2021/sharing-learnings-about-our-image-cropping-algorithm (accessed 27 October 2024). Luca Belli (2021), 'Examining Algorithmic Amplification of Political Content on Twitter', *X Blog*, 25 October, available at: blog.x.com/en_us/topics/company/2021/rml-politicalcontent (accessed 27 October 2024).

74 A lengthy description of this can be found at the whistleblower report about Twitter that was eventually given to Congress, which can currently be accessed at: s3.documentcloud.org/documents/22186683/twitter-whistleblower-disclosure.pdf

75 Andy Sullivan, David Morgan and Richard Cowan (2024), 'Elon Musk Brings Trump's Government Efficiency Push to Capitol Hill', *Reuters*, 5 December, available at: www.reuters.com/world/us/elon-musk-brings-trumps-government-efficiency-push-capitol-hill-2024-12-05/ (accessed 13 December 2024).

76 Transport for London (n.d.). *A Brief History of the Underground*, available at tfl.gov.uk/corporate/about-tfl/culture-and-heritage/londons-transport-a-history/london-underground/a-brief-history-of-the-underground (accessed 13 December 2024).

77 Gideon Skinner, Cameron Garrett, Laura King and Jordana Moser (2023), '3 in 5 Britons Would Prefer Utilities to Be Publicly Owned and Operated', *Ipsos*, 16 August, available at: www.ipsos.com/en-uk/3-in-5-britons-would-prefer-utilities-to-be-publicly-owned-and-operated (accessed 27 October 2024).

78 And there are lots of interesting and clever solutions. See the concept of the Public Commons Partnership, described here: Kai Heron, Mathew Lawrence, Keir Milburn and Bertie Russell (n.d.), 'Public-Common Partnerships: Democratising Ownership and Urban Development', *Common Wealth*, available at: www.common-wealth.org/interactive/a-new-model (accessed 13 January 2025). For digital platforms specifically see the ideas reviewed in some of these books: Robert Gorwa, (2024), *Internet Democracy: Musk, Zuckerberg, and Profits*, available at: jacobin.com/2024/12/internet-democracy-musk-zuckerberg-profits (accessed 13 January 2025).

79 Readers curious about ideas for a better web might consider the following sources (none of which I personally am endorsing, though many are interesting and promising): Nick Dowson (2023), 'What If ... Social Media Were Not Profit?', *New Internationalist*, 20 February, available at: newint.org/features/2023/02/20/what-if%E2%80%A6social-media-were-not-profit

(accessed 25 October 2024); Alex Krasodomski-Jones, Peter Pomerantzev, Harvey McGuinness and Ellen Judson (2022), 'The Good Web Project: Recognising and Realising Digital Democratic Infrastructure', *Demos*, available at: demos.co.uk/research/good-web-project/ (accessed 25 October 2024); Paul Rosenberg (2022), 'What's behind Elon's Twitter Disaster? A Fundamental Misunderstanding of Free Speech', *Salon*, 12 November, available at: www.salon.com/2022/11/12/whats-behind-elons-twitter-disaster-a-fundamental-misunderstanding-of-free-speech/ (accessed 25 October 2024); Nathan Schneider (2023), 'Exit to Community', *Noema Magazine*, 12 July, available at: www.noemamag.com/exit-to-community/ (accessed 25 October 2024); and Trebor Scholz and Sadev Parikh (2022), 'Saving the Socials: What if We Tried a Multipronged Approach?', *Platform Cooperative*, 5 July, available at: platform.coop/blog/saving-the-socials-what-if-we-tried-a-multipronged-approach/ (accessed 25 October 2024). See also Joe Bak-Coleman (2022), 'On Elon Musk's Vision of Twitter as a Hive Mind', *TechPolicy Press*, 3 November, available at: www.techpolicy.press/on-elon-musks-vision-of-twitter-as-a-hive-mind/ (accessed 25 October 2024).

80 Erin Blakemore (2021), 'Free School Breakfast and the Black Panther Party', History.com, available at www.history.com/news/free-school-breakfast-black-panther-party (accessed 13 January 2025).

81 This is a direct quote from a panel that was live-streamed by Al Jazeera on 14 March 2023.

82 Noah Kirsch, (2017), 'The 3 Richest Americans Hold More Wealth than Bottom 50% of the Country, Study Finds', *Forbes*, 9 November, available at: www.forbes.com/sites/noahkirsch/2017/11/09/the-3-richest-americans-hold-more-wealth-than-bottom-50-of-country-study-finds/ (accessed 13 December 2024).

83 As far as I can tell, her name is Tamara Vrooman. Found in this article: Carlos Teixeira (2023), 'Designing Capital Allocation', *LinkedIn*, 15 March, available at: www.linkedin.com/pulse/design-capital-allocation-carlos-teixeira/ (accessed 25 October 2024).

CHAPTER SIX: FIGHT SOCIAL ATROPHY

1 R. N. Spreng, E. Dimas, L. Mwilambwe-Tshilobo et al. (2020), 'The Default Network of the Human Brain Is Associated with Perceived Social Isolation', *Nature Communications* 11: 6393, doi.org/10.1038/s41467-020-20039-w (accessed 25 October 2024). J. T. Cacioppo and L. C. Hawkley (2009), 'Perceived Social Isolation and Cognition', *Trends in Cognitive Sciences*, 13(10): 447-54.

2 J. Holt-Lunstad, T. B. Smith, M. Baker, T. Harris and D. Stephenson (2015), 'Loneliness and Social Isolation as Risk Factors for Mortality: A Meta-analytic Review', *Perspectives on Psychological Science*, 10(2): 227-37.

3 Mary Beckman (2003), 'Rejection Is Like Pain to the Brain', *Science*, 9 October, available at: www.science.org/content/article/rejection-pain-brain (accessed 27 October 2024).

4 R. Waldinger and M. Schulz (2023), *The Good Life: Lessons from the World's Longest Scientific Study of Happiness*, Simon & Schuster.

5 N. Hirabayashi, T. Honda, J. Hata, Y. Furuta, M. Shibata, T. Ohara, Y. Tatewaki, Y. Taki, S. Nakaji, T. Maeda and K. Ono (2023), 'Association between Frequency of Social Contact and Brain Atrophy in Community-Dwelling Older People without Dementia: The JPSC-AD Study', *Neurology*, 101(11): e1108-e1117.

6 J. T. Cacioppo et al. (2000), 'Lonely Traits and Concomitant Physiological Processes: The MacArthur Social Neuroscience Studies', *International Journal of Psychophysiology*, 35: 143-54.

7 Spreng et al. 'The Default Network of the Human Brain is Associated with Perceived Social Isolation'.

8 A. Corbett, G. Williams, B. Creese, A. Hampshire, V. Hayman, A. Palmer, A. Filakovzsky, K. Mills, J. Cummings, D. Aarsland, Z. Khan and C. Ballard (2023), 'Cognitive Decline in Older Adults in the UK during and after the COVID-19 Pandemic: A Longitudinal Analysis of PROTECT Study Data', *The Lancet Healthy Longevity*, 4(11), e591-e599. See also

Alzheimer's Society (2020), 'The Impact of COVID-19 on People Affected by Dementia', 30 July, available at: www.alzheimers.org.uk/news/2020-07-30/lockdown-isolation-causes-shocking-levels-decline-people-dementia-who-are-rapidly (accessed 30 October 2024).

9   I. H. Gotlib, J. G. Miller, L. R. Borchers, S. M. Coury, L. A. Costello, J. M. Garcia and T. C. Ho (2022), 'Effects of the COVID-19 Pandemic on Mental Health and Brain Maturation in Adolescents: Implications for Analyzing Longitudinal Data', *Biological Psychiatry: Global Open Science*, doi.org/10.1016/j.bpsgos.2022.11.002.

10 For detailed data about American loneliness in particular, see U.S. Bureau of Labor Statistics (2023), 'American Time Use Survey', Bureau of Labor Statistics, available at: www.bls.gov/tus/ (accessed 27 October 2024). For an absolutely beautiful animated depiction of this crisis, see Alvin Chang (2023), 'The Invisible Epidemic: Understanding Loneliness in America', *The Pudding*, available at: pudding.cool/2023/09/invisible-epidemic/ (accessed 27 October 2024).

11 Mohsen Joshanloo (2024), 'Within-Person Associations between Personality Traits and Loneliness Controlling for Negative Affect', *Personality and Individual Differences*, 223: 112609. And an interview about this article: Mohsen Joshanloo (2024), 'Loneliness Leads to Changes in Personality over Time', *PsyPost*, 27 March, available at: www.psypost.org/loneliness-leads-to-changes-in-personality-over-time/ (accessed 27 October 2024).

12 Cacioppo et al. 'Lonely Traits and Concomitant Physiological Processes'; S. Cacioppo, S. Balogh, S. and J. T. Cacioppo (2015), 'Implicit Attention to Negative Social, in Contrast to Nonsocial, Words in the Stroop Task Differs between Individuals High and Low in Loneliness: Evidence from Event-Related Brain Microstates', *Cortex* 70: 213–33.

13 For the most part, I won't be looking at the obvious types of 'infrastructure for public reasoning' as described in the last chapter (that is, things such as schools and traditional media and social media, which are most obviously part of societal infrastructure for thinking). Much of what needs to be done in that area has already been discussed, especially funding and collective, democratic ownership. Moreover, others are already writing about this topic with greater expertise. Instead, I'll mostly look at the other two categories of infrastructure that I discussed, 'social infrastructure' and infrastructure that increases people's possibilities for actions.

14 U.S. Department of Health and Human Services (2023), *Our Epidemic of Loneliness and Isolation: The U.S. Surgeon General's Advisory on the Healing Effects of Social Connection and Community*, available at: www.hhs.gov/sites/default/files/surgeon-general-social-connection-advisory.pdf (accessed 27 October 2024). *The Economist* (2023), 'Five Years On, Is Britain's Strategy to Combat Loneliness Working?', 10 August, available at: www.economist.com/britain/2023/08/10/five-years-on-is-britains-strategy-to-combat-loneliness-working (accessed 27 October 2024).

15 World Health Organization (n.d.), 'Commission on Social Connection', *World Health Organization*, available at: www.who.int/groups/commission-on-social-connection (accessed 27 October 2024).

16 R. A. Mullen, S. Tong, R. T. Sabo, W. R. Liaw, J. Marshall, D. E. Nease, A. H. Krist and J. J. Frey (2019), 'Loneliness in Primary Care Patients: A Prevalence Study', *Annals of Family Medicine*, 17(2): 108–15, available at: https://pmc.ncbi.nlm.nih.gov/articles/PMC6411405/ (accessed 27 October 2024). Ellyn Maese (2023), 'Almost a Quarter of the World Feels Lonely', *Gallup News*, available at: news.gallup.com/opinion/gallup/512618/almost-quarter-world-feels-lonely.aspx (accessed 27 October 2024).

17 Esteban Ortiz-Ospina (2019), 'Is There a Loneliness Epidemic?', Our World in Data, available at: ourworldindata.org/loneliness-epidemic (accessed 27 October 2024).

18 There are differences between groups, of course; poorer, less educated people and non-white people do worse. So do young adults and old adults, compared with the middle-aged. Vincent La Placa and Julia Morgan (2023), 'Loneliness is a Major Public Health Problem, and Young People Are Bearing the Brunt of It', *The Conversation*, 24 May, available at: theconversation.com/loneliness-is-a-major-public-health-problem-and-young-people-are-bearing-the-

brunt-of-it-218391 (accessed 27 October 2024). Enghin Atalay (2023), 'How Time Spent Alone in the U.S. Has Changed over the Past Two Decades and Implications for Well-Being', Federal Reserve Bank of Philadelphia, available at: www.philadelphiafed.org/the-economy/macroeconomics/how-time-spent-alone-in-the-us-has-changed-over-the-past-two-decades-and-implications-for-well-being (accessed 27 October 2024).

19 U.S. Bureau of Labor Statistics (2023), 'American Time Use Survey'.
20 E. Ortiz-Ospina, C. Giattino and M. Roser (2020), 'Time Use', Our World in Data, available at: ourworldindata.org/time-use (accessed 27 October 2024).
21 Thomas O'Rourke (2023), 'The Decline of Trust and Neighborliness', *Institute for Family Studies*, 3 October, available at: ifstudies.org/blog/the-decline-of-trust-and-neighborliness (accessed 27 October 2024).
22 Much of the data on the American class divide and social isolation cited in this chapter comes from this excellent report: Daniel A. Cox and Sam Pressler (2024), 'Disconnected: The Growing Class Divide in American Civic Life. Findings from 2024 American Social Capital Survey', American Survey Center, 22 August, available at: www.americansurveycenter.org/research/disconnected-places-and-spaces/ (accessed 21 December 2024).
23 J. Mewes, M. Fairbrother, G. N. Giordano, C. Wu and R. Wilkes (2021), 'Experiences Matter: A Longitudinal Study of Individual-level Sources of Declining Social Trust in the United States', *Social Science Research*, 95: 102537.
24 Kimberlee D'Ardenne (2024), 'ASU Study Shows Middle-aged Americans Are Lonelier than Their European Peers', *Arizona State University News*, 18 March, available at: news.asu.edu/20240318-health-and-medicine-asu-study-shows-middleaged-americans-are-lonelier-european-peers (accessed 27 October 2024).
25 F. J. Infurna, N. E. Dey, T. Gonzalez Avilés, K. J. Grimm, M. E. Lachman and D. Gerstorf (2024), 'Loneliness in Midlife: Historical Increases and Elevated Levels in the United States Compared with Europe', *American Psychologist*, doi.org/10.1037/amp0001322.
26 Solability (2024), *Social Capital Index*, available at: solability.com/the-globalsustainable-competitiveness-index/social-capital, (accessed 9 Jan. 2025).
27 J. Mewes and G. N. Giordano (2017), 'Self-Rated Health, Generalized Trust, and the Affordable Care Act: A US Panel Study, 2006–2014', *Social Science & Medicine*, 190: 48–56.
28 E. D. Gould and A. Hijzen (2016), *Growing Apart, Losing Trust? The Impact of Inequality on Social Capital*, International Monetary Fund.
29 A. Alesina and E. La Ferrara (2002), 'Who Trusts Others?', *Journal of Public Economics*, 85(2): 207–34. E. Ortiz-Ospina, M. Roser and P. Arriagada (2016), 'Trust', Our World in Data, available at: ourworldindata.org/trust (accessed 27 October 2024).
30 J. Batsleer and J. Duggan (2020), 'Loneliness and Poverty', in *Young and Lonely*, Policy Press, 39–50. J. Cohen-Mansfield, H. Hazan, Y. Lerman and V. Shalom (2016), 'Correlates and Predictors of Loneliness in Older-Adults: A Review of Quantitative Results Informed by Qualitative Insights', *International Psychogeriatrics*, 28(4): 557–76.
31 See once again Daniel A. Cox and Sam Pressler (2024), 'Disconnected: the Growing Class Divide in American Civic Life'.
32 E. Ortiz-Ospina (2019), 'Are People More Likely to Be Lonely in So-Called "Individualistic" Societies?', *Our World in Data*, available at: ourworldindata.org/lonely-not-alone (accessed 27 October 2024).
33 Cacioppo and Hawkley, 'Perceived Social Isolation and Cognition'.
34 D. R. Carney, J. T. Jost, S. D. Gosling and J. Potter (2008), 'The Secret Lives of Liberals and Conservatives: Personality Profiles, Interaction Styles, and the Things They Leave Behind', *Political Psychology*, 29(6): 807–40.
35 D. H. Allcott, L. Braghieri, S. Eichmeyer and M. Gentzkow (2020), 'The Welfare Effects of Social Media', *American Economic Review*, 110(3): 629–76.
36 Those interested in the complexity of the question of 'loneliness' may be interested in the reporting of Derek Thompson at *The Atlantic*, who covers many relevant studies and compares them. See Derek Thompson (2024), 'Why Americans Suddenly Stopped Hanging

Out', *The Atlantic*, 14 February, available at: www.theatlantic.com/ideas/archive/2024/02/america-decline-hanging-out/677451/ (accessed 1 November 2024).

37 Eric Klinenberg (2024), *2020: One City, Seven People, and the Year Everything Changed*, Knopf, 179.

38 M. Ernst, D. Niederer, A. M. Werner, S. J. Czaja, S. Mikton, A. D. Ong, T. Rosen, E. Brähler and M. E. Beutel (2022), 'Loneliness before and during the COVID-19 Pandemic: A Systematic Review with Meta-Analysis', *American Psychologist*, 77(5): 660.

39 Thompson, 'Why Americans Suddenly Stopped Hanging Out.'

40 R. Kindred and G. W. Bates (2023), 'The Influence of the COVID-19 Pandemic on Social Anxiety: A Systematic Review', *International Journal of Environmental Research and Public Health*, 20(3): 2362.

41 Barratt, 'Social Infrastructure in Two Minutes'.

42 Klinenberg, *Palaces for the People*.

43 M. H. Lim, R. Eres and S. Vasan (2020), 'Understanding Loneliness in the Twenty-First Century: An Update on Correlates, Risk Factors, and Potential Solutions', *Social Psychiatry and Psychiatric Epidemiology*, 55: 793–810.

44 G. Meen (2005), *Economic Segregation in England: Causes, Consequences and Policy*, Policy Press.

45 Gallup (2023), 'The Power of Social Connection: A Conversation on the State of Connectedness and Loneliness in the World', *Gallup Analytics*, 20 April, available at: www.gallup.com/analytics/509675/state-of-social-connections.aspx (accessed 25 October 2024).

46 Ray Oldenburg (1999), *The Great Good Place: Cafes, Coffee Shops, Bookstores, Bars, Hair Salons, and other Hangouts at the Heart of a Community*, Da Capo Press. I am indebted to Sheila Liming and her book *Hanging Out* for her read of Oldenburg in this section of the book. Sheila Liming (2023), *Hanging Out: The Radical Power of Killing Time*, Melville House.

47 Robert Putnam (1995), 'Bowling Alone: America's Declining Social Capital', *Journal of Democracy* 6 (1), repr. in L. Crothers and C. Lockhart, eds. (2000), *Culture and Politics: A Reader*, 223–34.

48 G. C. Loury (1976), *Essays in the Theory of the Distribution of Income*, doctoral dissertation, Massachusetts Institute of Technology.

49 This is a quote from Putnam's recent film *Join or Die* (2024).

50 R. D. Putnam (1994), *Making Democracy Work: Civic Traditions in Modern Italy*, Princeton University Press.

51 See (among other places) a depiction of this in the aforementioned film.

52 Ibid.

53 Robert Putnam and Shaylyn Romney Garrett (2020), *The Upswing: How America Came Together a Century Ago and How We Can Do It Again*, Simon & Schuster, 327.

54 This is a quotation from the aforementioned film, and is based on/summarizing the data about churches, unions, clubs, dinner parties and more.

55 Daniel A. Cox and Sam Pressler (2024), 'Disconnected: the Growing Class Divide in American Civic Life.'

56 'Disconnected: The Growing Class Divide in American Civic Life. Findings from 2024 American Social Capital Survey', American Survey Center, 22 August, available at: www.americansurveycenter.org/research/disconnected-places-and-spaces/ (accessed 21 December 2024).

57 J. E. Sewell (2018), 'Public Space in North American Cities', in *Oxford Research Encyclopedia of American History*, doi.org/10.1093/acrefore/9780199329175.013.593. Alex Chapman (2022), 'Exposed: The Collapse of Green Space Provision in England and Wales', New Economics Foundation, available at: neweconomics.org/2022/05/exposed-the-collapse-of-green-space-provision-in-england-and-wales (accessed 1 November 2024). Matthew Adams (2022), 'Neighbourhood Green Space Is in Rapid Decline, Deepening Both the Climate and Mental Health Crises', The Conversation, 18 May, available at: theconversation.com/neighbourhood-green-space-is-in-rapid-decline-deepening-both-the-climate-and-mental-healthcrises-183389 (accessed 1 November 2024). Helena Horton (2022), 'Parks near New Homes Shrink 40% as Developers Say They Cannot Afford Them', *Guardian*, 3

May, available at: www.theguardian.com/cities/2022/may/03/green-space-decline-housing-developer-england-wales-plead-poverty-research-finds (accessed 1 November 2024).
58 Putnam and Garrett, *The Upswing*.
59 P. A. Neel (2018), *Hinterland: America's New Landscape of Class and Conflict*, Reaktion Books.
60 Stefan Szczelkun (2018), 'Document: Kennington Park – The Birthplace of People's Democracy', available at: www.kenningtonchartistproject.org/2018/04/20/document-kennington-park-the-birthplace-of-peoples-democracy/ (accessed 1 November 2024).
61 Kelly Intile (2007), *The European Coffee-House: A Political History*, doctoral dissertation, University of Oregon, available at: scholarsbank.uoregon.edu/xmlui/bitstream/handle/1794/7463/Kelly_Intile.pdf?sequence=1&isAllowed=y (accessed 1 November 2024).
62 Yasmin El-Beih (2020), 'How Coffee Forever Changed Britain', BBC Travel, 19 November, available at: www.bbc.com/travel/article/20201119-how-coffee-forever-changed-britain (accessed 1 November 2024).
63 Richard Wike and Alexandra Castillo (2018), 'International Political Engagement', Pew Research Center, 17 September, available at: www.pewresearch.org/global/2018/10/17/international-political-engagement/ (accessed 1 November 2024). See also Hansard Society, 'Audit of Political Engagement 16: The 2019 Report'.
64 Hansard Society, 'Audit of Political Engagement 16'.
65 World Health Organization Regional Office for Europe (2023), 'Widening Inequities, Declining Trust – They are Inextricably Linked, with Significant Impacts on Health, Finds New WHO Europe Report', available at: www.who.int/europe/news/item/12-07-2023-widening-inequities--declining-trust---they-are-inextricably-linked--with-significant-impacts-on-health--finds-new-who-europe-report (accessed 1 November 2024).
66 Peter Ganong and Daniel Shoag (2017), 'Why Has Regional Income Convergence in the US Declined?', *Journal of Urban Economics*, 102, pp.76–90.
67 Richard Fry (2017), 'Americans Are Moving at Historically Low Rates in Part Because Millennials Are Staying Put', Pew Research Center, 13 February, available at: www.pewresearch.org/short-reads/2017/02/13/americans-are-moving-at-historically-low-rates-in-part-because-millennials-are-staying-put/ (accessed 1 November 2024). Derek Thompson (2012), 'Generation Stuck: Why Don't Young People Move, Anymore?', *The Atlantic*, 12 March, available at: www.theatlantic.com/business/archive/2012/03/generation-stuck-why-dont-young-people-move-anymore/254349 URL (accessed 1 November 2024).
68 See the Cox and Pressler report cited earlier in this chapter for discussion of this in the US along both race and class lines. For the UK see for example Erica Meltzer (2024), 'School Segregation Increasing, Study Finds Charters Are One Factor', Chalkbeat, 6 May, available at: www.chalkbeat.org/2024/05/06/school-segregation-increasing-study-finds-charters-are-one-factor/ (accessed 1 November 2024). Anushka Asthana (2016), 'Britain More Segregated than 15 Years Ago, Race Expert Ted Cantle Warns', *Guardian*, 23 May, available at: www.theguardian.com/world/2016/may/23/britain-more-segregated-15-years-race-expert-riots-ted-cantle (accessed 1 November 2024).
69 Thompson, 'How America Lost Its Mojo'.
70 Fry, 'Americans Are Moving at Historically Low Rates'.
71 Liming, *Hanging Out*.
72 Chris Anderson (2024), 'Pub Closures in the UK', Company Debt, 5 August, available at: www.companydebt.com/articles/pub-closures-in-the-uk/ (accessed 1 November 2024).
73 Kabir Ahuja, Vishwa Chandra, Victoria Lord and Curtis Peens (2023), 'Ordering In: The Rapid Evolution of Food Delivery', McKinsey & Company, available at: www.mckinsey.com/industries/technology-media-and-telecommunications/our-insights/ordering-in-the-rapid-evolution-of-food-delivery (accessed 1 November 2024).
74 This is another point that Joshua Kalla made to me during our interview.
75 See, for example, United Nations (2014), '"Shrinking" Spaces for Citizens Threatened Democracy, Human Rights, Experts Tell Third Committee As It Considers Country Reports', available at: press.un.org/en/2014/gashc4112.doc.htm (accessed 1 November 2024).

76 You can even see it here: New York Public Library (n.d.), *The Green Book*, available at: digitalcollections.nypl.org/collections/the-green-book (accessed 1 November 2024).

77 Joyce Balls-Berry, L. C. Dacy and J. Balls (2016), '"Heard It through the Grapevine": The Black Barbershop as a Source of Health Information', *Western Journal of Nursing Research*, 38(10): 1409–17, available at: www.ncbi.nlm.nih.gov/pmc/articles/PMC4749262/ (accessed 1 November 2024).

78 Jeffrey Shantz (2016), *Constructive Anarchy: Building Infrastructures of Resistance*, Routledge.

79 Anton Jäger (2022), 'From Bowling Alone to Posting Alone', *Jacobin*, 5 December, available at: jacobin.com/2022/12/from-bowling-alone-to-posting-alone (accessed 1 November 2024).

80 Ibid.

81 BBC (2023), *Now Here*, available at: www.bbc.co.uk/programmes/p0h9wxmz (accessed 1 November 2024).

82 See both Putnam and Thompson on this.

CHAPTER SEVEN: LOVING AND LEAVING THE LIBERAL IDEAL (OR, TO MY FELLOW LOVERS OF IDEAS)

1 David Brooks (2024), 'My Unsettling Interview With Steve Bannon', *New York Times*, available at: www.nytimes.com/2024/07/01/opinion/steve-bannon-trump.html (accessed: 14 January 2025).

2 Meredith Whittaker (2022), 'Social Media Authoritarianism and the World As It Is', *LPE Project*, available at: lpeproject.org/blog/social-media-authoritarianism-and-the-world-as-it-is/ (accessed 1 November 2024).

3 This is the point made in König, 'Patterns of Movement Recruitment': that it is those with few strong ties who are most likely to join especially weird groups and shift their beliefs the most widely.

4 This phrase comes from a blog post by lexicographer Erin McKean (2006), 'You Don't Have To Be Pretty', *A Dress A Day*, 20 October, available at: dressaday.com/2006/10/20/you-dont-have-to-be-pretty/ (accessed 1 November 2024).

5 D. S. Hamermesh (2011), *Beauty Pays: Why Attractive People Are More Successful*, Princeton University Press.

6 For more evidence of all this, see L. David, E. Vassena, and E. Bijleveld (2024), 'The Unpleasantness of Thinking: A Meta-analytic Review of the Association Between Mental Effort and Negative Affect.' *Psychological Bulletin*, 150(9), 1070–1093. doi.org/10.1037/bul0000443.

7 For a summary of some of this research, see *The Economist* (2022), 'How Thinking Hard Makes the Brain Tired', 11 August, available at: www.economist.com/science-and-technology/2022/08/11/how-thinking-hard-makes-the-brain-tired (accessed 25 October 2024).

8 Karen M. Douglas. R.M. Sutton, and A. Cichocka, (2017), 'The Psychology of Conspiracy Theories', *Current Directions in Psychological Science*, 26(6), pp.538–42.

9 Hansard Society, 'Audit of Political Engagement 16: The 2019 Report', www.hansardsociety.org.uk/projects/audit-of-political-engagement (accessed 22 October 2024.)

10 Pew Research Center (2023), 'Americans' Dismal Views of the Nation's Politics.' *Pew Research Center – U.S. Politics & Policy*, available at: www.pewresearch.org/politics/2023/09/19/americans-dismal-views-of-the-nations-politics/ (Accessed 21 January 2025).

11 For discussion and evidence of the many studies on this, see: R. Petré (2023), 'Smile, You're an Activist', *In These Times*, 22 March, available at: inthesetimes.com/article/smileyoure-an-activist (accessed 25 October 2024); and Meredith Maran (2015), 'The Activism Cure', *Greater Good Science Center*, 20 January, available at: greatergood.berkeley.edu/article/item/the_activism_cure (accessed 25 October 2024).

12 See also Vestergren, Drury and Chiriac, 'The Biographical Consequences of Protest and Activism'.

13. Ibid.
14. For one such study on burnout, see J. O. Conner, E. Greytak, C. D. Evich and L. Wray-Lake (2023), 'Burnout and Belonging: How the Costs and Benefits of Youth Activism Affect Youth Health and Wellbeing', *Youth*, 3(1): 127–45.
15. Christian Jarrett (2009), 'Political Activism Is Good for You', *British Psychological Society Research Digest*, 30 September, available at: www.bps.org.uk/research-digest/political-activism-good-you (accessed 25 October 2024).
16. For a summary, see C. Peterson (1999), 'Personal Control and Well-Being', in D. Kahneman, E. Diener and N. Schwarz, eds., *Well-Being: The Foundations of Hedonic Psychology*, Russell Sage Foundation, 288–301.
17. There are a great many examples, but see, for example, Robert Putnam's suggestion of this in Lulu Garcia Novarres (2024), 'Robert Putnam Knows Why You're Lonely', *New York Times*, 13 July 2024, available at: www.nytimes.com/2024/07/13/magazine/robert-putnam-interview.html (accessed 21 Dec 2024).

INDEX

abortion 82–3, 140
abstractions 93, 98
activism, and happiness 242–3
affective context 121
Affordable Care Act ('Obamacare') 188
affordances (action-possibilities) 88–94, 98, 101, 105, 106, 189, 203, 240
  and infrastructure 149, 151–2, 161–5
African Americans 80
agency 24–6, 38, 79, 92, 131, 243, 245
Agmon, Shai 38
agonistic politics 63–4
agora 19
alien hand syndrome 89
Allport, Gordon 107–8, 120
American Time Use Survey 185
Andreas-Salomé, Lou 56
anti-racism 25
approval ratings 47–8
Arab Spring 100, 143
Arendt, Hannah 9, 222
Aristotle 33, 135
AT&T 158
attention spans 28–9
Aufhebung 241
austerity 200, 239

authoritarianism 12, 21, 93, 100, 168, 172, 174, 177, 190, 210, 214, 219, 222, 225, 231, 240

Baerthlein, Thomas 60
Balls-Berry, Joyce 211
Bannon, Steve 221–3
Barber, Melissa 59–60
barbershops 211–12
Basque separatists 69
BBC 61
belonging 24–6, 37, 128, 161–3, 192, 212–14, 216, 226–8, 245
  'behaviour, belonging, belief' model 95
Berlin 69–71
Bernays, Edward 130
Bevins, Vincent 143–4
Bezos, Jeff 142, 145
Biden, Joe 41, 44, 139–40
'bird-dogging' 72
Black Lives Matter 73–6
Black Panthers 173
Blair, Tony 52–3
Bloomberg, Michael 145
Bourdieu, Pierre 97
brain
  and affordances (action-possibilities) 88–92
  and ambiguity 236
  and debates 50–1, 66–7

predictive processing 89–90
and social isolation 181–4,
193, 215–16
Brexit 61
Broockman, David 125
Brookings Institution 41
Brooks, David 221–2
Buckley, Bill 221
Bueno, Avi 142
Bush, George W. 58, 72–3, 144
Bush, Stephen 36

cancel culture 2, 6, 231
Capitalist Realism 93
Carmichael, Stokely 212
Carnegie, Andrew 175
censorship 19, 37–8, 224
'champagne socialists' 122
Charles II, King 201
Chartists 201
Christianity 3–4
churches 36, 44, 76–7, 81, 160, 209, 212–13, 223, 244
Civil Rights Movement 102–4, 210–12
class structures 51
climate change 62–3, 73–4, 83, 85, 96, 125, 163–4, 174, 240, 244, 254n
climate-friendly behaviours 118
Clinton, Bill 197–8
clubs and associations 198–9, 202, 208, 213, 217
coffee houses 8–9, 201–2, 252n
coffee shops 149, 187, 196, 199, 201–2, 207, 215
cognitive dissonance 5, 23–4, 26, 44, 55, 77–80, 94, 96, 123, 131, 162, 166, 230–1, 236
and homophobia 111–12

cognitive load 235–6
cognitive science 5, 88, 97, 131
colonialism 5, 8–9
Comcast 158
commons 100
'tragedy of the commons' 156
community, romanticizing 225–9
confirmation bias 22–3, 44
consciousness-raising groups 133–4
Conservative Party leadership contest 41–2, 47
conspiracy theories 1–2, 22, 131, 137–8, 191, 222, 232, 236
Cooperation Town 86
Covid-19 pandemic 27, 152, 164, 174, 182, 184, 190, 193, 237
Cox Media Group 145
critical theory 10, 12, 251
critical thinking 4, 135, 176, 197, 234, 239
crowd psychology 129–30, 166
cults 95, 117, 223
cultural cognition 27
cystic fibrosis 59

de Tocqueville, Alexis 170
debate 6, 41–68, 95–6, 114, 146, 149, 170, 216, 231, 233–4, 244
and argument culture 49–50
and brain activity 50–1, 66–7
and Brexit 61
and climate change 62–3

Grand Débat 53–5
and medicine pricing 59–60
decision fatigue 236
deep canvassing 123–8, 134, 209
DellaPosta, Daniel 111
dementia 182
democracy (definition) 105–6
Democrats 73–4
depression 34
dinner parties 97, 198
disinformation 4, 131
diversity and inclusion training 32
domestic violence 59
Douglas, William, O. 18

echo chambers 2, 6, 29, 131, 231
Edison, Thomas 26
education 10, 37, 56–7, 59, 76, 81, 96, 98, 118, 150–1, 155, 157, 164, 177–8, 185, 187, 189, 197–8, 239
Elaboration Likelihood Model 92
election fraud 140
Eli Lilly 138
Enlightenment 9, 19
epistemic virtues 135
Euro crisis 60
evictions 87
experience and learning design 97

Facebook 28, 48
fact-checking 237–8
'false consciousness' 131
far right 45, 46, 151, 167–8, 178, 223

fascism 8, 170–1, 245
Faye, Shon 59
feminism 21, 25. 32, 39, 56, 133–4, 229–30
feminist witches 69
financial crisis 102
Financial Times 36
First World War 18
Fisher, Mark 93
flooding 85
'folk politics' 101
food co-operatives 86–8
Fox News 28, 145
free markets 240
free speech 2, 18–20, 35–6, 105, 138, 224, 234
French Revolution 130
Freud, Sigmund 130
friendships 109–23, 127–8, 132, 134–6, 160, 162, 243
and affective context 121
decline in 186, 190, 199
indirect friendships 121
political friendships 135–6
and voting behaviour 118–19

Ganong, Peter 205
gay marriage 21, 111
gay rights 39, 111, 134
Geuss, Raymond 61
Gezi Park protests 99
Gilded Age 200
Gimbel, Sarah I. 26
Ginsburg, Ruth Bader 110
Global North 12
Goldacre, Ben 62
Google 28
Graeber, David 32–3, 98
Granovetter, Mark 117

grassroots movements 53, 174, 214–15
Greeks, ancient 19, 45
'green book' 211
groupthink 100, 116, 228
gun ownership 26, 73

Habermas, Jürgen 7–10, 52, 196, 207, 215
habitus 97
Haiven, Max 65, 69, 70
Haley, Nikki 41
Hansard Society surveys 203–4, 236–7
Harris, Kamala 140
Harris, Sam 26
Harvard Happiness Study 181
hazing 94
Hegel, G. W. F. 56–7, 241
Heidegger, Martin 8
Henk, Mandy 100
Hewstone, Miles 110
hierarchies 195–6
high-speed rail 64
Hitler, Adolf 130
Hitler Youth 7
Holmes, Oliver Wendell 18
'home beliefs' 29
homophobia 111–12
House Un-American Activities Committee 169
housing activists 128–9
housing crises 204–6, 239
Huertas, Aaron 62
'hyperloop' 175
hyper-specialization 132

identity 25–7, 39, 236, 242
independent thinking 129–31, 135, 167

individualism 132, 189, 198, 200, 242
inequality 20–1, 31, 37, 80, 99–101, 151, 155, 163, 187–8, 190, 193–5, 204–5, 232, 239–40
infrastructure 143–78, 223–4, 228–9, 232–4, 239
   and affordances (action-possibilities) 149, 151–2, 161–5
   civic infrastructure 199
   and collective intelligence 177
   in decline 199–200, 213–14
   and interdependent thinking 150, 157–9
   privatization 154–5, 158, 161, 175–6, 206
   social infrastructure 150–1, 159–62, 173–4, 183–4, 194–5, 199, 202, 206, 208–10, 214, 216–19
Infurna, Frank 187
Ingber, Stanley 20, 267
Instagram 88, 144
insulin 59, 138
interdependent thinking 6, 114–15, 132, 135, 150, 157–9, 183, 224, 228
internet 28–9, 49, 109, 144–5, 149–50, 154, 156–8, 161–2, 175–6, 186, 191, 193, 195
   'net neutrality' 145, 158
   as network of networks 161
   and radicalization 222
Iraq war 72–3, 100
Israel–Palestine 140, 226
Ito, Tiffany 51

INDEX

Jackson, Andrew 169
Jameson, Fredric 130
Japanese–Mexican Labor
    Association 198
Jefferson, Thomas 19
Joshanloo, Mohsen 182
Jost, John T. 80
journalism jobs 28
Judaism 226

Kahan, Dan 27
Kahneman, Daniel 253n
Kalla, Joshua 125–6, 209
Kaplan, Jonas T. 26
Kennedy, John F. 42–4
Kenney, Jason 46
Keytruda 59
Klee, Miles 46
Klinenberg, Eric 159–60, 192
Kristof, Nicholas 143
Ku Klux Klan 19

Lakoff, George 58
Laurin, Kristin 78–9, 81, 83
Le Bon, Gustave 129–30, 166
le Pennec, Caroline 43
left-wing people 242–3
Legg, David Knight 46
leisure time 163–4
Liberal Democrats 11
liberal economists 35
liberalism 11–12, 241–4
libraries 100, 175, 207
Lichtenberg, Georg
    Christoph 67
Liming, Sheila 206
lived experience 83, 98, 126, 223
Lockheed Martin 17
London Underground 172

loneliness 180–2, 184–9, 192, 194–5, 204, 217, 222–3
    see also social isolation
Loury, Glenn Cartman 197
low-wage earners 206
lynchings 169, 211

McRaney, David 35, 124, 253n
Macron, Emmanuel 53, 55
Maitlis, Emily 61
male vulnerability 21
manipulation 224–5
Marcus Aurelius 130
marketplace of ideas 6, 17–22, 32, 35–40, 66, 68, 110, 117, 167–8, 224, 231, 233–4, 244
    and digital media 27–31
    as 'frictionless'
        competition 38, 46
    and Twitter/X 137, 139, 143, 146–7, 149, 170–1, 175
Marshall, Douglas A. 95
Marxists 69, 97
Matthews, Dylan 43
Maxwell Air Force Base 85
medicine pricing 59–60
Medina, José 135
Meta 144–5
#metoo 21
Metropolitan Police 140
Metzinger, Thomas 88–9
migration 73, 153, 244
Mill, John Stuart 19, 130
Millennials 205
Millgram, Elijah 132–3
Mills, Quincy T. 212
miners' institutes 214
Mormon missionaries 77
Murdoch, Rupert 145

music festivals 70
Musk, Elon 137–43, 146, 148–9, 155–6, 159, 161, 165–6, 170–1, 175–7
Muslims 108
Mussolini, Benito 130

narrative exchange 126
neoliberalism 92, 200, 214
Netflix 143
New Data Project 119
New Left 21
New York Times 221
Newhouse, Donald and Samuel 145
NGOs 214
NHS 59
Nixon, Richard M. 42–4
Northrop Grumman 17
Now Here podcast 214
nuclear weapons 25

Obama, Barack 11, 48, 197
Ocasio-Cortez, Alexandria 11, 46
Occupy 99, 100, 143
Oldenburg, Ray 195
Orkambi 59
Ortiz-Ospina, Esteban 184
Overton window 11

paranoia 170, 180, 189–91, 208, 215
Paris Commune 130
Parks, Rosa 85
patriarchy 32, 81, 92
patriotism, American 198
paywalls 27, 155, 158, 171
Pentagon 16
People's Libraries 100

Perry, Katy 31
Pfeifle, Mark 144
Phillis Wheatley clubs 198
plastic water bottle ban 78–9
polarization 1, 6, 49, 52, 73, 146, 155, 160–1, 171, 190, 197, 209, 216, 231, 236, 244
police 128–9
Politico 47
Pons, Vincent 43, 73
Popper, Karl 168
Portnoy, Dave 46
post-natal depression 22
praxis 98
Prime Minister's Question Time 53
privacy 227
protest movements 69–77, 85, 95, 98–104, 106, 257n
    biographical impacts 75
    networked protests 100–3
    'paid protests' and 'astroturfing' 103
    and public opinion 71, 73–6, 103
    and Twitter 143–4
public bathroom legislation 124
public health 160, 211
public opinion 13, 21, 71, 73–6, 103, 111
public service 163–4
public spaces 8, 78, 164, 201, 203–4, 210, 216, 239
public sphere 1–2, 5, 7–10, 21–2, 38, 72, 183, 196, 207, 216, 232–4, 241, 243
    and barbershops 211–12
    and Euro crisis 60
    and infrastructure 153, 156–7, 173

public transport 149, 154, 160, 164
pubs, decline in 207
Putnam, Robert 196–201

'race science' 63
racism (racial oppression) 33, 73, 81, 113, 133, 164, 170, 222, 266n
rail privatization 158, 172
Ramirez, Louis 85
Rawls, John 32
Raytheon 15, 16n, 17
reactance 34, 83, 126, 131
reactionary centrism 62
reasoning
  errors of 24–7, 39–40, 253n
  reasoning-as-commerce 6, 13–14, 18, 36, 40, 68
  reasoning-as-war 6, 13–14, 46, 51–2, 55, 58, 63–4, 66–8
relational organizing 119
remote working 217
Republicans 1, 23–4, 41, 48, 74, 221–2
Requerimiento 2–3, 5, 13, 15, 141, 169
Richardson, Samuel 8
right-wing people 190–1, 224, 242, 245
  see also far right
Roberts, Alasdair 101–2
Romans 45, 148
Romeo and Juliet 122
Roosevelt, Theodore 130

Sabato, Larry 42
Saint-Exupéry, Antoine de 122
Scalia, Antonin 110
School of Life 50
Sciences Po 259n
screen time 163–4, 191
Second World War 85, 107
self-efficacy 92
self-interest 32, 122
sewage management 152, 154
sexism 108, 133
sexual harassment 34, 134
Shalmy, Shiri 86–7
Shantz, Jeff 213
Shoag, Daniel 205
Silicon Valley 140, 161, 175
Sky News 47
smoking ban 78–9
social atrophy 7, 180–3, 185, 188–94, 206–8, 217–18, 228
social capital 183, 188, 196–202
social contact theory 107–11, 120–1, 196
social isolation 12, 180–9, 193–4, 198, 207, 217
  see also loneliness
social media 22, 24, 27–30, 50, 52, 58, 109, 131, 144, 150, 157, 166, 172, 177, 191, 212, 222–4, 236
  as 'digital town square' 161
  and protest movements 99–102
  and 'wokeness' 203
'social robots' 108
social trust 12, 38, 133, 186–90, 197, 203–4, 239
solar panels 96, 151
space programmes 175
'spectrum of allies' 66
Srnicek, Nick 101

standpoint theory 32
Star, Susan Leigh 147
Starmer, Keir 53
student loans 59
suburbanization 204
Sullivan, Andrew 143
Sun 28
Sunak, Rishi 42, 47, 53
System Justification Theory 79–81

Tahrir Square 99
Táíwò, Olúfẹ́mi O. 19
Tannen, Deborah 49
tax policy 9, 58–9, 93, 116, 158
Tea Party 257n
Terence 114
Tesla 139
third spaces 8, 194–6, 200, 205, 207
TikTok 145
'tolerance, paradox of' 168
town squares 161–2, 169
trade unions 85, 101–2, 102–3, 198, 213–14
traffic jams 153–4
trans people 59, 70, 124
Trump, Donald 1, 24, 41, 48, 110, 138–42, 166, 175, 177, 221
Truss, Liz 41–2, 47
Tufekci, Zeynep 76, 99, 100, 101, 104
Twitter/X 2, 18, 30, 109, 137–49, 155–6, 165–7, 169–73, 176–7, 216, 238
    Black Twitter 148, 212
'tyranny of the majority' 170

unemployment 187
university campuses 203
US Capitol riot 138
US Congress 58, 72, 169, 221
US Constitution 21
US Department of Government Efficiency 171
US military 107
US Supreme Court 6, 18, 110
US Surgeon General 184
'user experience design' 154

van Stekelenburg, Jacquelien 118
van Zomeren, Martijn 122
Vance, J. D. 140
Vancouver Airport Authority 178
Varol, Ozan 25
Vote with Me app 119

Wall Street Journal 145
Washington Post 43, 48, 145
Weizman, Eyal 176
white supremacists 169
Whittaker, Meredith 223
Williams, Alex 101
women's suffrage 21
working hours 34
World Health Organization (WHO) 59–60, 184
World Trade Organization (WTO) 60

xenophobia 170, 190

Zaleski, Luke 142
Zapatistas 99
Zuckerberg, Donna 45
Zuckerberg, Mark 45, 142, 175